CHELSEA HOUSE PUBLISHERS

Modern Critical Views

Further titles in preparation.

Modern Critical Views

TOM STOPPARD

Modern Critical Views

TOM STOPPARD

Edited and with an introduction by

Harold Bloom

Sterling Professor of the Humanities
Yale University

1986
CHELSEA HOUSE PUBLISHERS
New York
New Haven   Philadelphia

PROJECT EDITORS: Emily Bestler, James Uebbing
ASSOCIATE EDITOR: Maria Behan
EDITORIAL COORDINATOR: Karyn Gullen Browne
EDITORIAL STAFF: Perry King, Bert Yaeger
DESIGN: Susan Lusk

Cover illustration by Mark Sparacio

Library of Congress Cataloging in Publication Data

Tom Stoppard.
      (Modern critical views)
      Bibliography: p.
      Includes index.
      Summary: Fourteen critical essays on the works of
the famous English playwright.
      1. Stoppard, Tom—Criticism and interpretation—
Addresses, essays, lectures. [1. Stoppard, Tom—
Criticism and interpretation—Addresses, essays,
lectures.   2. English drama—History and criticism—
Addresses, essays, lectures]   I. Bloom, Harold.
II. Series.
PR6069.T6Z89   1986   822'.914   85–25523
ISBN 0–87754–671–1

Chelsea House Publishers
Harold Steinberg, Chairman and Publisher
Susan Lusk, Vice President
A Division of Chelsea House Educational Communications, Inc.
133 Christopher Street, New York, NY 10014

Contents

Editor's Note

This volume gathers together what, in its editor's judgment, constitutes the best literary criticism yet published on the plays of Tom Stoppard, arranged in the chronological order of its publication. It begins with an attempt in the "Introduction" to come to a judicial estimate of the relative eminence of Stoppard's achievement, with an emphasis upon his mode of interlacing his precursors, Beckett and Wilde in particular.

The chronological sequence of criticism begins with Allan Rodway's exposition of Stoppard's comic philosophy, called here a metaphysics of *Perhaps*. Brian M. Crossley's investigation of *The Real Inspector Hound* emphasizes the inward turnings of Stoppard's rebellion against both dramatic convention and the genre of detective literature. *Lord Malquist and Mr Moon*, Stoppard's one novel, is briefly examined by Ronald Hayman as a mingling, like the plays, of outrageous entertainment and relatively abstruse argument.

With the next group of essays, we move to Stoppard's three major works (to date): *Jumpers*, *Travesties* and *Rosencrantz and Guildenstern Are Dead*. John A. Bailey and G. B. Crump are juxtaposed here as very diverse analysts of *Jumpers*; Bailey reading the play as an ironical theism, and Crump presenting it as cosmological murder mystery, resulting only in the "sound of closure." A kind of Stoppardian freeplay of further antithetical readings follows, with two essays on *Travesties* interlaced with two on the sorrows of Rosencrantz and Guildenstern. Howard D. Pearce centers on the mirror image and its relation to the doublings and redoublings of *Travesties*, while John William Cooke discusses the "excess of forms" in the play, which unsettles any imaging of truth. June M. Schlueter works back from *The Real Inspector Hound* to *Rosencrantz and Guildenstern Are Dead*, showing the difference in mimetic concepts between the two plays, with the earlier one further away from classical mimesis, while William E. Gruber rather surprisingly concludes that the mimetic concept of *Rosencrantz and Guildenstern* is quite classical, rejecting absurdist modes of irony.

A consideration of Stoppard's later work begins with Jim Hunter's account of *Night and Day*, read as a Chekhovian "well-made play." Thomas R. Whitaker provides an overview that takes us through *Dirty Linen* and

New-Found-Land and on to Every Good Boy Deserves Favour and Professional Foul. Whitaker insists upon the moral and political maturation Stoppard manifests in this sequence. In a defense of The Real Thing, Hersh Zeifman reminds us that "Stoppard's ambushes never cease," even in his ostensibly more "serious" phase. Something of the same conviction is voiced by Richard Corballis in his comments on Dirty Linen and New-Found-Land, where the dialectic between what Corballis calls "the mystery and the clockwork" is seen to be a continuing one.

The final essay, by Keir Elam, applies semiology to Stoppard's "reflexive poetics," in an attempt to illuminate the oxymoronic pain and pleasure of Stoppard's ambiguities. Just as Stoppard himself is in mid-career, even so we can expect that the criticism devoted to him will augment in the intensity of its quest to illuminate his parodistic jumpings and ambiguous travesties.

Introduction

A character in a play, when removed from his setting, ceases to exist; everything he said in his original context, at least when related to that context, would be meaningless in a different context. Hence the part would have to be rewritten afresh. The dramatist would have to write the new words himself. This is not borrowing, but original composition.

—WILLIAM BEARE, *The Roman Stage*

I

The ancient Roman stage trope, *contaminatio*, which could be called a kind of interlacing between an old play and a new one, has found many distinguished uses in modern drama, particularly by Shaw, Pirandello, and a host of French revisers of the ancients. Tom Stoppard can be called an almost obsessive contaminator, since perhaps no other dramatist relies so crucially upon the trope of interlacing. *Rosencrantz and Guildenstern Are Dead* (1967) was the first of Stoppard's successes, contaminating *Hamlet, Prince of Denmark* with *Waiting for Godot*. The best of Stoppard, *Jumpers* (1972) and *Travesties* (1974), contaminate with more agility, *Jumpers* interlacing Shaw and Robert Dhery (among others), *Travesties* courageously mixing Shakespeare with Wilde's *The Importance of Being Earnest*, with Tristan Tzara, Joyce and Lenin appearing in their proper persons.

Interlacing, depending upon the reader's or playgoer's critical perspective, can be regarded either as a dramatist's defense against precursors (and contemporary rivals) or as the same dramatist's joyous disregard of the literary force of the past. Contamination is another term for influence (which after all began as *influenza,* a supposedly astral disease) except that true literary influence is an involuntary process. A willed influence, or contamination, does seem to me essentially apotropaic, and intends to ward off involuntary influx. Stoppard, a superb theatrical craftsman, sometimes subtly masks his true anxiety of influence (always Samuel Beckett) by seeming to accept the influence, as *Rosencrantz and Guildenstern Are Dead* seems to hold itself open to *Waiting for Godot*. But usually he evades *Endgame* and

Beckett's giant shadow by travestying W. S. Gilbert, Shaw, Wilde, contemporary drama, and (endlessly) Shakespeare.

Thomas Whitaker, Stoppard's best critic, has offered the most generous overview of Stoppard's achievement, in a judgment that almost persuades me:

> At mid-career, Tom Stoppard has amply demonstrated what can be done by a self-styled entertainer who has assimilated the recent tradition of British comedy and learned much from the formal discoveries of the avant-garde. Like W. S. Gilbert, he can parody with ease the absurdities of his time. Like Noel Coward, he keeps his eye on the popular stage as he attends to "those weary, Twentieth Century Blues." Like Bernard Shaw, he knows that the stage at its best does not set before us photographs of "real people" but invites us to participate in stylised explorations of our intellectual and emotional life. And like Oscar Wilde, who was himself far more than an aesthete, Stoppard knows what it means to write "a trivial play for serious people." His wit is often touched by an intellectual chill, a mordant fantasy, or an inarticulate pang that suggests the presence of Samuel Beckett. But his plays also complicate their artifice with various strategies that invite our intimate approach. Eliciting from actors and witnesses a more various participation than either Wilde or Beckett would have endorsed, they begin to turn the theatre itself into the model of a playful community. They ask us to accept as a finality neither Wilde's delightfully brittle world of masks nor Beckett's exhilaratingly austere world of fragmentation and deprivation. Alert to the possibility of dwelling in those worlds among others, they invite us to rediscover the humane balance and freedom that constitute the open secret of play.

Myself a disciple of Wilde and Walter Pater, I do not know what it is to be "far more than an aesthete." Pater and Wilde teach us that an aesthete is "one who perceives," and so the aesthetic critic is necessarily the true critic of her or his time, as the aesthetic poet is the authentic poet of that time. Whether Stoppard merits Whitaker's implicit evaluation as the peer of Wilde and Beckett seems to me very problematic, but Whitaker is certainly accurate in portraying Stoppard's ambitions. When Whitaker names the Player in *Rosencrantz and Guildenstern Are Dead*, Sir Archibald Jumper in *Jumpers*, Tristan Tzara in *Travesties* as Stoppard's "anxious stylists" who "dazzle us with their panache," he avoids the overt statement that they truly are Stoppard's own surrogates. Stoppard himself, in my view, is an anxious stylist who dazzles us with his panache. Such an achievement is already considerable, but whether it is likely to prove permanent is a puzzling matter, which is to say that Harold Pinter, rather than Stoppard, might prove to be Beckett's true son.

II

The study is hardly the proper context even for reading the intensely theatrical Stoppard, since the nature of Stoppard's text always is deliberately somewhat provisional. My own experience is that I benefit more by seeing a new Stoppard play before I read it, though even that procedure did not rescue *The Real Thing* for me, despite the lingering aura of the performances of Glenn Close and Jeremy Irons. In an "author's note" to *Jumpers*, Stoppard asserts that he can give only a "basic version" rather than a "definitive text." Presumably this is related to the antithetical style of discourse that moves him in Beckett. He once spoke of:

> . . . a Beckett joke which is the funniest joke in the world to me. It appears in various forms but it consists of confident statement followed by immediate refutation by the same voice. . . . That sort of Beckettian influence is much more important to me than a mere verbal echo of a line of a parallelism at the end of *Jumpers* . . .

Surely the most important influence is the very idea of the Stoppardian play, which is a Beckettian idea. If there could be a Gnostic drama (and there cannot), then Beckett would write it, as only Kafka could write a Gnostic story (but there is no Gnostic story). The essential tenet of Gnosticism is that the Creation of the world and of mankind, and the Fall of the world and of mankind, were one and the same event. Stoppard, who writes well only in the shadow of Beckett, gives us Gnostic farce (which also barely can be). Whatever my doubts about Stoppard's ultimate eminence, he compels wonder and respect because he too, like Beckett and Kafka, courageously and obsessively attempts what cannot be done.

There is another Stoppard, celebrated by Whitaker as an affirmer of "freedom and moral sensitivity," and by the more positivistic Richard Corballis as a celebrator of "the flux of reality" over "an abstract, artificial view of the world." This Stoppard exists, but he is rather mediocre when compared to the parodist, comedian, and disciple who inherits Beckett's sense of what the Gnostics called the *kenoma*, the cosmic emptiness into which we have been thrown. Here is the last of Rosencrantz and Guildenstern, fading out into that emptiness:

> ROS.: That's it, then, is it?
> *No answer. He looks out front.*
> The sun's going down. Or the earth's coming up, as the fashionable theory has it.
> *Small pause.*
> Not that it makes any difference.

Pause.
What was it all about? When did it begin?
Pause. No answer.
Couldn't we just stay put? I mean no one is going to come on and drag
us off . . . They'll just have to wait. We're still young . . . fit . . .
we've got years . . .
Pause. No answer.
(*A cry.*) We've done nothing wrong! We didn't harm anyone. Did we?
GUIL.: I can't remember.
ROS. *pulls himself together.*
ROS.: All right, then. I don't care. I've had enough. To tell you the truth,
I'm relieved.
And he disappears from view. GUIL. *does not notice.*
GUIL.: Our names shouted in a certain dawn . . . a message . . . a summons
. . . There must have been a moment, at the beginning, where we
could have said—no. But somehow we missed it. (*He looks around
and sees he is alone.*)
Rosen—?
Guil—?
He gathers himself.
Well, we'll know better next time. Now you see me, now you— (*and
disappears*).

It is admirable, but not contaminated enough, since all too clearly
we are in the abyss of Beckett's *Endgame.* And it is not so much Shakespeare's timeserving courtiers who are thrown into that abyss as it is Vladimir
and Estragon, so that the true title might as well be *Rosencrantz and Guildenstern Are Waiting for Godot.* But the true title of *Jumpers* is *Jumpers,*
perhaps because the theaters of W. S. Gilbert and of Ionesco so pungently
contaminate the theater of Beckett. Absurdist farce proves to be Stoppard's
best mode, as in the first encounter of Sir Archibald Jumper and Inspector
Bones:

ARCHIE: Ah! Good morning!
(ARCHIE *moves to come out from the bed. Meanwhile* DOTTY *looks over the
top.*)
DOTTY: Lunch! And Bonesy!
(ARCHIE *picks his coat up and hands it to* BONES, *and then readies himself to
put his arms in the sleeves, as though* BONES *were a manservant.*)
ARCHIE (*slipping on his coat*): Thank you so much. Rather warm in there.
The lights, you know.
DOTTY: Isn't he sweet?
ARCHIE: Charming. What happened to Mrs. Whatsername?
DOTTY: No, no, it's Bonesy!
BONES: Inspector Bones, C.I.D.

DOTTY (*disappearing*): Excuse me!

ARCHIE: Bones . . . ? I had a patient named Bones. I wonder if he was any relation?—an osteopath.

BONES: My brother!

ARCHIE: Remember the case well. Cognomen Syndrome. My advice to him was to take his wife's maiden name of Foot and carry on from there.

BONES: He took your advice but unfortunately he got interested in chiropody. He is now in an asylum near Uxbridge.

ARCHIE: Isn't that interesting? I must write him up. The Cognomen Syndrome is my baby, you know.

BONES: You discovered it?

ARCHIE: I've got it. Jumper's the name—my card.

BONES (*reading off card*): "Sir Archibald Jumper, M.D., D.Phil., D.Litt., L.D., D.P.M., D.P.T. (Gym)" . . . What's all that?

ARCHIE: I'm a doctor of medicine, philosophy, literature and law, with diplomas in psychological medicine and P.T. including gym.

BONES: (*handing back the card*): I see that you are the Vice-Chancellor of Professor Moore's university.

ARCHIE: Not a bad record, is it? And I can still jump over seven feet.

BONES: High jump?

ARCHIE: Long jump. My main interest, however, is the trampoline.

BONES: Mine is show business generally.

ARCHIE: Really? Well, nowadays, of course, I do more theory than practice, but if trampoline acts appeal to you at all, a vacancy has lately occurred in a little team I run, mainly for our own amusement with a few social engagements thrown in—

The Cognomen Syndrome is worthy of Ionesco, and Archie's voiced qualifications are from the world of W. S. Gilbert. Perhaps only the trampoline is Stoppard's own, but in farce at so sublimely exuberant a level all indebtedness can be discounted. Alas, *Jumpers* is unmatched elsewhere in Stoppard. *Travesties* comes closest, particularly in the agon of James Joyce and Tristan Tzara, where most critics have given the victory to Tzara, who speaks with the exuberance of Shaw's surrogates, as he denounces Joyce's aestheticism:

Your art has failed. You've turned literature into a religion and it's as dead as all the rest, it's an overripe corpse and you're cutting fancy figures at the wake. It's too late for geniuses! Now we need vandals and desecrators, simple-minded demolition men to smash centuries of baroque subtlety, to bring down the temple, and thus finally, to reconcile the shame and the necessity of being an artist!

In contrast, Stoppard's Joyce is a failure, and his credo lacks a countervailing eloquence:

An artist is the magician put among men to gratify—capriciously—their urge for immortality. The temples are built and brought down around him, continuously and contiguously from Troy to the fields of Flanders. If there is any meaning in any of it, it is in what survives as art . . .

Though we are told that Stoppard regards this as the most important moment in his play, it is clearly a failure in contamination, an interlacing that does not work. *Travesties* is a splendid notion not properly worked through, though its triple agon of Modernism against Dada against Lenin's ardor has given it an inevitable panache. Stoppard remains one of the most audacious legatees of Modernism, and at forty-eight is hardly to be judged as being beyond the centerpoint of his theatrical quest.

ALLAN RODWAY

Stoppard's Comic Philosophy

In *Rosencrantz and Guildenstern Are Dead* (1967) and even more in *Jumpers* (1972) both themes and subject-matter are philosophical. The questions they ask suggest a need to get back to base: What is it to be "human"? What is identity, and its relation to impersonal structures or manipulation? Is there any place for idealism in a scientific, rationalistic world? Above all, how do we know if the answers are right? What, indeed, is knowledge: how do we know we really *know* what we think we know?

In the first play, these questions are not quite clearly sorted out. Like *Hamlet* itself it conveys a sense of the author's having bitten off a little more than he can chew; nor does the triple-perspective structure (of *Hamlet*, the Players, and the world of Rosencrantz and Guildenstern) help in such realisation. It does, however, help to emphasise the difficulty of knowing what is "real" or what "reality" is; and this is valuable, for Stoppard's comedy mainly purports to demonstrate the absurdity of dogmatic assurance. Like Joyce's, his work is balanced, but in a different way, and for a different reason.

Joyce made an immense effort to "prove on the pulses"—by sharing the experience of deeply explored, finely rendered characters—that certain values *were* better than others, though man-made not God-given. Stoppard's "distance" carried him further from humanity, not to cynicism or hardhearted amorality like Waugh, but to the philosophical problems underlying human ones. Stoppard has crystallised the modern writer's incertitude into the clear recognition that there is *a problem of knowledge*, perhaps insoluble. He is a genuine, thoughtful "Don't-know" of a humane tem-

From *English Comedy: Its Role and Nature from Chaucer to the Present Day*. Copyright © 1975 by Allan Rodway. University of California Press.

perament. Naturally such comedies of incertitude carry no positive message, but rather the implicit negative one that cocksure manipulation of others, systematic or dogmatic, regardless of their feelings, seems unwarrantable. However, his philosophic neutrality does seem to incline just a little to one side, enough to suggest that scientific rationalism has no better claim to cocksureness than metaphysical idealism had.

The distance established between themes and characters, and between the author and both, means that Stoppard's comedy, like Waugh's in this one respect, can tolerate a great deal of farce and divertisement. Deep questions can be, and are, combined with a surface capable of rolling an audience in the aisles. *Rosencrantz and Guildenstern*, for example, brings in the question of pragmatism and metaphysics in the guise of Bloomian (and Everyman's) scientific thinking:

> GUILDENSTERN (*clears his throat*): In the morning the sun would be easterly.
>   I think we can assume that.
> ROSENCRANTZ: That it's morning?
> GUILDENSTERN: If it is, and the sun is over *there* (*his right as he faces the audience*) for instance, *that* (*front*) would be northerly. On the other hand, if it is not morning and the sun is over *there* (*his left*) . . . *that* . . . (*lamely*) would *still* be northerly. (*picking up*). To put it another way, if we came from down there (*front*) and it is morning, the sun would be up there (*his left*) and if it is actually over *there* (*his right*) and it's still morning, we must have come from up *there* (*behind him*), and if *that* is southerly (*his left*) and the sun is really over *there* (*front*), then it's the afternoon. However, if none of these is the case—
> ROSENCRANTZ: Why don't you go and have a look?
> GUILDENSTERN: Pragmatism?!—is that all you have to offer? You seem to have no conception of where we stand! You won't find the answer written down for you in the bowl of a compass—I can tell you that. (*Pause.*) Besides, you can never tell this far north—it's probably dark out there.
>
>   (Act II)

A paradigm of the official rebuke is imagined so:

> ROSENCRANTZ: To sum up: your father whom you love, dies, you are his heir, you come back to find that hardly was the corpse cold before his young brother popped on to his throne and into his sheets, thereby offending both legal and natural practice. Now why exactly are you behaving in this extraordinary manner?
>
>   (Act I)

And very naturally then the logic of uncertainty is theatrically conveyed in this flippant way:

ROSENCRANTZ: He has moods.
PLAYER: Of moroseness?
GUILDENSTERN: Madness. And yet.
ROSENCRANTZ: Quite.
GUILDENSTERN: For instance.
ROSENCRANTZ: He talks to himself, which might be madness.
GUILDENSTERN: If he didn't talk sense, which he does.
ROSENCRANTZ: Which suggests the opposite.
PLAYER: Of what?
    (*Small pause.*)
GUILDENSTERN: I think I have it. A man talking sense to himself is no
    madder than a man talking nonsense not to himself.
ROSENCRANTZ: Or just as mad.
GUILDENSTERN: Or just as mad.
ROSENCRANTZ: And he does both.
GUILDENSTERN: So there you are.
ROSENCRANTZ: Stark raving sane.

        (Act II)

What is common to these examples, and to all other cases of this comic philosophy, is that any hint of a solution to the problem implied is immediately undermined. Thus the coin business raises the possibility that they are outside natural law, the creations of some god-Shakespeare, but the logic leading to that conclusion patently collapses and leaves the question open. So, too, the business of interpenetrating stage-worlds leaves open the questions whether we are all actors ("the opposite of people"), whether the manipulators ("Wheels have been set in motion, and they have their own pace, to which we are . . . condemned") are themselves manipulated, or whether we are all puppets in a deterministic machine, and whether we can know when we are being authentic, real, as against performing for an audience. So too the swiftness with which the two protagonists cease to know which is which, leaves open the question whether or not personal identity depends on one's habitat.

By setting *Jumpers* in a recognisable modern environment and making the chief characters professional university philosophers of different schools of thought, Stoppard has been able to clarify the questions, and even hint at an answer. It is in this play that the slight inclination of his balance becomes noticeable. Recognisable environment and characters, however, by no means make it a realistic play. In keeping with the philosophic preoccupation and the need for distance—so that we see the problems rather than feel with the characters—its mode is that of metaphorical and highly fictional comedy, the mood, satirical and humorous—satirical about Archie, dandy leader of the scientific rationalists (as we may stereotype the Jumpers), humorous about George Moore (the Third), dishevelled metaphysician fighting a losing battle against these acrobats. It is in this difference of mood that the inclination of Stoppard's comic balance is most evident. The chief method is that of travesty: texturally of philosophic debate, structurally of the detective story, the two being mutually supporting, since both are concerned with trying to *find out* (neither, however, in this comedy of incertitude, being successful). What is to be found out, essentially, is whether the metaphysical standpoint is still tenable. And closely connected with this is the problem of knowledge . . .

Like the mystery of who murdered McFee, the metaphysical theme and the truth theme come to no clear conclusion—unless it is a clear conclusion that neither is an open-and-shut case. George's contorted attempt to prove the existence of God by adapting Zeno's mathematics—doomed to failure anyway as math's is a world of ideas (which, like wishes, are not horses) and existence is an empirical matter—reaches a triumphant, logical, but self-cancelling conclusion in the proposition that God exists but is nought. On the other hand, when be abandons logic, he does make a telling point or two, thus:

DOTTY: Archie says the Church is a monument to irrationality.
GEORGE: . . . The National Gallery is a monument to irrationality! Every concert hall is a monument to irrationality!—and so is a nicely kept garden, or a lover's favour, or a home for stray dogs! You stupid woman, if rationality were the criterion for things being allowed to exist, the world would be one gigantic field of soya beans! . . . The irrational, the emotional, the whimsical . . . these are the stamp of humanity which makes reason a civilizing force. In a wholly rational society the moralist will be a variety of crank, haranguing the bus queue with the demented certitude of one blessed with privileged information—'Good and evil are metaphysical absolutes!'

(Act I)

But of course this is no answer to Archie's rational linguistic analysis of the problem of moral absolutes, as reported by Dotty in reply:

. . . Things do not *seem*, on the one hand, they *are*: and on the other hand, bad is not what they can *be*. They can be green, or square, or Japanese, loud, fatal, waterproof, or vanilla-flavoured; and the same for actions, which can be *disapproved of*, or comical, unexpected, saddening, or good television, variously, depending on who frowns, laughs, jumps, weeps, or wouldn't have missed it for the world. Things and actions, you understand, can have any number of real and verifiable properties. But good and bad, better and worse, these are not real properties of things, they are just expressions of our feelings about them.

What in fact calls the Jumpers' viewpoint in question is the practical effects their logic leads to. Dotty, for instance, seems to have been driven dotty by *science*, which has bleached out romance for her (signified by her horror at the astronauts on the moon who render her no longer capable of singing her spoony Juney moon songs), and by *reason* (George's philosophical remoteness having made her frigid, Archie's glib management having corrupted her into conniving at murder and supporting the sinister Rad.-Lib. Party). Her next speech, in fact, well conveys a sense of inescapable loss, and a deep need for something that nevertheless has to be abandoned since it cannot be justified by science or reason:

> . . . If you like I won't see him. It'll be just you and me under that old-fashioned, silvery harvest moon, occasionally blue, jumped over by cows and coupleted by Junes, invariably shining on the one I love; . . . *Keat's* bloody moon!—for what has made the sage or poet write but the fair paradise of nature's light—and *Milton's* bloody moon! rising in clouded majesty, at length apparent queen, unveiled her peerless light and o'er the dark her silver mantle threw—And Shelley's sodding maiden, with white fire laden, whom mortals call thee—(*weeping*) *Oh yes, things were in place then!*

The very last words of the play are Dotty's "Goodbye spoony Juney Moon" "and," one inwardly seems to hear by that time, "Hail, cost-efficiency!"

The play begins with a brilliant *coup de théâtre*: the Secretary, at the Rad.-Lib. victory party, swinging by her legs from a trapeze "*between darkness and darkness . . . into the spotlight and out*" doing a striptease. In retrospect, surely, a symbol of Truth, the naked truth, seen only in glimpses, flashes of illumination, and never quite whole (she crashes into the butler before the strip is completed). She never speaks during the whole course of the play (the truth is not self-explanatory). She is the mistress of McFee the arch-rationalist and the secretary of George Moore. Both press her into service, as it were, but in different ways, or, she "takes down" for both, but in different senses. Both sides, that is to say, are theatrically seen to possess part of the truth, but neither knows the Whole Truth. There really is a problem of knowledge; and that is why nothing in the play is resolved: not the murder, not the status of Archie (glib self-seeker or necessary clever cynic?), not his relationship with Dotty (doctor or lover?). Indeed the whole movement of the work is appropriately Zeno-like, always approaching a conclusion, never reaching it. The two acts and the coda abound in uproarious slapstick (e.g. with the body), travesty (of police business and, in the Coda, of Justice), and of psychological and logical wit—and almost all of it, when examined, turns out, like the striptease, to be relevant to the main themes. The action, too, is clever, funny, and relevant. Indeed, since there is no answer in theory to the metaphysical problem—poised between arguments contradictorily entailing "that though an arrow is always approaching its target, it never quite gets there, and Saint Sebastian died of fright," and that ". . . the first term of the series is not an infinite fraction but *zero*. It exists. God, so to speak, is nought"—the answer, or rather tendency, has to be given in practice, reality, where action naturally looms large.

The Party victory and the affair of the astronauts (in which the up-to-date rational Captain Oates clobbers his companion, climbs into the damaged spacecraft, and gets to safety), together with their consequences, represent *applied* philosophy and *applied* science. It is these which cause McFee to doubt his own standpoint (and, perhaps, bring about his murder as a traitor):

> CROUCH: It was the astronauts fighting on the Moon that finally turned him, sir. Henry, he said to me, Henry, I am giving philosophical respectability to a new pragmatism in public life, of which there have been many disturbing examples both here and on the moon . . . he kept harking back to the first Captain Oates . . . Henry, he said, . . . if altruism is a possibility, my argument is up a gum-tree . . . Duncan, I said, Duncan, don't you worry your head about all that. That astronaut yobbo is good for twenty years hard. Yes, he said, yes *maybe*, but when he comes out, he's going to find he was only twenty years ahead of his time. I have seen the future, Henry, he said; and it's yellow.
>
> (Act II)

Human emotions, it would seem, are not easily to be *permanently* caught in the web of rationalism and science. A point confirmed by one argument of George's that is subtle without being self-cancelling or muddled—though it does have to concede *most* of the case against goodness as an absolute. The speech, too long to quote in full, comes in a theatrically insistent place at the end of Act I:

> . . . Professor McFee . . . goes on to show . . . that the word "good" has also meant different things to different people at different times, an exercise which combines simplicity with futility in a measure he does not apparently suspect, for on the one hand it is not a statement which anyone would dispute, and on the other, nothing useful can be inferred from it. It is not in fact a statement about value at all; it is a statement about language and how it is used in a particular society. . . . Certainly a tribe which believes it confers honour on its elders by eating them is going to be viewed askance by another which prefers to buy them a little bungalow

somewhere, and Professor McFee should not be surprised that the notion of honour should manifest itself so differently in peoples so far removed in clime and culture. What is surely more surprising is that notions such as honour should manifest themselves at all. For what *is* honour? What are pride, shame, fellow-feeling, generosity, and love? If they are instincts, what are instincts? . . . what can be said to be the impulse of a genuinely altruistic act? Hobbes might have answered self-esteem, but what is the attraction of thinking better of oneself? What is *better*? A savage who elects to honour his father by eating him, as opposed to disposing of his body in some—to him—ignominious way, for example by burying it in a teak box, is making an ethical choice in that he believes himself to be acting as a good savage ought to act. Whence comes this sense of some actions being better than others?—not more useful, or more convenient or more popular, but simply pointlessly *better*? What, in short, is so good about *good*? Professor McFee succeeds only in showing us that in different situations different actions will be deemed, rightly or wrongly, to be conducive to that good which is independent of time and place and which is knowable but not nameable. It is not nameable because it is not another way of referring to this or that quality which we have decided is virtuous . . . The irreducible fact of goodness is not implicit in one kind of action any more than in its opposite, but in the existence of a relationship between the two. It is the sense of comparisons being in order.

A subtle and profound conclusion not undermined by the ivory-towerism that leads George to ignore Dotty's cries of Help, Rape, Murder; whereas Archie's cool attention to it does undermine his human credibility as a man to follow:

ARCHIE: It's all right—just exhibitionism: what we psychiatrists call 'a cry for help.'

BONES: But it *was* a cry for help.

ARCHIE: Perhaps I'm not making myself clear. *All* exhibitionism is a cry for help, but a cry for help *as such* is only exhibitionism.

Such speeches, and such actions as his Pooh-Bah manipulation of a multiplicity of official positions to get away with murder (perhaps), do tend to discredit him as logic is not able to.

Nevertheless, the Coda forms a Conclusion in which nothing is concluded. George Moore's concern for absolute values, universal truths, is once again shown to be a sort of fiddling while Rome burns, Clegthorpe's conversion may, but equally may not, show hope in humanity's capacity for transcending self-interest. Like Thomas à Becket, he changes character with the office, but also like Becket he is disposed of, as was the other renegade Radical Liberal, McFee. The final word—apart from Dotty's one-line song—is left with Archie; and a very callous, sane, and balanced statement it seems to be. But it gets a hint of taint from all we have seen of the Jumpers before, and its own conclusion. "Wham, bam, thank you Sam," suggests a cynical theatricality. In fact it has to be taken in some degree ironically. The audience is balanced not, in the end, between two viewpoints, as in the beginning, but between belief and scepticism: belief in the facts (or most of them) and scepticism about the speaker:

> ARCHIE: Do not despair—many are happy much of the time; more eat than starve, more are healthy than sick, more curable than dying; not so many dying as dead; and one of the thieves was saved. Hell's bells and all's well—half the world is at peace with itself, and so is the other half; vast areas are unpolluted; millions of children grow up without suffering deprivation, and millions, while deprived, grow up without suffering cruelties, and millions, while deprived and cruelly treated, none the less grow up. No laughter is sad and many tears are joyful. At the graveside the undertaker doffs his top hat and impregnates the prettiest mourner. Wham, bam, thank you Sam.

So does the play finally imply that "the great human comedy in which each has share" may still have a happy ending, that under the dominion of the three thick-skinned giants of our day, totalitarianism, technology, and bureaucracy, we may still make life worth while, aided by the weapon of wit, the resilience of humour, the mockery of laughter, the critical distance of comedy? Well, accordant to a time even more menaced than his, the last word is clearly not a Joycean *Yes*, but something more appropriate to a comedy, and time, of such incertitude. Perhaps *Perhaps* . . .

BRIAN M. CROSSLEY

An Investigation of Stoppard's "Hound" and "Foot"

... All the plays that have ever been written, from ancient Greece to
the present day, have never been anything but thrillers. Drama's
always been realistic and there's always been a detective about. Every
play's an investigation brought to a successful conclusion.

—from *Victims of Duty*

It is the parodic and satirically self-referential quality of Tom Stoppard's plays that sets him apart from the Juvenalian playwrights of the fifties. Whereas Osborne uses anger as a means of attack upon the world, Stoppard remains the theatrical critic and aims his derision at the mores of drama, and especially at the age-old detective figure of Sophocles' Oedipus. Turning the tradition against itself is the main thrust of his aesthetic attack. Using the modern preoccupation with absurdity and *Angst*, he strikes home at such figures as T.S. Eliot and his "overwhelming question," which is not to be asked, which one dare not ask, for perhaps there is no answer or only such an answer as it would be better not to know. Stoppard makes games of these notions by the old theatrical trick of inverting them. Throughout his plays the serious forms of the dramatized detective story are reduced to cartoon-like scenes which

From *Modern Drama* 1, vol. 20 (March 1977): 77–86. Copyright © 1977 by University of Toronto.

humorously strip away the conventions on which they are founded. Even the highly visual comic effects appear to mock both blind justice and the Oedipus myth.

Questions of recognition and reality provide the central mystery of *The Real Inspector Hound.* In terms of the detective story, the title appears to make it plain what this work is to be about. The sleuth as a kind of "bloodhound" is a hunting phrase long since ridden to death. Yet beyond this cliché is the title's ambiguous suggestion of an inspector who is, somehow, not real. By creating a play-within-a-play, Stoppard produces a kind of double vision which challenges the validity of the real itself.

Whatever the play's classical antecedents, as a parody of the murder-mystery form, *The Real Inspector Hound* finds its target in a contemporary play, that most famous of all stage whodunits, Agatha Christie's *The Mousetrap.* Stoppard's work parallels this popular play at virtually all its crucial points. For example, we are invited to discover "who done it?" only to find that the detective plays two roles, sleuth and slayer. The situation is further complicated in Stoppard's version by the dual roles of Moon and Birdboot as audience and players. And in the travesty of an ending, the order-bringing figure of the detective unleashes bloody anarchy on both the innocent and the guilty. As lame ducks, Moon and Birdboot are shot down with the kind of relish found mainly in fairground shooting galleries.

Stoppard repeatedly sets up the standard classical thriller situations with the deliberate intention of knocking them down. For example, the action of the play takes place in an isolated country house. Mrs. Drudge, the servant, in answering the telephone summarizes the play and a thousand others like it:

> Hello, the drawing-room of Lady Muldoon's country residence one morning in early spring? . . . Hello!—the draw—Who? Who did you wish to speak to? I'm afraid there is no one of that name here, this is all very mysterious and I'm sure it's leading up to something. I hope nothing is amiss for we, that is Lady Muldoon and her houseguests, are here cut off from the world, including Mangus, the wheelchair-ridden half-brother of her ladyship's husband Lord Albert Muldoon who ten years ago went out for a walk on the cliffs and was never seen again—

Added to this scene, with its convenient French window, are an unexpected guest (the cad Simon), an all-enveloping mist, and a police message over the radio. Apart from the pseudo-serious tone of the announcement, the call emphasizes terminal situations, death, and lunacy, all of which are undercut by the final, incongruous use of the word "madman" and the ridiculous appeal to his *reason*:

Essex county police are still searching in vain for the madman who is at
large in the deadly marshes of the coastal region. Inspector Hound, who
is masterminding the operation, is not available for comment but it is
widely believed that he has a secret plan. . . . Meanwhile police and
volunteers are combing the swamps with loud-hailers, shouting, "Don't
be a madman, give yourself up." That is the end of the police message.

The terminal situations are clearly self-referential, as we discover; and the
fact that the play takes place over a dead body adds to the farce. In a more
serious vein, the underlying figure of the corpse on stage makes the gyrations
of the actors those of the dance of death, preparing us for the final macabre
event when their bodies clutter the stage as the curtain falls. The situation
of the old house reinforces this point: strangely, it has no roads leading
from it; set among the marshes, it too is a dead end. Stoppard is leading
us all up the garden path in order to show us that the detective play has
come, in every sense, to the end of the road. Thus, the well-made thriller
is nominally and theatrically "Hounded" to death, while the kind of fatuous
critiques of *The Real Inspector Hound,* especially those of the critic Birdboot,
are shown to be a dead letter.

Watching this play-within-a-play are two typical drama critics,
Moon and Birdboot. We hear in the facile proclamations of these two
critics, a language which is no longer vital. For Birdboot the play they
witness is "A rattling good evening out," including "a performance which
I consider to be one of the summits in the range of contemporary theatre.
In what is possibly the finest Cynthia since the war—" For Moon, symbolic
searches are rewarding: "I think we will find that within the austere frame-
work of what is seen to be on one level a country-house week-end, and
what a useful symbol that is, the author has given . . . us the human
condition—." The critical language they use throughout merely echoes the
hackneyed dialogue of the play they review. The fact of their actual involvement on stage thereafter is, in effect, an extension in deed of their
semantic complicity.

The semantic satire in implicating the internal audience of *The Real
Inspector Hound,* that is Birdboot and Moon, is most clearly evident in the
kinds of praise they lavish on the play and its players. Birdboot's ravings
about Cynthia inform us that she has "More talent in her little finger—"
and that in her case it is "—a public scandal that the Birthday Honours
to date have neglected—." Caught up in Birdboot's personal enthusiasm,
Moon, as his name implies, waxes eloquent, though the tenor of his speech
wanes into an absurd kind of library catalogue. In exaggerated terms he
declares his critical assessment of this trite detective drama:

> Faced as we are with such ubiquitous obliquity, it is hard, it is hard indeed, and therefore I will not attempt, to refrain from invoking the names of Kafka, Sartre, Shakespeare, St. Paul, Beckett, Birkett, Pinero, Pirandello, Dante and Dorothy L. Sayers.

Thus, Birdboot and Moon are a travesty of the kind of critic that William Empson types as "barking dogs," in that "they merely relieve themselves against the flower of beauty." Stoppard, in parodying the detective form, is like the other sorts, who, like Empson himself, "afterwards scratch it up." The play, then, does not gain added existential or humanistic significance from the flowery phrases Moon utters; rather, it sends up the notion of such notions, makes game of the question "Where is God?" or reminders of Voltaire.

Lineal descendants of Rosencrantz and Guildenstern, Moon and Birdboot become fatally involved in the action they too have been called on to unravel. The dramatic irony in *Hound* works in much the same perverse way as it does in *Rosencrantz and Guildenstern are Dead*. When Birdboot condescendingly remarks that the play on stage will have "a startling denouement," that "it has a beginning, a middle, and I have no doubt it will prove to have an end," he is unaware of the enormity of this platitude as it will affect him. Moon is also more of a Cassandra-like figure than he realizes, and although his opening piece of professional opinion is more applicable to *Hamlet* than to the play in question, he too will be a victim of his own prophecy:

> Already in the opening stages we note the classic impact of the catalystic figure—the outsider—plunging through to the centre of an ordered world and setting up disruptions—the shock waves—which unless I am much mistaken, will strip these comfortable people—these crustaceans in the rock pool of society—strip them of their shells and leave them exposed as the trembling raw meat which, at heart, is all of us. But there is more to it than that—

Satirically, the play does just that; it exposes and undermines both critics as they become an integral part of the action, the private off-stage philandering of Birdboot leading to public exposure on stage.

Both off and on stage, Birdboot and Moon try to detect "who done it." As detectives they are about as competent as they are as critics, and in searching for what is true within the play, they reveal what is false about themselves. Beguiled into the Inspector's role, Moon attempts to solve the mystery and put "the final pieces of the jigsaw" into place. Yet Moon himself has no firm place in the play. Three times he changes roles. As critic turned actor turned detective, Moon is always playing a losing part. As detective, he gives a long "conclusive" summary of events which is as fatuous as his critical appraisal earlier. On the other hand, the triple role-playing of Puckeridge, disguised as Mangus, reveals him to be the successful Inspector Hound. If the well-meaning Moon is the Polonius of the play, Puckeridge, throwing off his disguise and invalid disposition, is its Hamlet, who stage-manages his own murders. Like *Hamlet*, this play ends with corpses littering the stage. In this burlesque of tragic endings, the final resolution is that provided by the summary justice of the gun.

In *The Real Inspector Hound* Stoppard has dissolved the distinction between stage and stalls, and though the play's novelty appears to rest, for the most part, on the fact that his critical audience venture onto the stage and become embroiled in the action, as the rhetoric used on and off stage has shown, the division is an artificial one in the first place.

The division between Moon's failure and Birdboot's success as critic, between players and audience, between mystery and solution, furthers a kind of Platonic dualism and the concept of question and answer. Yet the numerous questions the two critics raise during the course of the play, questions which Moon claims they are "entitled to ask," are not finally answered but confounded and nullified. Their attempts to define into reality a lunatic situation are as farcical as they are futile. The very notion of "entitlement" is itself a false prerogative founded upon conventions of order which the play deliberately reduces to nonsense. With Felicity's "huff," Mangus's "ruff," and Birdboot's "bluff," they succeed in blowing down a play which is as fragile as a house built of playing cards, and which, crazily enough, falls on their heads with deadly consequences.

The personal desires and aspirations of Moon and Birdboot become interchangeable parts in the language and mechanisms of the thriller. For all their righteousness, Moon and Birdboot are caught in an endgame situation in which they unwittingly implicate and condemn themselves. "Certainly the same could be said of Rosencrantz and Guildenstern and *Hamlet*. When they grasp the artist's metaphor it is too late. The script is written; there is nothing to be done. Like Rosencrantz and Guildenstern, Moon and Birdboot are dead because the play calls for their death." Both the detective play and its commentators have confounded each other at last, and generically Stoppard has brought about a mercy killing.

In so far as *After Magritte* is a search for some kind of veracity by a detective figure, it is a sequel to *Hound*, but unlike the previous play it is wholly comic. However, Stoppard's concern and formal approach remain unchanged. Instead of the sinister implications of an Inspector named Hound, we have, in Foot of the Yard, a schoolboy pun which nominally implies a "flat-foot" and a smaller unit of measurement within a larger one. The name Foot also parodies, on both the thematic and generic levels, the name of the theatre's first great detective, Oedipus. Moreover, the name Foot, in this play, is wildly exaggerated for comic effect. For example, Mother's "burnt foot," "football," and "ballroom dancing" steadily maintain an emphasis on this member, with ridiculous consequences for Inspector Foot. Harris asks, "Is something the matter with your foot, Foot?/ Inspector, Foot?/ You wish to inspect your foot, Inspector?" The parody of the detective genre is carried through to both the name and the misguided actions of Foot's assistant. When the rationalizing Guildenstern assured the more elementary minded Rosencrantz that their dilemma could be resolved, we were reminded of the postures of Holmes and Watson. In *After Magritte*, the roles of Holmes and Watson are not simply inverted; in case the point is missed, Stoppard calls his police constable Holmes.

The recurrent theme of investigation becomes again more than a vehicle for exploration, identification, and resolution; it manifests itself in the form of a total dramatic construct. *After Magritte* asks questions of life's apparent absurdities; it seeks for explanations which in turn raise more questions than they answer. The circularity of this domestic comedy plays with the nature of point of view, and the reliability of witness and testimony. It is a detective story which turns its satiric aim at the authority figure of the police Inspector and at this inquisitor's methodology. The self-revelatory and self-defeating nature of Foot's investigation parallels and parodies the Oedipus myth which it tantalizingly evokes. But the setting and characters belong to what might be called the low mimetic reminiscent of Aristophanes.

Police Constable Holmes is, initially, like Moon and Birdboot, an onlooker to the scene on stage. The extraordinary scene he witnesses through the Harris window sets the tone for the rest of the action in which he too becomes inextricably involved. Stoppard gives the following stage directions about the Harris family of this Magritte-like household:

> MOTHER *is lying on her back on the ironing board, her head to Stage R, her down-stage foot up against the flat of the iron. A white bath towel covers her from ankle to chin. Her head and part of her face are concealed in a tight-fitting black rubber bathing cap. A black bowler hat reposes on her stomach. She could be dead; but is not.*

Thelma Harris, her daughter-in-law, "is dressed in a full-length ballgown," and she "is discovered on her hands and knees . . . staring at the floor," and occasionally sniffing. Reginald Harris is seen "standing on the wooden chair. His torso is bare, but underneath his thigh-length green rubber fishing waders he *wears his black evening dress trousers."* He is preoccupied with *"blowing slowly and deliberately up into the recess of the shade"* of the lamp he is fixing. To complete this surreal tableau, *"Most of the furniture is stacked up against the street door in a sort of barricade."*

By the time P.C. Holmes's report has brought Inspector Foot racing onto the scene, the "bizarre spectacle" of the Harris household is back in order; normality has been resumed. Deflated, but not defeated, Foot begins his search for clues. The first of the various searches is the ludicrous one for the search warrant Foot claims to have "dropped." Added to the physical search are Foot's imaginative re-creation and explanation of the scene witnessed by P.C. Holmes. It is these flights of fancy based on circumstantial evidence that introduce a note of absurdity into the dialogue: "I have reason to believe that within the last hour in this room' you performed without anaesthetic an illegal operation on a bald nigger minstrel about five-foot-two. . . . " Foot goes on to warn a bemused Harris that: "The D.P.P. is going to take a very poor view if you have been offering cut-price amputations to immigrants." This line of questioning leads directly into the quarrel between Harris and his wife, and thematically becomes the main focus of the play's inquiry.

The mysterious figure seen by the family earlier in the day is the cause of bitter argument between Harris and his wife. What Harris has witnessed with his "own eyes" is:

> . . . an old man with one leg and a white beard, dressed in pyjamas, hopping along in the rain with a tortoise under his arm and brandishing a white stick to clear a path through those gifted with sight—

The same apparition appears to Thelma as a "one-legged footballer" wearing a striped shirt and "carrying a football under his arm" while "waving an ivory cane." Harris claims the man had a white beard; Thelma claims his face was covered in shaving foam. Mother's version adds to the confusion; her eye-witness account of this mock kind of Tiresias figure intrigues Foot in an unexpected way:

> He was playing hopscotch on the corner, a man in the loose-fitting striped gaberdine of a convicted felon. He carried a handbag under one arm, and with the other he waved at me with a cricket bat.

Added to this, it appears that the man in question "was wearing dark glasses, and a surgical mask." Detective Foot conjectures from other information received that:

> . . . shortly after two o'clock this afternoon, the talented though handicapped doyen of the Victoria Palace Happy Minstrel Troupe emerged

from his dressing-room in blackface, and entered the sanctum of the box-office staff; whereupon, having broken his crutch over the heads of those good ladies, the intrepid uniped made off with the advance takings stuffed into a crocodile boot. . . .

Foot's labored illustrations and the theoretical observations which accompany them destroy the coherence of an argument which they do nothing to further; as so often in this play, there is no recognizable development of thought to justify the verbal complexity. This verbal shadow-boxing is a shadow without a substance, and ultimately self-defeating. Foot is floored, in every sense of the word, during the cross-examination, as the search for Thelma's lost needle goes on. He too is reduced to crawling around in "hunt the needle" after the search for the search warrant proves to be fruitless. The deliberate use in *After Magritte* of the needle–hunting game makes fun of the play's own attempts at self-referential subplots and motifs. Here is an instance, then, of the play parodying both itself and the structural metaphors germane to the activity of the detective play. Foot, too, like Moon and Birdboot in *Hound*, is drawn into the action he has come to solve. He finds himself unwittingly changing the light bulb, and thereby re-enacts Harris's part; and his hypothetical reconstruction of the crime is also discredited. The light, as symbol of enlightenment, is constantly swinging before our eyes; the blackouts and dimly lit episodes are all obvious commentaries on the state of the investigation in progress.

Reinforcing the structural metaphors, Stoppard makes flagrant use of the theatre's props as a means of showing up the fact that they are merely devices. For all its idiosyncrasies, *After Magritte* is more than a well-made play, and although the timing may be perfect, the crazy clockwork is deliberately exposed. The props serve multiple purposes: overworked and juxtaposed incongruously they function as a challenge to our well-made sense of perception and flaunt our conditioned responses to the conventions of the theatre.

As Foot's role is gradually reduced to that of the play's fool, tuba-playing mother Harris assumes the role of detective. It is her pertinent questions which prove that the detective is, like Oedipus, the man he is looking for. Ironically, it is the detective's confession that solves the mystery about the antics and attire of the one-legged man. Illegally parked, after a night out, Foot hurried out to remove his car when he saw a traffic warden approaching:

I flung down my razor and rushed into the street, pausing only to grab my wife's handbag containing the small change and her parasol to keep off the rain— . . . and I couldn't move fast because in my haste to pull up my pyjama trousers I put both feet into the same leg. So after hopping about a bit and nearly dropping the handbag into various puddles, I just thought to hell with it all and went back in the house.

If all the odd circumstances finally fit into a pattern of events, the surreal tableau of the finale appears to deny the rationality of such a scheme. The end of the play is another version of the opening pose. Thus, there is a deliberate attempt to re-create in the audience the sense of "this is where we came in." This circularity of design therefore denies in *After Magritte* the sense of an ending.

Stoppard's drawing of the play's close is similar to its opening. Mother's stance is again very odd, to say the least: "*standing on her good foot only, on the wooden chair which is placed on the table; a woollen sock on one hand; playing the tuba.*" Foot's attempts to relieve his migraine consist of wearing sunglasses and "*eating banana.*" He wears his sock on the other hand in order to hold the hot light bulb, thus leaving detective Foot "*with one bare foot.*" Harris, in order to prove whether a one-legged blind man can actually stand unaided, is "*blindfolded with a cushion cover over his head, arms outstretched, on one leg, counting.*" Thelma is repeating her search: in a state of undress, she is "*crawling around the table, scanning the floor and sniffing.*" This, then, is the bizarre scene Holmes witnesses when he reenters the living room and turns on the light. Foot's demand to his amazed constable, "I think you owe us all an explanation," is the question the play has been demanding consistently and denying circumstantially. The farcical action of the play is, whatever its explanations, contained within the surreal tableau described. As a result, Thelma's opening rebuke to Harris that "there's no need to use language" takes on broader connotations, for we see in the revealing light that one picture speaks a thousand words.

Self-possessed, the play makes conscious reference to its own language and technique as a detective drama. Admitting that he does not have a television licence, Harris says to Inspector Foot: "All right! Can we call off this game of cat and mouse?" Thelma's confusion over the artist Magritte's name and the fictional French detective Maigret conflates the play's pictorially inspired title and its tableau quality with the detective genre of which the play itself forms a part. Harris's last speech is wholly referential and carries the overtones of a theatrical critic, a choric figure, and an outraged suspect:

The activities in this room today have broadly speaking been of a mundane and domestic nature bordering on cliché. Police Constable Holmes obviously has an imagination as fervid and treacherous as your own. If he's found a shred of evidence to back it up then get him in here and let's see it.

Here the wider implications of this diatribe gesture toward the room as stage, and as the theatre of the absurd itself, which has become in the end a form of artistic cliché fit only for ridicule. Whereas the action of *The Real Inspector Hound* was played out over the corpse of Higgs, *After Magritte* first presents the seemingly dead body of "Mother," bowler hat incongruously at rest on the winding-sheets, and then resurrects an absurd detective play in order to make game of it.

Thus Stoppard turns his derision inwards at the mainsprings of dramatic conventions in general and at the detective genre in particular. His plays are saved from the esoteric "in jokes" of côterie theatre, which an introspective drama about drama can produce, by his broad-based humour. The humour of the plays in question derives mainly from popular forms, such as the *Goon Show* of B.B.C. radio and the satirical magazine *Private Eye*, the latter being an appropriate title in terms of the plays discussed if ever there was one. Not for Stoppard the black comedy and frightening economy of Pinter's dialogue, nor the "successful conclusion" of the detective form as proclaimed by Ionesco, for all its irony. His reply is to question constantly the notion of *the answer* itself, in a dialogue rich and extravagant with question marks and verbal gymnastics. The figure of the detective is the epitome of the problem solver par excellence who brings order and reassurance because he brings answers. These plays are a mock celebration of such a character, of all who believe in him, and of the concept of drama which defines itself in terms of the enactment of a riddle and its answer.

RONALD HAYMAN

"Lord Malquist and Mr Moon"

Rosencrantz and Guildenstern Are
Dead was premiered at Edinburgh during the same week that Lord Malquist
and Mr Moon was published, so, as Stoppard has said, "I was very light-
hearted about the whole thing . . . there was no doubt in my mind what-
soever that the novel would make my reputation, and the play would be
of little consequence either way." It is not, in fact, unnatural that he should
have had more confidence in the novel, which is the more elaborate of
the two artefacts. Like the mid-sixties novels of Iris Murdoch and John
Fowles, it is very much the work of a fabulator, to use Robert Scholes's
word. The fabulator is more concerned with intricacy and ingenuity of
design than with reproducing a lifelike surface of appearances. Ideas and
ideals become more important than objects or actions. Signalling the writer's awareness of his own limitation, comedy and irony license him to
embark on absurdly ambitious schemes. Parody and self-parody have become
inseparable.

"Nothing to be done," says Estragon at the beginning of Waiting for
Godot, meaning that it is no use trying to take his boots off; Vladimir replies
as if they were discussing whether action can ever be worthwhile.
"Nothing," says the ninth Earl of Malquist on the first page of the novel,
"is the history of the world viewed from a suitable distance." He praises
Louis XVI for writing "Rien" in his private diary on the day the Bastille

---

From Tom Stoppard. Copyright © 1979 by Ronald Hayman. Fourth edition, Heinemann,
1982.

fell, and, within a page, the earl is arguing about boots. Wellington never had an original idea in his life, and the boots he wore should have been called Malquist boots.

In his useful *Encounter* article, Clive James suggests that Stoppard's universe is Einsteinian: he abandons fixed viewpoints. "What looks odd when you stand over There is perfectly reasonable if you stand over Here . . ." he says, "and now that you're Here, you ought to know that Here is on its way to somewhere else, just as There is, and always was." We do not need to understand this conception of the time-space continuum: "it exists to be ungraspable, its creator having discovered that no readily appreciable conceptual scheme can possibly be adequate to the complexity of experience."

The novel resembles the plays in mingling abstruse argument with gaudy entertainment. Built into the plot is an infallible device for engendering suspense: Mr Moon, who is hired as Lord Malquist's Boswell, carries a bomb in his pocket. He also has a beautiful and magnetic wife. But these simple means of hooking the reader's interest are woven into an extremely complex design which involves literary parody. As in James Joyce's *Ulysses*, style is one of the main subjects, and amusing reverberations are set up between the style of the narrative, the life-style of the characters and their prose-style, both in conversation and in what they write. Lord Malquist is a Wildean creation: his epigrams, his clothes, his horse-drawn carriage, and his outlook belong gloriously to the 1890s, and there is nothing sneaking about Stoppard's admiration for the panache to which privilege was conducive. He amuses himself and his readers by revelling in the style that Malquist incarnates, but he pits it against the austerities of the more democratic sixties.

Churchill is never named but his funeral procession winds its way through the narrative in almost the same way as *Hamlet* does through *Rosencrantz and Guildenstern*. Lord Malquist's comments are filtered to us through Moon's unreliable summary:

> the extravagant mourning exacted from and imposed upon a sentimental people is the last flourish of an age whose criteria of greatness are no longer applicable . . . his was an age that saw history as a drama directed by great men. Accordingly he was celebrated as a man of action, a leader who raised involvement to the level of sacred duty, and he inspired his people to roll up their sleeves and take a militant part in the affairs of the world . . . the funeral might well mark a change in the heroic posture—to that of the Stylist, the spectator as hero, the man of inaction who would not dare roll up his sleeves for fear of creasing the cuffs.

Do we catch a faint echo of Prufrock's

I shall wear the bottoms of my trousers rolled.
Shall I part my hair behind? Do I dare to eat a peach?

There is some direct quotation from "Prufrock" and a reference to *Hamlet*:

> (That is not it at all,
> that is not what I meant at all.
> But when I've got it in a formulated phrase, when I've got it
> formulated, sprawling on a pin, when it is pinned and wriggling on the
> wall, then how should I begin . . . ?)
> *And how should you presume?*
> (He's got me there, cold. How should I presume?)
> All the same Moon knew that there was something rotten.

The funeral procession sometimes reminds us of the funeral procession that
winds its way through James Joyce's *Ulysses*, but, as in *Travesties*, the voice
we most often hear behind Stoppard's is that of Oscar Wilde:

> He puffed delicately on Turkish tobacco papered in a heliotrope cylinder,
> and blew a perfumed wreath for the fading light.
> "One must keep a dialogue of tension between the classes, otherwise
> how is one to distinguish between them? Socialists treat their servants
> with respect and then wonder why they vote Conservative."
> "I told you, dear boy. It is the duty of an artist to leave the world
> decorated by some trifling and quite useless ornament."

Equally Wildean is the languid indifference to casualties. "I am always
bumping into people," says Lord Malquist after a motorcyclist has been
killed by his coach.

The most extreme stylistic antithesis is provided by the cowboys.
A confrontation between two characters can be a confrontation between
two styles almost as contrasted as Elizabethan and modern English. Later,
in writing dialogue for the cowboys, Stoppard will demonstrate his expertise
as a mimic of theatrical and filmic clichés. He is also fluent in stage Irish
and stage Jewish, the languages spoken by the donkey-rider who thinks he
is the Risen Christ and the coloured coachman who works for Lord Malquist:

> "Holy Mother, is it me papers ye're after, yer honour?"
> O'Hara jeered from his box: "Papers-schmapers! A mile off I can smell
> a Yid!"
> "O'Hara," reproved the ninth earl, "enough of this papist bigotry."
> "A Roman, are you?" asked the Risen Christ.
> "I'm a Holy Catholic already!" shouted O'Hara. "I should tell a lie!"

Almost as if Stoppard were throwing down a challenge to himself,
the first chapter gives us flashes of events which seem not only improbable
but disconnected: will he ever be able to make them cohere into a plausible

story? Moon travelling in the earl's coach, inefficiently scribbling notes of his epigrammatic observations; Long John Slaughter moseying down a slope on his chestnut mare, a gun slung from his left hip; a lion watching a woman from behind a scrub of thorn; a dark man with thick matted curls riding side-saddle on a donkey; a slim girl with hair like spun gold ordering her French maid to tell Monsieur Jones that she is not at home; Moon conducting an interview with himself about why he carries a bomb. Can threads like these ever be interwoven convincingly? No one knows better than Stoppard that anything can be made convincing if it is made sufficiently stylish. The earl complains about other people's

> "utter disregard for the common harmonies of life." . . . We live amidst absurdity, so close to it that it escapes our notice. But if the sky were turned into a great mirror and we caught ourselves in it unawares, we should not be able to look each other in the face. He closed his eyes. "Since we cannot hope for order let us withdraw with style from the chaos."

Instead of withdrawing, Stoppard stylishly creates a chaos he can tidy up. We soon learn that Jane is Moon's wife, that the cowboys, who are not really cowboys, may have something to do with the promotion of Western Trail Pork 'n' Beans, that Malquist is liable to let his lion run loose in Hyde Park, and so on.

Nor are the narrative shifts mere devices for dizzying the reader. The vertigo of the short stories is being developed into something more meaningful—more communicable. Tormented by circumstantial but inconclusive evidence of Jane's infidelity, the desperate husband questions her.

> Every response gave Moon the feeling that reality was just outside his perception. If he made a certain move, changed the angle of his existence to the common ground, logic and absurdity would separate. As it was he couldn't pin them down.

All the nonsense in the novel makes sense if the absurdities are construed as problems that demand a solution. Stoppard, like Moon, is the struggling victim of a vision which presents all the phenomena of the present and the past as somehow interconnected:

> The rest of the world intruded itself in a cause-and-effect chain reaction that left him appalled at its endlessness; he experienced a vision of the billion connecting moments that lay behind and led to his simplest action, a vision of himself straightening his tie as the culminating act of a sequence that fled back into pre-history and began with the shift of a glacier.

This is one way the spectator can be a hero: to keep one's eyes unflinchingly open calls for almost heroic courage.

As in the best of Stoppard's plays, extreme seriousness co-exists happily with extreme frivolity. Even his private doubts about the value of his activity as a writer are fed back into the comic dialogue. Lord Malquist talks to Jane about Beau Brummell:

> "You see, he understood that substance is ephemeral but style is eternal . . . which may not be a solution to the realities of life but it is a workable alternative."
>
> Jane pressed against him as they wheeled back into Park Lane and headed south.
>
> Lord Malquist brooded on. "As an attitude it is no more fallacious than our need to identify all our ills with one man so that we may kill him and all our glory with another so that we may line the streets for him. What a nonsense it all is."

Stoppard's artistic self-consciousness may have been highly developed before he began the novel, but it was apparently sharpened to an even finer point by the experience of writing it. Moon tells the coachman:

> "I distrust attitudes . . . because they claim to have appropriated the whole truth and pose as absolutes. And I distrust the opposite attitude for the same reason. O'Hara . . . ? You see, when someone disagrees with you on a moral point you assume that he is one step behind in his thinking, and he assumes that he has gone one step ahead. But I take both parts, O'Hara, leapfrogging myself along the great moral issues, refuting myself and rebutting the refutation towards a truth that must be a compound of two opposite half-truths. And you never reach it because there is always something more to say. But I can't ditch it, you see O'Hara."

In manner this is remote from John Donne, but the Metaphysical poets also leapfrogged themselves along the great moral issues, defiantly holding to untenable premises, decorating absurdity with logic, transforming logic into drama. Stoppard shares their delight in teasing out ideas to such an extreme that they almost break, casually breathing an autobiographical cloud of cigarette smoke over the abstracting construction. He is bothered, for instance, as every writer is, by the knowledge that each sentence he puts down on paper represents a commitment which may be premature. Wouldn't it have been better to go on thinking about it until later in the evening? Moon is given a vision of himself "as pure writer who after a lifetime of absolutely no output whatever, would prepare on his deathbed the single sentence that was the distillation of everything he had saved up, and die before he was able to utter it."

Stoppard is also reminiscent of the Metaphysical poets in the pleasure he takes from wordplay and in the richness of the harvest he gathers from paradoxes. He even plays dialectical leapfrog with his deflations. Some of them become gestures that themselves ask to be deflated, and the narrative bloodstream is so infected with parody that the characters begin to feel guilty about literary echoes. "*Good grief,*" Moon reprimands himself, "*Wooster to the life.*" But he is talking to Birdboot, the butler, who is rather like a Wildean Jeeves. The parodies pile up against each other strongly enough for the resultant fiction to be appealingly original.

Peter Handke's title *The Ride across Lake Constance* recalls a legend about a horseman who crosses the frozen lake in safety, only to die of fright when he realizes that he might not have survived the ride. The existence of Stoppard's characters is equally precarious. "My dear fellow," says Lord Malquist, "the whole secret of life is to carry on as if nothing has happened." But he is better than Moon is at ignoring the symptoms of impending disaster: "He felt the shell of human existence ballooning to a thinness that must give way at some point, and his whole nervous system was tensed for the apocalyptic moment." The big power station is "a constant threat to his peace of mind for it sat by the river, monstrous and insatiable, consuming something—coke or coal or oil or something—consuming it in unimaginable quantities, and the whole thing was at the mercy of a million variables any of which might fail in some way."

Moon is "afraid of all of the people some of the time and some of the people all of the time." Malquist seems more confident. When asked what he stands for, he answers "Style." But his style is elegantly self-destructive: "You know, Mr Moon, I could not bear to outlive my wealth, and since I am spending it more quickly than I am aging, I feel my whole life is a process of suicide." But it is Moon who is spectacularly killed by the husband of the woman who was killed at the beginning of the novel, knocked down by the coach and pair. Moon is mistaken for Lord Malquist because he is riding in the coach. An accident, yes, but it fits beautifully into the design.

JOHN A. BAILEY

"Jumpers": The Ironist as Theistic Apologist

In *Jumpers*, not his most recent but his most important play to date, Tom Stoppard has written a farce with strongly surrealistic overtones. *Jumpers* is about a professor who uses a bow and arrow and hare and tortoise as visual aids in his lectures. He is married to an ex-musical comedy actress, and the action takes place in the near future in their stylish London flat. One of the walls of the bedroom consists of a giant television screen. A murder occurs and is investigated by a police inspector infatuated with the chief suspect, the actress; the body is put into a large plastic bag by a group of philosopher-gymnasts (the Jumpers) and spirited away. The play culminates in an academic symposium which is in reality a kind of judgment scene presided over by a porter, at which among others an astronaut and the Archbishop of Canterbury appear as witnesses; the archbishop is choreographed by the Jumpers into a position where he is shot and killed.

Such a synopsis gives one some idea of the zaniness of the comedy, its madcap surrealist humor and energy. But there is more to it than that. The professor, George, holds the chair of Moral Philosophy, and is passionately concerned to expound and defend a theistic position. God is creator and first cause, good and evil are objective realities, and man is more than an animal. George develops this position at length in the course of preparing a paper for the symposium. With wit and subtlety he attacks

From *Michigan Academician* 3, vol. 11 (Winter 1979). Copyright © 1979 by Michigan Academy of Science, Arts, and Letters.

the linguistic analysts, the atheists, the behaviorists, and the moral relativists who dominate the field. Arguing for the element of irrationality, of the emotional, the whimsical, the beautiful in life, his is the passionately antireductionist voice in the play. But George is also a ridiculous figure. Preparing his lecture by a method of stream of philosophical consciousness (dictated to his secretary), he is the funniest caricature of a professor, verbose, mannered, and eccentric, in English literature.

George is not only funny. He is also futile. He has apparently little or no effect on his students, and is not respected by his fellow academicians. He is insensitive to others, being unable to cope with any feelings but his own. Hardly related to his younger, beautiful wife Dotty, he often does not listen to her. She has had a serious nervous breakdown, and again and again she appeals to him, but he is unable to give her emotional support. The way in which they talk to, or rather by, each other, is very funny, but it nevertheless constitutes a brilliant portrait of a failed marriage. Though interested above all in arguing for the existence of good and evil, George is unable to put his theory into practice; he is unconcerned with practical ethics. He has no interest in politics, and mouths fashionable banalities about the totalitarian Radical-Liberal Party which has just come into power ("It is, after all, a radical idea to ensure freedom of the individual by denying it to groups"), and he watches passively while the archbishop is set up for assassination at the end. What little practical ethical interest he has focuses on a concern for dumb animals, for his pets, the hare Thumper and the tortoise Pat, and for his wife's goldfish. He is more affectionate with them than with people. Yet even here he is unable to act in accord with his feelings. Furious when Dotty carelessly allows the goldfish to die, he himself unwittingly kills both his pets, in a manner symbolizing his futility.

Dotty is completely unlike George. She was his student, who seduced and married him; then, bored with being a housewife, she became a West End star. Her career waxed until the first men reached the moon. "When they first landed, it was as though I'd seen a unicorn on the television news. . . . It was very interesting, of course. But it certainly spoiled unicorns!" For Dotty the moon symbolizes the heavenly, the inaccessible, the transcendent—and as such the romantic, the unconditional, and significant aspect of human love. Man's reaching the moon therefore meant for her the death of wonder, and with it the loss of a sense of meaning (and love) in life. The result was a serious breakdown; she was unable to continue to live a normal life believing in nothing. As the play opens, the first two Englishmen (delicious touch!) have just landed on the moon, and, after a partial mechanical failure, the one of them in command, Scott, selfishly sacrifices the life of the other, Oates, in order to return to earth. In a remarkable speech, Dotty says that this amoral act calls into question and indeed undermines all moral codes by indicating their lack of universality and therefore their relativity, and that it will bring in its wake moral chaos on earth. For Dotty the moon (heaven) and earth are both spoiled by men's reaching the moon. Man's technology therefore has as reductionist an effect for Dotty as do in his eyes the philosophies which her husband opposes; but, unlike George, Dotty finds no alternative.

So she stays in her bedroom, sees a psychiatrist and leads a life not fully clear in relation either to death or to sex. One of the Jumpers, McFee, is shot at the party she gives in celebration of the Radical-Liberal victory. It is generally believed she was responsible, though the gun is never found and no one actually saw her do it. Her behavior in not at once informing the police and in concealing the body in the room makes it almost certain that she was responsible, as do several of her remarks (for example, her "God help me" in response to her husband's statement "Everything comes out in the wash sooner or later"). Yet it remains not quite certain, because she feels no remorse and also because she apparently had no motive— except perhaps that violence for her is an anodyne in a situation which is no longer viable (as is for Moon in Stoppard's only novel *Lord Malquist and Mr Moon*).

So also with sex. Though incapable of responding sexually to her husband since her breakdown, she is involved with the psychiatrist, Archie, whom she receives in her bedroom every day and who photographs her naked while running his hand over her body supposedly as part of his psychiatric treatment. (Here again we find a parallel in Stoppard's novel in Lord Malquist's relation to Moon's wife Jane, whose navel he "reads," whose breast he examines, and with whose body he entwines his in an elaborate yoga posture. It is virtually certain the two are having an affair, but not absolutely so; Stoppard never makes it fully clear.) Dotty also succeeds by the use of her charms in causing Inspector Bones to forget about the corpse he has seen and about his intention to determine if she is responsible, whether or not by actually seducing him is not clear. Her relationships with both men are the occasion of much of the bawdy humor which is a part (though only a part) of Stoppard's comic stock in trade, particularly in relation to Dotty's suspicious and sexually frustrated husband, George. In neither case is it clear that Dotty has been unfaithful; one feels that in both cases, as in that of McFee's killer, Stoppard wishes it to remain uncertain—a point to which I shall return.

George's foil, as far as Dotty is concerned and in other ways, is Archie, the vice-chancellor of the university. He is also a psychiatrist, a lawyer, a philosopher, and a gymnast, a man as many-sided as George is one-sided, as practical as George is impractical, and completely cynical. He agrees with the Radical Liberals in their advocacy of technology and their atheism; their lack of genuine democracy does not bother him, and he is quite willing to destroy the archbishop when he disagrees with him. Dorothy, having had a breakdown and finding George inaccessible, has turned to him for treatment and perhaps for solace. Stoppard chooses to lampoon in him not one but two professions. The first is psychiatry. "When did you first become aware of these feelings?" he asks Dotty when she says she finds mashed potatoes and gravy very consoling. More chillingly, he reacts to Dotty's offstage cry for help "It's all right—just exhibitionism: what we psychiatrists call a 'cry for help.' " And his treatment of Dotty seems to have more to do with response to her charms than anything else. The second profession is that of the academic administrator. Archie has organized a team of gymnasts from the philosophy staff, which calls itself Jumpers. The team members work well together—whatever individuality they might have doesn't interfere with that, and in that sense is not significant; they are one in their intentness on advancement. Theirs is the fashionable relativistic antimetaphysical philosophy of the day, sometimes linguistic, sometimes behavioristic, which Archie shares; and their real focus is hardly on truth, in which they don't strictly speaking believe, but on conformity and professional success. The symbolization of their aspirations and methods in terms of gymnastic jumping is one of the most successful things in the play. As their leader, Archie is completely unprincipled, ready (hilariously) to bribe the inspector with the offer of one of several academic chairs. His mass of academic degrees (itself a parody) has nothing to do with knowledge in the grand disinterested sense and everything to do with the amassing of professional expertise useful in acquiring power. Archie believes in nothing, which is to say he agrees with Dotty, but whereas this brings her to an only intermittently forgotten despair, he thrives on it. He is the most consistent relativist in the play. Not believing in truth but in process (as his closing speech makes clear), he also does not believe in ascertainable fact (and in that sense not in history): "Anybody could have fired the shot [that killed McFee], and anybody could have had a reason for doing so, including, incidentally, myself."

Archie has isolated Cognomen's Syndrome—by which the names of people not only characterize but influence their character and actions; indeed, as he says, he has it: his last name is Jumpers. Names are significant in Stoppard; the title of one of his plays, which has at least two meanings, is *If You're Glad I'll Be Frank*. The importance of names highlights Stoppard's positively Shakespearean love of puns. Dotty's name—the usual English spelling of the woman's name is Dottie—is an obvious play on her condition. The porter whose station is modest though his knowledge is not is called Crouch. George's name is the most interesting, George Moore. For it is also the name of the noted philosopher of the first half of the twentieth century. George is condemned to live in the shadow of a brighter light, at times even being confused by students with the other, though the latter has been dead for years. His name, one might say, is as anachronistic as his philosophy is generally taken to be.

The plot of *Jumpers* hinges on McFee, the Jumper who is killed at the beginning. It is only after he is dead that we learn about him, first from George and then from Crouch, who alone knew him well enough to understand the significance of his life. McFee as a pragmatist held a position within the spectrum of philosophical views currently acceptable and therefore open to a Jumper; indeed. Archie calls him the "guardian and figurehead of philosophical orthodoxy." Originally, therefore, he is parallel to Archie, at least a member of his team. But the doings on the moon affected him, Crouch says after his death, as deeply as they did Dotty; in this he is parallel to her. According to Crouch, he contrasted the selfish act of Scott with the altruistic behavior of Captain Oates who on an expedition to the South Pole led by another Scott in 1912 sacrificed his life to give his companions a chance of survival. (Note that the name of this man who died for others is the same as that of the man who has just been left to die an unwilling victim of—or sacrifice to—Scott's selfishness on the moon. The two men are not the same, but their deaths are variations on a single theme. So too the lunar Scott, who saves himself but only at the cost of morality, has the same name as the heroic leader of the 1912 expedition who perished.) McFee, struck by the contrast between the altruism of the past deed (for which his philosophy left no room) and the moral cowardice of the present one, suddenly threw over his position and decided to become a monk. Like Dotty he was haunted by the men on the moon, but unlike her he is able to take a positive step as a result, and so becomes parallel to George, though hardly fully so. For George's life, fired by philosophical passion in the defense of the existence of good but pretty much devoid of good in the sense of selfishness, is a far cry from that of a monk.

But—one of the many ironies in *Jumpers*—the last word as regards McFee is ironic. Hoping to live his life for others in a monastery, he lost it—senselessly?—at the hands of an unknown killer. Archie, before Crouch tells him of McFee's conversion and the reason for it, tells the inspector that had McFee done just what in fact he did do ("decided that he was St. Paul to Moore's Messiah") he himself in the cause of philosophical orthodoxy would have killed him. After the fact he turned out to have a reason for killing McFee such as Dotty never had. Yet he cannot have known this when McFee was killed, unless (which is conceivable) he already knew what Crouch told him—though there is no other indication in the play that he did so, and it is exceedingly unlikely. Was Archie nevertheless responsible? Did, in this case, the crime not follow the motive for it but rather produce in its wake the motive? Was the motive not cause but effect? This is the kind of surrealistic twist with which Stoppard's plays are laden, often (as also in the case of The Real Inspector Hound) in connection with a whodunit plot. (One is reminded of the work of Nabokov, Stoppard's fellow Eastern European. Stoppard, whose name originally was Straussler, was born in Czechoslovakia in 1939, left when he was two, lived in Singapore and India and arrived in England in 1946.) McFee, in dying, may have been a martyr, in which case he was parallel to the archbishop.

Finally, the archbishop, Sam Clegthorpe. As a veterinarian, he was the Radical-Liberal spokesman for Agriculture, and when at the time of the Radical-Liberal victory the see of Canterbury is made a political appointment, he is appointed to it, though an agnostic, as part of the program of rationalization of the church. Yet, once appointed, he finds himself sufficiently impressed by the faith of the flock which looks to him for leadership that he protests at the speed with which the government is moving against the church. He pays for his protest with his life, dying an (agnostic) martyr.

There is at least one martyr, and quite possibly two, in Jumpers, not to mention the two animals and the goldfish which are also killed. Death is a theme not without importance in the play, and not only because the plot turns on it. This is true here, and also in Lord Malquist and Mr Moon, in Rosencrantz and Guildenstern Are Dead, and in The Real Inspector Hound. George confesses to being afraid, not of dying but of death, and so once more shows his old-fashioned colors. Death is not like love, which is rare in Stoppard; there is in all his oeuvre no portrait of a happily married couple, as there is no woman who has children—the family is not a part of his world. Sex in contrast to love is a frequent topic, though not necessarily itself frequent; its signs are everywhere, but in ambiguous fashion. But death is certain—perhaps the most certain thing, or even the only certain thing, in life.

This has to do with the characteristic convergence of two themes in Jumpers. One is the theme of truth: whether or not God exists, whether or not good and evil are objective realities, whether life has meaning. To anticipate, there is no certainty on these subjects in the play. Related to this is the issue of the uncertainty of fact, which is the obverse of the other theme. What happened? Who killed McFee? Why was he killed? These questions are never answered in the play. The two themes are in fact related. George's "How the hell does one know what to believe?" applies initially to an issue of fact, that of whether Dotty has committed adultery with Archie, but he then realizes it applies equally to matters of faith. Archie's statement also applies to both:

> The truth to us philosophers, Mr. Crouch, is always an interim judgment. We will never even know for certain who did shoot McFee. Unlike mystery novels, life does not guarantee a denouement; and if it came, how would one know whether to believe it?

He here seems to be speaking for Stoppard, who would appear to be agnostic both about history (facts) and the meaning of history. A story told by George is also illuminating in this context:

> Meeting a friend in a corridor, Wittgenstein said: "Tell me, why do people always say it was *natural* for men to assume that the sun went around the earth rather than that the earth was rotating?" His friend said, "Well, obviously, because it just *looks* as if the sun is going round the earth." To which the philosopher replied, "Well, what would it have looked like if it had looked as if the earth was rotating?"

The story makes the point that appearances are deceptive; it is interesting that it is made by George and not, as we would expect, by Archie.

The issue of fact is hardly new in Stoppard. In *After Magritte* Stoppard sets up a surrealist situation including a supposed crime, only to account for every detail realistically, including the crime, which turns out never to have been committed. In *The Real Inspector Hound* the two theatre critics, Birdboot and Moon, begin by watching a whodunit in their capacity as critics, only to become involved in it (Moon turns out to be the *raison d'être* for it, the hinge of the real-life plot which lies beneath its fictional plot) and to be murdered by the killer, while their place as critics is taken by two of the actors in the play, one of whom, Simon, has been shot and killed during it. What happened here? What is the play really about? Did Simon die or not? Is Birdboot Simon? One is reminded of the well-known aphorism quoted by Guildenstern about the Chinese philosopher who dreamed he was a butterfly, never henceforth to be certain that he was not a butterfly dreaming he was a Chinese philosopher. In *The Real Inspector Hound* the situation of changing identity and role is so extreme that it is hard to take the issue of fact seriously. Nevertheless, one sees the same hand at work there as in *Jumpers*, though in *Jumpers* working in a less extravagant way, and dealing in addition with philosophical issues lacking in the earlier play.

Words are important to any writer. To Stoppard they have a special quality because the reality they describe (or mask) is opaque. But another factor also enters in at times, for instance in connection with names. Many of Stoppard's characters (though none in *Jumpers*) are named Moon or Boot. (Two of his unpublished radio plays are titled *The Dissolution of Dominic Boot* and *M is for Moon among other Things.*) When asked about this, Stoppard (in an interview published in the program of the original National Theatre production) pointed to the arbitrariness of the names of many of his characters. "I can't help it if [a character's name] keeps turning out to be Moon or Boot. In fact, the chief characters in [*Jumpers*] are masquerading under false names. Moon and Boot is what they are really called. . . . I keep writing about the same double-act." Whereas the name Boot is derived from Evelyn's Waugh's novel *Scoop*, Moon comes (according to the *Observer* drama critic Robert Cushman) from the name of the victim in the Paul Newman film *The Left-Handed Gun*. Cushman therefore maintains that there is no lunar significance to the name in Stoppard, hence no connection between the name and the heavenly body which is of such importance to both Dotty and McFee. But that is surely an oversimplification. In conversation with Cushman, Stoppard has said, "Moon is a person to whom things happen. Boot is rather more aggressive." One might add that Moon is more articulate and less successful with women than Boot. Not all the principal male characters of Stoppard's plays fall neatly into these categories—Rosencrantz and Guildenstern come to mind in this regard—though they are useful. In *Jumpers* George is clearly Moon (or, as Stoppard would say, a Moon), heir to the mantle of Moon in *Malquist*, of George in *Enter a Free Man* and of Moon in *The Real Inspector Hound*. Archie is a Boot, like Malquist in the novel, Birdboot in *Inspector Hound* and Harry in *Enter a Free Man*. That is not to say that all these characters are identical (despite Stoppard's statement), though Michael Hordern has played the parts of George in the London productions of both *Enter a Free Man* and *Jumpers*—but they *are* all variations on the same theme—which gives Stoppard's different plays something of the same almost musical quality in their relation to one another that Ingmar Bergman's movies have. In the same way, Dotty, the wife of the Moon George, has a number of similarities with Jane, Moon's wife in *Malquist*, who is a prostitute working in the home of her unsuspecting husband. Jane has never slept with her husband, and is almost certainly having an affair with Lord Malquist. Dotty is also akin to Lady Malquist, a childless siren who has lost her way in alcoholism but who takes a passing interest in Moon and enables him, after years of unconsummated marriage, to discard his virginity. These themes recur with the fluidity of details in dreams. Indeed, it is in large measure because Stoppard is able, in his use of the comic mode, to draw on the reaches of his subconscious mind that his work has such extraordinary vitality.

As if to compensate for the ambiguity of what he writes about, in order to contain that ambiguity, Stoppard gives his plays, including *Jumpers*, a tight and balanced form. *Jumpers* begins and ends with a scene involving singing and dancing, and with a man's being shot, and the first act also ends with the combination of singing and dancing. These three scenes frame—at once breaking up and resolving—action which occurs on a stage divided into three areas. That action begins with Dotty's cry to George "Help! Murder!" and ends with the identical cry on George's part directed to Dotty. The three areas are on either side the bedroom and study of the flat, and in the center the hall. The two side areas are both tenanted by a woman. The bedroom is occupied by Dotty who never leaves it and dominates it; it is for all intents and purposes her room, not George's and hers, despite the double bed. The study is occupied almost the entire time by George's secretary, who in contrast to Dotty never says a word. George, endlessly dictating notes for his lecture, dominates this area as clearly as Dotty does the other, a situation reflecting the state of their marriage. In between is the hall, a kind of no-man's, or rather, no-woman's land. In the hall men talk to each other—first George and the inspector, then Archie and the inspector and finally Archie and Crouch. This area might be called McFee's area, for he is the primary topic of conversation. And perhaps it should be called the area of communication, because of the final speech here, when Crouch tells Archie the true story, the denouement of McFee's life. In the other two areas communication is rare. In the bedroom there is very little between George and Dotty, though some (mostly nonverbal) between Dotty and Archie. And in the study George dictates to, but in no way communicates with, his secretary.

In its form *Jumpers* therefore has many of the elements of the old-fashioned well-made play; but it also has the looseness which comes from the song-and-dance frame, which "springs" and opens up the well-made play. And its wordiness—Stoppard is often, like Shaw, a wordy play-wright—is beautifully relieved by the music and dancing of the frame; the ideas of the one part are set off by the rhythmic, melodic vigor of the other. The result is a play highly original in form, pointing to the future in that it shows one way in which the drama can survive without repeating the past: by taking on a hybrid form.

Jumpers is not the first of Stoppard's plays which concerns itself with metaphysical issues. *Albert's Bridge* is a play about space; *If you're Glad I'll be Frank* is a play about time. *Jumpers* is, however, Stoppard's first work to focus on the theistic issue. There are in previous works theological references, but they are more or less fleeting. One is in *Malquist:* the figure of the Risen Christ, the Irishman on a donkey with a weakness for sex and the bottle, not above using racially bigoted slang, who is selling salvation and looking for a multitude to whom to preach the Word. A charlatan, he is mad enough to believe in the claim he makes. One may also mention Gladys in *If you're Glad I'll be Frank* who before she turned to the telephone office and the telling of time wanted to become a nun ("it was the security I was after, that and the clean linen") but was turned down because she didn't believe that Jesus was the son of God—a reference noteworthy because of the total absence of Christological interest in *Jumpers.* Lastly, there is a speech of Guildenstern's in *Rosencrantz and Guildenstern Are Dead* sufficiently important to warrant its citation in full.

> A man breaking his journey between one place and another at a third place of no name, character, population, or significance, sees a unicorn cross his path and disappear. This in itself is startling, but there are precedents for mystical encounters of various kinds, or to be less extreme, a choice of persuasions to put it down to fancy; until—"My God," says a second man, "I must be dreaming, I thought I saw a unicorn." At which point, a dimension is added that makes the experience as alarming as it will ever be. A third witness, you understand, adds no further dimension but only spreads it thinner, and a fourth thinner still, and the more witnesses there are the thinner it gets and the more reasonable it becomes until it is as thin as reality, the name we give to the common experience. . . . "Look, look!" recites the crowd. "A horse with an arrow in its forehead! It must have been mistaken for a deer."

We have here an interesting description of what could be called the demythologizing process. What is significant is that Stoppard skillfully posits but does not answer the question whether there is another reality besides that of the common experience, the reality of the unicorn (the transcendent). The implication of the story's beginning seems to be that there is, but the matter is left open. The story is in fact in its lucidity a textbook illustration of the nature and *Problematik* of the transcendent.

In contrast to these plays, the theological issue is sufficiently central to *Jumpers* so that the question inevitably arises, where does Stoppard stand in relation to it? As we have seen, he leaves the issue open, undecided in the play, but more can be said about his position than that. To be sure, *Jumpers* is a comedy, indeed a farce, and to ask this question involves taking the play more seriously than might seem to be justified. Yet many of the best comedies conceal, however skillfully, a serious substratum, and *Jumpers* is one of these.

The place to begin is with the fact that George, the tireless apologist for theism and objective morality, is the play's central figure. For him the issues of the existence of good and of God are *the* philosophical issues, and they are in the play also. All other positions are more or less equated, being represented by George and the Jumpers; in this way Stoppard allows the theological issue to emerge. To be sure, George's position, based on natural theology (proofs for the existence of God) is old-fashioned (as he admits). George—and through him Stoppard—shows no awareness of the criticism of natural theology made by many twentieth-century theologians (e.g. Karl Barth); continental philosophy (Heidegger) with its influence on theistic existentialism is never mentioned. Perhaps more surprisingly, George has as little interest in religion (Christian or any other) as in practical ethics or politics. His statement "If God exists, he certainly existed before religion" is orthodox from a Judeo-Christian point of view, but his remark "I'm not at all sure that the God of religious observance is the object of my faith" is not. Related to this is his lack, so far as one can tell, of piety; he is not a man of prayer any more than he is of love. George cannot be taken strictly speaking as a spokesman for the Christian position—but only for the philosophical position that Christianity is a valid possibility.

Several of George's remarks have such bite that one unmistakably hears the voice of Stoppard himself speaking. "Of all forms of wishful thinking, humanism demands the greatest sympathy" is an example. So too the response of George (who never learns about McFee's conversion) to Archie's dissimulating suggestion that McFee committed suicide "Where did he find the despair? I thought the whole *point* of denying the Absolute was to reduce the scale, instantly, to the inconsequential behavior of in-consequential animals; that nothing could ever be that important." To which Archie replies "Including, I suppose, death. . . . It's an interesting view of atheism, as a sort of *crutch* for those who can't bear the reality of God!" These remarks are not undercut but put into perspective by George's saying "I'm lumbered with this incredible, indescribable, and definitely shifty God, the trump card of atheism." Furthermore, George's finest state-ment, a cogent and beautiful argument of perfection as the limiting curve of life just as a circle is the limiting curve of regular polygons with innu-merable edges, is underlined by Stoppard who indicates that George is to be spotlighted during it against an otherwise dark stage. Here, for once, George is no longer mannered, or ridiculous, but speaks with eloquent authority—and Stoppard, one senses, speaks with him.

Stoppard allows George to argue—at times as finely as this—for his position. Stoppard also shows a keen awareness, through Dotty, of the threatening, reductionist nature of modern technology—and therefore of the need, one might say, for a gospel. Just as significant is Stoppard's critique of psychiatry and its lack of compassion, a critique implied in what Archie says and does, and his critique of the university as a force for either real communication or enlightenment. (One thinks in the context of the Watergate affair of Yale Chaplain William Sloane Coffin's remark that Jeb Magruder, admitted perjurer, must have failed the ethics course he took with Coffin at Williams College.) The significance of this is that technology, psychiatry, and the university (education) are among the most popular soteriological alternatives to religion today. Stoppard indicates with his usual bite an awareness of their incapacity to fulfill such expectations. His sense of the seriousness of the modern dilemma is clear in his choice of an act of amoral selfishness on the part of a contemporary explorer to contrast with Oates' altruistic act of 1912. And Archie's justification of that act of selfishness in the final symposium indicates Stoppard's awareness that modern non-Christian philosophy by and large does not foster, and often cannot even comprehend, the noblest human behavior—again, an indication of the need for a gospel.

But this is not the whole story. A number of factors which point in a different direction remain to be mentioned. George, in his very self-centered futility, represents a salutary reproof to a moralistic interpretation of theism (as being rooted or inevitably resulting in moral improvement). Yet one wonders if this is not related, in the play, to a lack of any sense of redemption, a lack of a sense of either sin or grace, and a lack of Christology. McFee reaches out at the end of his life to the church and a vocation as a religious, but he dies before this could become a reality. Indeed, no one knows about McFee's final decision except Crouch and Archie to whom Crouch speaks, and one senses that neither of them will reveal the secret. McFee's Christian commitment, his intended witness will never be known; the appearances of his life will remain deceptive.

What of the others? George and Dotty never get together. He continues unresponsive, she remains inaccessible. There is a dark undercurrent in almost all of Stoppard's work which sets off the brilliance of his wit and vitality, and it is not lacking in Jumpers. George, after his best speech, inadvertently kills both his pets; it is hard to see the hand of God in his life, unless, in the fashion of Isak Dinesen, one sees God as having a sense of humor, and not a gentle one. After that, in the symposium, George makes a final speech (containing, as usual, a good point—against the linguistic analysts), but it ends in confusion. And it is not the last word. Archie speaks next, summing up his worldly wise position in a speech which is a modern equivalent of Ecclesiastes. (Note the unexpected, and effective—typically Stoppard—reference to the thief crucified with Christ.)

> Do not despair—many are happy much of the time; more eat than starve, more are healthy than sick, more curable than dying; not so many dying as dead; and one of the thieves was saved. Hell's bells and all's well— half of the world is at peace with itself, and so is the other half, vast areas are unpolluted; millions of children grow up without suffering deprivation, and millions, while deprived grow up without suffering cruelties, and millions, while deprived and cruelly treated, none the less grow up. No laughter is sad and many tears are joyful. At the graveside the undertaker doffs his hat and impregnates the prettiest mourner. Wham, bam, thank you Sam.

But Archie, no more than George, has not the last word. The last word is Dotty's. She is able to sing in the last scene as she was not in the first— so it is possible (though by no means certain) that her nervous breakdown is over. But its cause, her sense of isolation, is not over, as her final words make clear: "Goodbye spoony Juney Moon."

A final clue to Stoppard's position may lie in a passing use by George of the word which gives the play its title. "McFee jumped, and left nothing behind but a vacancy." In the context of Archie's gymnasts, jumping refers to professional advancement. Here, however, it refers to death—and one wonders if there is not the implication that jumping also refers to life, that for Stoppard living is jumping, from one position to another, finally from life to death. Dr. Berndt Schaller, a German theologian who saw the play, suggests that jumping is Stoppard's image of life and its situations as not to be comprehended in terms of one system, as unsystematic. This accords well with what is certainly a major theme of the play (as of much of Stoppard's work), the deceptiveness of appearances, their ambiguity. There is no one system, including the Christian, which can account for all of reality, and, perhaps because of this, the appearances of that reality are deceptive. Stoppard's understanding of reality does allow for the existence of transcendence and ultimate value, though not as illuminating all of reality, and therefore not as certainties but as possibilities. This finding does not negate the fact that, in *Jumpers*, he, the dazzling ironist, *is* an apologist for God and meaning, but his must be seen (and assessed) for what it is, a limited apology.

G. B. CRUMP

The Universe as Murder Mystery: "Jumpers"

The reaction of reviewers to Tom Stoppard's *Jumpers*, produced in England in 1972 and in America in 1974, reflects the critics' suspicion that in his plays Stoppard indulges in startling stage antics, erudite allusions, and involved puns in order to disguise deficiencies in insight and make shallow plays appear profound. A comment in a recent handbook of modern writers typifies this attitude: "Stoppard's plays reveal good ideas theatrically well developed but intellectually unexplored (reflecting a lack of grasp of his material), a clever ear for merging his predecessors' . . . effects, and a frothy, infectious, vacuous excitement." Much the same assessment is discernible in an extended critique of *Jumpers* by John Weightman. He complains that, although the play is striking and theatrical, "quite a bit of the action did not seem necessary." He singles out the murder of McFee, the central incident in the plot, claiming that it has no relation to the play's ideas and is merely a convenient stratagem for sustaining audience interest: "You only have to kill a character pointlessly in Act I to have a corpse to play about with for the rest of the evening and to run a gratuitous thread of suspense through the whole action."

The image of Stoppard as a superficial dilettante is at odds with his friend Derek Marlowe's account of the pains the author takes in his work. "For Tom, writing a play is like sitting for an examination. He spends ages on research, does all the necessary cramming, reads all the relevant books,

From *Contemporary Literature* 3, vol. 20 (Summer 1979). Copyright © 1979 by the Board of Regents of the University of Wisconsin Press.

and then gestates the results." Nevertheless, the real issue is not Stoppard's industry in studying his sources but whether his labors lead to a meaningful and aesthetically satisfying whole or merely to a "vacuous" exercise in showing off. *Jumpers*, one of Stoppard's most erudite works, illustrates the problems his use of research can pose for the reviewer. The philosopher-protagonist, George Moore, spends most of his time arguing for a belief in God and moral absolutes and against the materialism and moral relativism of the "jumpers," the logical positivists who compose the philosophical establishment at his university. Besides being uncertain about the relevance of the murder plot to this argument, reviewers were unsure about the very basic question of which side, if either, Stoppard intended to have win the argument. In an article on Stoppard, Kenneth Tynan has asserted that "there is no question where Stoppard stands" in the debate. He "votes for the spirit," and indeed the "main purpose" of *Jumpers* is "to affirm the existence of God," to defend "transcendent moral values," and to attack the "pragmatic materialism" of the jumpers. In support of his interpretation, Tynan quotes Stoppard's public endorsement of "Western liberal democracy . . . based on a moral order derived from Christian absolutes." But it does not necessarily follow that the playwright is arguing for the validity of a Christian moral order in *Jumpers*. Other difficulties posed by the play are why Stoppard chose to name his hero G. E. Moore after the British in-tuitionist philosopher, and whether Bones, a major character, is merely an appendage to the mystery plot or relates to the philosophical debate in a significant way.

An explication of *Jumpers* in the light of the major tenets of logical positivism will show that the murder of McFee is integral to George's debate with the materialists, that the debate also includes Bones, that nothing in the play is gratuitous or pointless, and that, far from adding complications or allusions solely for the sake of dazzling the audience, Stoppard fashions the language and action of *Jumpers* into a highly particularized and apt portrait of the intellectual and moral uncertainty modern man feels when confronting his world. An integral part of this portrait is the implication that George, however sympathetic his character and attractive his beliefs, fails in his efforts to give life a satisfying meaning through philosophy. . . . Further, since *Jumpers* does form a unified and meaningful whole, not all of Stoppard's works may be dismissed as shallow displays of stage pyrotech-nics.

Although George classifies his antagonists as "Logical positivists, mainly," he also includes in their number "a linguistic analyst or two, a couple of Benthamite Utilitarians . . . lapsed Kantians and empiricists generally . . . and of course the usual Behaviourists"—that is, nearly all the groups prominent in the "orthodox mainstream" of British philosophy in the forty years since, in George's view, "it went off the rails." Much of the satire in *Jumpers* extends beyond logical positivism to materialistic philosophy in general. Logical positivism originated in Vienna in the 1920s but, with the rise of Hitler, its center shifted to England, where it merged with a well-established tradition of British analytic philosophy represented in the early twentieth century by G. E. Moore, George's namesake, and Bertrand Russell, whose Theory of Descriptions is mentioned in *Jumpers*. One might argue that the roots of logical positivism are British since Ludwig Wittgenstein, the Austrian whose *Tractatus Logico-Philosophicus* (1921) was one of the most powerful influences on the movement, had studied with Moore and Russell at Cambridge. In addition to Moore, Russell, and Wittgenstein, *Jumpers* alludes to British philosophers A. J. Ayer and Gilbert Ryle and it is the British branch of the movement Stoppard satirizes.

The world of *Jumpers* is carefully constructed to give dramatic form to some of the questions pondered by the logical positivists. For instance, a distinguishing trait of logical positivism is its focus on language. This focus was inspired by Wittgenstein's *Tractatus*, which is concerned with the relation between a logical language and the world of which that language purports to give us a picture; distortions in the language that shapes the picture, Wittgenstein believed, can lead to an unclear picture of reality. Similarly, Russell has described the British branch of logical positivism as a "school of linguistic analysis," which holds "that all philosophical perplexities are the outcome of slovenly use of language." In *Jumpers*, much of the action and humor hinges on linguistic ambiguities and confusions. These confusions mirror larger ambiguities present in the reality represented in the drama. For instance, the double meaning implied in Dorothy's remark that "she's all right in bed" (which may mean that she feels secure as long as she is in bed or that she is sexually adroit) and Archie's reply that "there's something in that" reflects the uncertainty about whether he is Dorothy's lover or her doctor. The play is constructed of a whole tissue of such uncertainties, which the language compounds and perpetuates.

The most pervasive verbal joke in *Jumpers* is the "cognomen syndrome," a psychological condition in which one's name corresponds to one's role in life. Archie (archer) Jumper is a gymnast. Crouch is a servant aspiring to become a jumper-philosopher. Duncan McFee suffers the fate of the murdered king in *Macbeth*. Inspector Bones tries to deal directly with the bare bones of reality. Dotty is "dotty." George seems doomed to embrace some of the ethical principles of G. E. Moore because he has the same name. Although the convention of descriptive names stretches back in English drama as far as Jonson and the morality plays, its use here alludes to an indirect consequence of Russell's Theory of Descriptions—"that ordinary proper names function as descriptions [in Russell's sense]"—and to such philosophical concerns as the relation between names and descriptive phrases, between names and what they denote, and between the reference and the sense of a word. Similarly, George's gibe that it is for "reasons which will be found adequate by logical spirits" that G. E. Moore was never in when George called points to what P. F. Strawson, in an attack on Russell's theory, calls "the lingering superstition that a name is logically tied to a single individual." If this were true, then Stoppard's George Moore would actually be G. E. Moore, an adequate reason why he cannot be in two places at once. Bones's remark that "there's only ever been one Dorothy Moore" repeats this joke, the wife of G. E. Moore having also been named Dorothy. Thus Stoppard's tricks with language in *Jumpers* are not purposeless games or incidental flourishes of wit but part of his depiction of logical positivism.

The best known statement of the logical positivist position in English is *Language, Truth and Logic*, published in 1935 by A. J. Ayer, and Stoppard almost certainly consulted it in preparing to write *Jumpers*. In addition to its having virtually the status of a textbook, Stoppard alludes to it in the title of George's work *Language, Truth and God* and Archie's initials suggest Ayer's famous first and middle initials. One of Ayer's illustrations in the revised introduction of 1946 may have supplied Stoppard with the seed of the idea for his play: "The statement that I have blood on my coat may, in certain circumstances, confirm the hypothesis that I have committed a murder, but it is not part of the meaning of the statement that I have committed a murder that I should have blood upon my coat." That is, a man may kill without getting bloody or have blood on his coat without being a murderer. At the end of *Jumpers*, we are invited to conclude that George's secretary murdered McFee because of the blood on her coat, but we immediately learn the coat is actually stained with the blood of Thumper, the rabbit (a fact which would nevertheless not preclude her being the murderer); further, Archie, George, Crouch, and Dorothy also have motives for shooting McFee. The central tenet of logical positivism is the principle of verification, which holds that no statement is "literally significant" or "meaningful," no statement is truly about the world unless its truth or falsity can be empirically verified. As Ayer puts it, "We say that a sentence is factually significant to any given person, if, and only if, he knows how to verify the proposition which it purports to express—that is, if he knows what observations would lead him . . . to accept the proposition as being true, or reject it as being false."

As the secretary's coat demonstrates, however, observations can be ambiguous, untrustworthy, and inconclusive. Ayer's coat illustration may have brought home to Stoppard the limits of what can be affirmed about life if one adheres to the principle of verification and also have suggested a means of dramatizing the limits of various philosophical approaches to reality. "To begin at the beginning," George reasons, is to ask "is God?" Just as the universe and George's argument begin with God, *Jumpers* begins with the murder of McFee and its mysterious perpetrator. This congruence signals that the mystery of McFee's murder is a metaphor for the essential mysteries of creation. In a murder mystery, the chief questions are "Who done it?" and "Why?" Some of our fundamental questions about life are the same: Who done it? Who created the universe and to what purpose? The ways that Archie, Bones, and George set about solving the murder represent various philosophical approaches to answering these larger questions.

Dorothy plays a special role in the murder investigation. Although at times she herself expresses a pragmatic philosophy of sorts—"Here is my consistent proposition / Two and two make roughly four"—Dorothy is chiefly concerned with the consequences of the murder rather than its solution and therefore must be distinguished from the three philosopher-detectives. Moreover, she forms the center of emotional interest for the men. For these reasons, Dorothy occupies a unique position in the play's structure. In one sense, she represents man's nature uncomplicated and unrefined by intellect, his emotions and appetites: she is an entertainer and spends most of the play in the bedroom, a place of sleep, sexual intercourse, and luncheon trays. Dorothy has been psychologically traumatized by the triumph of rationalistic materialism in the modern world, epitomized by the ascendancy of logical positivism in philosophy and radical-liberalism in politics and by technological achievements such as moon landings. A symptom of the trauma is her loss of the ability to croon romantic songs about the moon after man's lunar landing destroyed the planet's aura of poetry and romance. Her collapse into insanity signifies the persistence of emotional and spiritual needs which seem irrational viewed from a "sane" and materialistic perspective. She longs for something incredible rather than the "credible and all too bloody likely" acrobatics of the jumpers. She wants to believe in God, the soul, or right and wrong, absolutes incredible to the philosophically up-to-date jumpers, who accept as credible only what is verifiable.

Dorothy's plight, symbolized by her need to dispose of McFee's body, corresponds to that of modern man, caught with life and death on his hands and in need of a reason for continuing to function in a grim and chaotic world from which the spiritual consolations of the past have been withdrawn. The moments of most intense feeling in the play are those in which she pleads for the emotional support that might make life worth living. Her involvements with George, Bones, and Archie betoken three types of personal relations from which one might extract such support and also three stages in the historical development of the relationship between man and woman. George offers traditional married love, involving physical and emotional connection and a fair amount of realism about one's partner. Bones's idealistic love is callow and romantic in the nineteenth-century style, while Archie offers a crassly physical relationship of the modern type. All the men fail Dorothy in varying degrees, both as lovers and as philosopher-detectives trying to give her a convincing and sustaining picture of reality.

Dorothy, along with the secretary, also forms part of the puzzling reality the men strive to interpret. Both women play scenes in the nude; a metaphor for the *ding an sich,* this physical exposure hides more than it reveals. Stoppard invests the women with an air of enigma which, like the world, defies male ratiocination. The opening scene makes this point in a parable: all the party guests but Crouch are aware of the secretary's strip-tease, but each time he turns her way, she has just swung her trapeze into the darkness. Elsewhere in the play the secretary is stolid and *"poker-faced"*, never speaking and registering little emotion. The conclusions of Bones and George that Dorothy is a murderess are never verified, and the play leaves unanswered questions about her relations with the three leading men. It is not clear, as George himself says, "what on earth made *her* marry *him*", or whether Dorothy's charge of rape against Bones is true or concocted in order to blackmail him. Although the available evidence suggests the hypothesis that Dorothy is having an affair with Archie, the same evidence could conceivably support her explanation that Archie is her psychiatrist. As the anecdote about Wittgenstein's comment on the rotation of the earth shows, a single observed fact may have more than one possible explanation, and the most obvious is not necessarily correct. Faced with such ambiguity, George asks the question the entire play poses: "How the hell does one know what to believe?"

The answer Inspector Bones gives to that question represents that of the man on the street, for he embodies the intellectual processes of ordinary people while Dorothy expresses their emotional need. Bones's approach to solving the murder (and, by extension, the mystery of reality) is direct but altogether too simple for the complex issues involved. It is that of a detective whose main interest is show business (in other words, appearances). The precise analytical methods and elaborate distinctions of philosophy are mumbo-jumbo to him: when George introduces himself as a logician, Bones thinks he has said *magician*. Differences between schools of philosophy are likewise lost on him: "You bloody philosophers are all the same," he says of George and McFee. Bones's habit of scrambling names sometimes shows an intuitive grasp of the truth—as when he calls Archie Sir Jim (gym) and Sir Archibald Bouncer. But it also suggests the lack of precision in sense and reference to which everyday language is prone and which formal philosophy strives to avoid.

Bones's hope of arriving at a correct solution to the murder rests with his sentimental faith in a lover's insight into the motives of Dorothy and his adherence to the detective's code of integrity and disinterestedness. "This is a British murder enquiry," he says, "and some degree of justice must be seen to be more or less done." Because circumstantial evidence implicates Dorothy, Bones will go only so far to get her off, in spite of his crush on her; he looks for signs of temporary insanity but will not buy a phony suicide. Nevertheless, his passion wars with his integrity and prejudices his conclusions. When he describes Dorothy as "a delicate creature, like a lustrous-eyed little bird you could hold in your hand, feeling its little brittle bones through its velvety skin—vulnerable . . . highly strung," his language, hopelessly compromised by maudlin sentiment, reveals that he does not clearly perceive even her, let alone the crime. After all, the presence of the corpse does not in itself prove guilt, and Bones may want Dorothy to be guilty so that he can come to her rescue with the insanity plea. Asked why he suspects her, he can only reply that "I have a nose for these things." The example of Bones demonstrates that no tenable conclusions about reality can be reached by relying, as the average man does, on instinct and emotion bolstered by casual observation.

The logical positivist perception of reality is reflected in Archie's handling of the murder. In *Jumpers*, Stoppard depicts logical positivism as providing the intellectual impetus behind the modern drift toward materialism, utilitarianism, and state socialism. Archie is a composite figure embodying various prophets of this secular drift—psychiatrist, lawyer, bureaucrat, and physical culturist as well as philosopher. Under the leadership of jumpers like Archie, the radical liberals embark on their program to "rationalize" all social and religious institutions and even patterns of thought. God and the soul, their existence unverified, no longer have any reality. The fear of temporal law having therefore replaced respect for divine authority, the Chair of Divinity is offered to a policeman. Archie regards Dorothy's soul-sickness as a neurosis to be treated by a machine that examines her skin: in much the same way, logical positivism holds that the basic nature of the world can be understood by studying its "skin," the language through which we perceive it. The socialists appoint as Archbishop of Canterbury an agricultural minister who will feed bodies rather than save souls. Since statements of moral principle are viewed as expressions of the speaker's feelings rather than the setting forth of absolutes, the university's Chairs of Ethics and Logic are kept separate.

Using one of G. E. Moore's favorite reasoning tactics, *reductio ad absurdum*, George ridicules the materialism of the jumpers with a one-sentence summary of their philosophy: " 'No problem is insoluble given a big enough plastic bag.' " Archie's response to McFee's murder proves this summary to be accurate: he disposes of the corpse in a large plastic bag, blackmails Bones with the alleged rape of Dorothy, and certifies in his capacity as coroner that McFee crawled into the bag and shot himself. Archie is ruthlessly efficient in coping with life's immediate contingencies and therefore more immediately helpful to Dorothy than George and Bones. But the riddle of "who done it" he ignores. His final pronouncement about the murder rests on the logical positivist principle that no question about reality is worth asking unless one knows how to answer it: "We will never even know for certain who did shoot McFee. Unlike mystery novels, life does not guarantee a denouement; and if it came, how would one know whether to believe it?" Logical positivism can offer answers to the questions of life because it excludes unanswerable questions. In *Language, Truth and Logic*, Ayer designates all propositions that are neither "tautologies" (definitions) nor empirical hypotheses as "metaphysics." Any propositions about non-material reality (such as God, the soul, or the ideal) are metaphysics, including almost all statements made by theologians, poets, and even philosophers. For Ayer, such questions about the universe as "who done it" are not the proper concern of philosophy, which "as a genuine branch of knowledge, must be distinguished from metaphysics", and he does not conceal his contempt for those who have tried to answer them: "The labours of those who have striven to describe . . . [a transcendental] reality have all been devoted to the production of nonsense."

Jumpers demonstrates some of the drawbacks to the logical positivist attitude toward reality. For one thing, treating McFee's death as a problem of waste disposal leaves no room for sorrow over McFee the man, the unique individual who will never again know life on this earth. Archie's first reaction to his colleague's death is glib and callous: "It's a great pity,"

Dorothy quotes him as saying, "but it's not as though the alternative were immortality." The play ties this careless devaluation of life to the "emotive theory of ethics," the logical positivist doctrine that ethical statements are expressions of the speaker's feelings, not of absolutes, and the corollary principle that morality is the totally relative product of one's culture. As Ayer puts it in *Language, Truth and Logic*, "in so far as [statements of value] are not scientific, they are not in the literal sense significant, but are simply expressions of emotion which can be neither true nor false." Thus, curiously, "a strictly philosophical treatise on ethics should . . . make no ethical pronouncements." Stoppard represents this position as leading to the abandonment of ethics altogether. In this way, McFee's espousal of the emotive theory of ethics contributed to a climate of amorality in which his own murder became more likely.

A second drawback is that logical positivism cannot, by virtue of its materialistic assumptions, give Dorothy the spiritual comfort and reassurance she craves. It can dispose of the body but not of the spiritual dilemma of needing to believe and being unable to. Dorothy's need is reflected in her lament for the loss of our absolutes: "We are no longer the still centre of God's universe . . . and all our . . . thou-shalts and . . . thou-shalt-nots . . . look . . . like the local customs of another place. When that thought drips through to the bottom. . . . There is going to be such . . . gnashing of unclean meats, such covetting of neighbours' oxen and knowing of neighbours' wives. . . . Because the truths that have been taken on trust, they've never had edges before." Archie's response is that required by his logical positivism, the cliché response of the psychiatrist—"When did you first become aware of these feelings?" It is inadequate because it treats Dorothy's agony as purely subjective, ignoring the madness of the external world, the historical crisis of belief that triggered it. In the same way, Archie's materialism means that he can offer Dorothy sex but not love. This is why she turns to George for comfort both here and elsewhere in the play.

As a philosopher, George proposes to "set British moral philosophy back forty years," to restore it to its pre-Wittgenstein views. He counters the emotive theory of ethics by arguing that although men have believed various things to be good at different times and places, their particular beliefs have meaning only in relation to the concept "good" whose existence all men have intuitively recognized. This argument resembles that of G. E. Moore in his *Principia Ethica;* there Moore argued that good is an unanalyzable quality like the color yellow. Good is good; yellow, yellow. We cannot define these qualities, but we can recognize them when we experience them and can therefore legitimately ask such questions as "What things are good in themselves?" and "What things can produce good?"

Although the original George Moore could find no convincing evidence that God exists, the George of *Jumpers* affirms God's existence on several traditional grounds—that He is a first cause, that He is needed as an authority for moral absolutes, and that His existence can be inferred from life just as the existence of a circle can be inferred from the idea of a polygon with an infinite number of sides. George would prefer a "philosopher's God, logically inferred from self-evident premises" and independent both of organized religion and man's emotional need to believe. But, unlike Archie, he also possesses an authentic passion to know, even in matters where complete knowledge is not possible; he fears more than anything the unknown—death, for instance, rather than dying. In his argument that God can be inferred from life, at the furthest boundary to which reason can carry him George abandons rationality and makes a jump of his own, an existential leap of faith: "Now and again . . . in some quite trivial moment, it seems to me that life itself is the mundane figure which argues perfection at its limiting curve. And if I doubt it, the ability to doubt, to question, to *think*, seems to be the curve itself. *Cogito ergo deus est.*"

Even to George himself, it sounds like he believes because he believes: "All I know is that I think that I know that nothing can be created out of nothing, that my moral conscience is different from the rules of my tribe, and that there is more in me than meets the microscope—and because of *that* I'm lumbered with this incredible, indescribable, and definitely shifty God." In these passages, George speaks to and for that element in man's nature which craves sureties in spite of reason and evidence. He is not so out-of-step with his contemporaries after all. Wittgenstein summarizes "the whole sense" of the *Tractatus* in these words: "What can be said at all can be said clearly, and what we cannot talk about we must pass over in silence." Chiefly concerned with the limits of what can be said and reasoned, Wittgenstein was also something of a mystic, aware that things exist "we cannot talk about," things beyond the limits reached by reason. George's convictions about God lie beyond the boundary where analytical philosophy halts and mystical theology takes over.

As a result, George, though he may not have a more rational argument than the logical positivists, has more of what we might call soul. He contrasts with McFee, who "never put himself at risk by finding mystery in the clockwork," and whose death, for that reason, "left nothing behind but a vacancy," a gap in the pyramid of jumpers. Stoppard has said that

Jumpers originated with the image of a pyramid of acrobats with one missing. The appropriateness of the image to characterize the logical positivists is evident, for it connotes not their momentary defiance of material laws in the act of intellection but their ultimate subjection to them.

Several details of *Jumpers* testify to George's philosophical competence. His ability to interpret Dorothy's mimes in their running game of charades signifies a grasp of reality which goes beyond the narrowly literalist range of logical positivism. In her first charade, for instance, she actually appears to be dead, but he correctly recognizes she is miming, in spite of her earlier cries of "murder." In the dream-like *Coda*, where George and Archie debate their philosophical positions, Archie's presentation is a paragraph of gobbledy-gook, a parody of the formal languages devised by logicians to insure the precision of their statements (it is, in fact, a highly ambiguous conglomeration of interwoven puns). After the audience at the debate cheers Archie's nonsense, George offers a spirited and cogent refutation of logical positivism in which he argues that the principle of verification is a two-edged sword. In practice, the logical positivists make many value judgments which cannot be verified—that socialism and technological progress offer the best hope for feeding the world and that gymnastics is healthy, to name only two. But how can they be sure that a well-fed world and good health are to be desired? If they can agree to the relatively simple proposition that the Bristol train left from Paddington only "if they were actually there when it left—and even then only on the understanding that all the observable phenomena associated with the train leaving Paddington could equally well be accounted for by Paddington leaving the train," how can they "claim to *know* that life is better than death, that love is better than hate," both very complex propositions? Given their strict requirements for affirming a truth, what cannot finally be doubted?

These details favorable to George are undercut by others which suggest that he fails as a husband and as a detective. The nature of the failure is implied in Stoppard's choice of G. E. Moore as a model for his hero. Although respected as a philosopher, Moore was notorious among his acquaintances for what one writer calls "an almost childlike naiveté concerning ordinary affairs." In *Russell and Moore*, A. J. Ayer quotes J. M. Keynes on Moore's "unworldliness and his indifference to the 'qualities of a life of action' " and points out that Moore himself conceded that his work took its "main stimulus" not "from direct reflection of 'the world or the sciences' but rather from what other philosophers had said about them." All these traits are displayed by the George of *Jumpers*. The self-reflexive nature of his thought is represented by his lecturing before a mirror; he is talking only to himself. The opening stage directions stipulate that either Dorothy's bedroom (which looks out on the world through French windows and television) or George's study must be blacked out, thereby dramatizing the radical separation between the abstract conceptual world of his philosophizing and the "real" world of her breakdown and McFee's corpse. Because of his isolation, George consistently learns of developments in the public drama of the radical-liberal coup and the private drama of the murder indirectly, through others.

George's love for the rarefied atmosphere of abstract logic results in a destructive indifference to human concerns. He dismisses political events as insignificant, yet they have great influence on the actual lives of people. In the *Coda,* he is unwilling or unable to defend the new Archbishop of Canterbury, who, like Thomas à Becket, faces martyrdom when he begins to take his role as spiritual leader seriously. In view of Dorothy's special role in the play, the fact that George is her husband rather than a mere lover like Bones or Archie suggests that he has a closer relationship to "reality" and ought to better comprehend the trauma she suffers. But George repeatedly fails Dorothy as a husband. When she cries first "Murder!" and then "Rape!" Bones and Archie go to her aid, but George disregards her cries for help, responding only when they get so loud that they disrupt his train of thought. In the larger sense, he overlooks her crisis of unbelief: "*Please don't leave me!* I don't want to be left, to cope," Dorothy begs him (almost as if George himself were God), but belief in God is for him a philosophical issue, not a pressing human need. When Dorothy promises to stop seeing Archie and weeps on George's breast, his heart is described in the stage directions as "*uncomprehending,*" and he returns to his study rejecting her invitation. George's eloquence in the *Coda* is unable to restore Dorothy's lost sense of romance, and the play ends with her farewell to the "spoony Juney moon," a symbol for the ideal of undying marital love and fidelity. This gesture suggests that she will turn from her husband to her lover. George's indifference helps to destroy his marriage and, by extension, the civilizing forces of moral tradition and social stability that the institution of marriage embodies.

In the instance of George, philosophy has degenerated into sterile academic debate divorced from the issues actually troubling man. For this reason, he cannot fill Dorothy's need for spiritual assurances, and she must perforce turn to Archie, who can at least help in disposing of the corpse. George's misordering of human priorities is epitomized by the fact that he is more worried about Thumper and Pat, the rabbit and tortoise he uses to refute Zeno's paradoxes, than about Dorothy and McFee.

As a detective, George is no more astute than Bones. He is the last person in the play to learn there has been a murder, his ignorance continuing through several scenes in which others discuss the killing with him but he misunderstands because of various linguistic confusions: for George as for Bones, language is a trap. At one point, he accepts Archie's improbable suicide story. George's eventual solution to the murder is cast in the same language and issues from the same arbitrary intuitive leap as his conclusions about God: "There are many things I know which are not verifiable but nobody can tell me I don't know them, and I think that I know that something happened to poor Dotty and she somehow killed McFee, as sure as she killed my poor Thumper." The last part of this deduction undercuts the reliability of George's overall solution, for the audience eventually learns that George himself shot the rabbit by accident when he mistook Dorothy's cry of "fire" (a noun) for a command to fire (imperative verb) his bow and arrow.

Going to answer the door and expecting to greet Archie, George says to his turtle, "Now might I do it, Pat." The line echoes that of Hamlet as he passes up his chance to stab the praying Claudius. Like Hamlet, George is guilty of thinking too much, and because he is so absorbed in resolving issues solely on the conceptual plane, he is never able to dispatch his rival Archie and regain Dorothy's affections. When George discovers Thumper impaled on his arrow, he utters his own cry for help, for the emotional support he has denied Dorothy. Though a final humanizing touch, that cry once more emphasizes George's ineffectuality in the realm of action.

Whatever may be Stoppard's personal views about God, *Jumpers* does not endorse George's position at the expense of those of Bones and Archie. It does not show a brilliant Sherlock Holmes outwitting the bumbling representatives of Scotland Yard and triumphantly proving that the murderer is the one person we would never suspect. At the end, we have not discovered the identity of the murderer or the nature of his motive, but have merely listened to several inconclusive speculations and received some inkling of the plethora of possible culprits, the variety of their motives, and the ambiguities of the evidence. McFee's puzzling murder forms a dramatic image of a reality as striking, as full of menace, and as enigmatic as the sharp sound made by the closing of the secretary's purse. That sound of closure is all the answer man gets when he seeks knowledge of life's ultimate mysteries, yet the presence of the detectives in *Jumpers* testifies that he will never stop seeking.

HOWARD D. PEARCE

Stage as Mirror: "Travesties"

$\mathbf{I}$n Tom Stoppard's *Travesties*, Lenin
and Tzara stand opposed, Lenin living at Number 14 *Spiegelgasse*, Tzara
meeting his associates at the Meierei Bar, Number 1. The name of the
street comments on the two historical figures' thematic and structural relationship in the play. They mirror one another as revolutionaries, but they
differ in that one is transforming the world, the other art. This fundamental
structure of sameness and difference is essential to the design of the play.
It is an imaginative form, not simply conceptual or analytical. It functions
as metaphor, and is a metaphorical principle underlying particular images.

I

The mirror image posits sameness and difference. It is, of course, tied up
with the traditional *topos* of theater-dream, one of the perennial embodi-
ments of the epistemological question. Life and dream reflect one another
with sameness and difference. Without difference life and dream, stage and
world, would flow into one another indistinguishably. The sense of difference discomforts us, and our imaginations, wakened to the life-dream distinction, play upon it. This is not to say that the difference between dream
and reality is an absolute dimensionalization of real as opposed to unreal.
The very distinction sets up reflections that open into other reflections.
We may look for and discover the ironic inversion of dream and reality,
life becoming dream, dream becoming reality. Then the problematic of

From *Modern Language Notes* 5, vol. 94 (December 1979). Copyright © 1979 by Johns
Hopkins University Press.

dream within dream, play within play, multiplies the images, and our meeting with the question of reality becomes manifold reflection. But the exploration of differences is grounded in similarity. We always operate metaphorically, always stand ready to relate the new to the familiar. A *topos* itself gives the clues that make it recognizable as type. We already have the dream and the reality, the stage and life, and if one refers itself to the other, the two together nevertheless manifest a dimensionalizing activity and a dimensionalized world. Together they present an element of the structure of experience. Temporally the theater-dream *topos* recalls for us the old epistemological and ontological problem. Theater and dream are reflective of the real waking world we take for granted, and they function to call our attention to the question of its reality. Univocity is shattered by echo. We pursue unity through multiplicity. We delight in discovering the old form in the new experience. We smile when we recognize that the other we see is actually ourselves in the mirror. But even the recognition provokes us to reflect upon self as if the mirrored image were the reality, to consider how others see us as we appear there. . . .

We shall be concerned to observe how parodies, specifically *Travesties*, reflect their objects and establish relationships between worlds, reflections, and viewers. The viewer is decidedly a factor in *mimesis*, and his perspective too must be taken into account. The premise that he sees only the mirror-image of the absent world need not be granted. His perspective may include mirror and reflected object at the same time, thereby complicating any idea of *mimesis* that gives rise to the mirror metaphor. Given both the imitation and the object imitated as presence, we are brought nearer to the mirror's essential function as equipment. The mirror is not merely an object reflecting but serves as our means of gaining perspective on reality. It gives us *relations* rather than *simple images of objects*. And herein lies the mimetic principle of interpretation. Mirror and mirrored object standing before us are in a relationship that we recognize to be not mere surface reflection but interdependence. Mere perception of object leaves us in the absolute flow of experience, perhaps the unquestioning acceptance of that experience and its reality. Mirror lifts us to contemplation of difference and similarity. And experiencing this function of the mirror brings us into complex relationship with objects in the world. Mirror bespeaks interpretation. The mirror brings to the thematic level the question of reality. The mirror is not, then, mere reflector of surfaces, but causes us to be engaged in a way that we pay attention to similarity and difference. It provokes us to fulfill our nature as interpreters of reality, as Heidegger's *Da-sein*.

This engagement in the dimensions of image and appearance reflects back upon ourselves and calls us into play as interpreting agents. The mirror functions, certainly, not simply to show us the world. The world, as a matter of fact, stands there before us without practical need, in most everyday actions, of mirror at all. Except when the mirror aids in our apprehending the obstructed object, as when the periscope or the rear-view mirror in an automobile serves us, we do not desperately need the mirror to show us the world. It is there. We are here. We are subject and object. But our interpreting nature calls for the shifting perspective of the mirror, a capability that becomes a questioning. Is the surface we see true, or can the mirror show us another angle that hides some contradiction from us? How does our hair look from the back? The mirror plays us up as interpreter.

But in playing us up, the mirror calls us into view. We are reminded that, if the mirror is not necessary merely to see the world, it is indeed absolutely necessary to see ourselves. We are all Narcissus. We cannot fully realize ourselves without the mirror. It is essential to us, and its essential nature encompasses our need to see ourselves in it. Again the mirror reveals itself as something other than the two-dimensional reflection of an object caught in the Platonic gaze. We bring our temporality to it, and bestow upon it the power of the imagination that invites it to transcend time— for and with us. We do not stand apart from the mirror but interpenetrate, share self and Being with it. We become both subject and object. We project ourselves into it and it yields our selves back from its own nature. Narcissus, self-absorbed in his reflection, totally united with image of self, becomes a victim of time and himself. We look for our old selves, the past, in it; and we anticipate the future. Young, we wonder at the past and hope for the future. Old, we long for the past and fear for the future. Time is essential to the mirror, as we use it in interpreting reality. The mirror functions in a temporality that we cannot deny. As equipment, it is far more to us than Plato allowed.

But Plato let us appear as object in the mirror, as artist reflecting himself. The mirror reflects what it itself is not, that is, the spatially absent, when we look at only the mirror and relate it in simplest terms to some unseen. Similarly, it reflects a temporal what-is-not, as we make use of it. Our own images are present in the mirror. But the selves we encounter there are no more the entire "object" than is the partial image the mirror gives us of the totality of world. We are provoked by the mirror to see both the temporally and the spatially absent. The mirror presents a narrowly perspectival image, and we relate that image, which bears as part of its statement to us something of its own limited perspective, to the structures of the world we already know as temporal and spatially constituted. The mirror's image, as a presence, appears as a structure of the world. But the mirror's imitative function is not merely to present an image, as Plato pretends. By its very referentiality it draws us into relationships and interpretative acts of relating. The very absence of its objects, temporal or spatial, appears as an element in the structure of relations. The what-is-not of the image instigates acts of the imagination, the imagination as both image-presenting and relation-drawing faculty. The mirror presents the utterly surface image and provokes us to see beyond into temporal-spatial relationships and, importantly, subject-object relationships.

Here again subject and object are not to be taken as philosophically irreconcilable dimensions. "Being-in-the-world" involves the obvious assumption of subject and object. "But while this presupposition is unimpeachable in its facticity, this makes it indeed a baleful one, if its ontological necessity and especially its ontological meaning are to be left in the dark." Attempts to "prove" the existence of a material world "outside" our subjectivities err in failing to see the circularity of their arguments and in the presupposition of an "isolated subject" rather than "Being-in-the-world." The relationship between subject and object requires their being seen in terms of the subject as *Da-sein*, interpreter of world already in the world, and objects in the world as standing already and always in structural relationships. The world is known through relationships and references. Equipment is known not as simply present object but as object ready-to-hand. It is something *toward* which we are related and beyond which an edifice of relations rises. *Da-sein*, interpreter, grasps the mirror *as* mirror in those relationships. It may be possible with a blank start to free the mirror of relationships to ourselves and the world, to grasp it *"free, as it were, of the 'as'."* But such a "privation" only points up the preconditions of experiencing the mirror and of our fundamental relationships to it in the world.

The mirror functions, then, in presenting images and drawing relations between those images and ourselves and the world. The mirror is the objective pole of metaphor. It is not only utilizable as metaphor but also reflects the very structure of metaphor. E. H. Gombrich suggests that, instead of merely using a metaphorical language loosely and unreflectively, we might open ourselves up to the fundamental structures of metaphorical relationships. Of Lotto's painting, "*Allegory*," he says, "The very metaphors of our language that we use in describing this picture still preserve the basic relationships on which its symbolism is grounded." We need to discover the "keyboard of relationships," the "matrix or scale that has intelligible dimensions." Such "intelligible dimensions" are the referential systems of mirror and its metaphorical double, stage.

The imaginative structures of mirror and metaphor present images and relate them, with the effect of our seeing sameness and difference, presence and absence, self and other. The stage clearly functions as mirror, and mimetic theory of drama has assumed this premise. But the metaphor of mirror-stage has been too easily simplified, stage and reflected world being taken to be merely object and object. And the referential relationships themselves are precisely the problem with the stage metaphor. Even in Aristotle there is a certain ambiguity about reflector and reflection. The imitative act might even be taken by interpreters of Aristotle to be an act of the playwright, though Aristotle clearly talks of two other dimensions of imitation. He never reconciles his discussion of the stage as imitation of reality with that of the tragic experience of the audience as imitation. But fortunately Aristotle's unresolved treatment of *mimesis* leaves us open to the multiplicity of stage as mirror. The multiple reflections, the interpenetrating of subject and object, the referentiality of experience, all complexly there in mirror relations, are the essence of *mimesis*. And this manifold of reflection is only complicated by the stage metaphor, since reflections are of not only subject and object but also subject and subject. The relationship between two human beings is different than that between human being and object, even equipment. The mirror is a special kind of equipment in that, though in a tool's scheme of references other human beings are implicit, the mirror brings us directly into relationships of self and others. As a matter of fact, the mirror manifests the essential relationship we have with others. We ordinarily assume that some psychological condition, "none too happily designated as 'empathy,' " is the "bridge from one's own subject . . . to the other subject." But, Heidegger suggests, the relation we have with others is essential to our being and we already have "an understanding of Being" that involves our own relatedness toward others. Our relationship toward them is then "a Projection of one's own Being-towards-oneself 'into something else.' The Other would be a duplicate of the Self." Heidegger is suggesting that there is an essential, underlying *structure* of relationship between ourselves and others, a structure of doubling, that makes possible such apprehensions of our relationships as "empathy" or "identification with." Wordsworth may be cited to exemplify such a mimetic theory. In imitating the passions of others, the poet may "let himself slip into an entire delusion, and even confound and identify his own feelings with theirs." Here again the mirror serves to clarify that relationship, to point up the structure of duplication. The doubling of world images produces the structure of sameness and difference. The doubling of human images effects the same forms but opens up as well into manifold interior landscapes as imaginative structures.

II

Stoppard's Lenin and Tzara are such a stage image of mirroring. *Spiegelgasse* is the appropriate setting for their revolutions in art and the world. Stoppard's play is like a hall of mirrors, character mirroring character, art mirroring world, stage mirroring art reflecting world, artist reflecting world reflecting artist, present reflecting past. In the tradition of memory play or dream play, *Travesties* raises the fundamental question of whether reality lies in dream or in life. Old Carr controls the action, as remembering and reflecting agent. From the first he is undependable, and Old Cecily's final correction of his fiction only underlines the fact that his is a problematical image of reality. The dream play raises its own doubt about the validity of its own reality. Henry Carr's dream—the major action of the play, as it frees itself of historical document—reflects upon itself. Carr's final speech in Act I declares the compelling motive of the action—Carr's ambivalence toward the successful artist, James Joyce, and toward himself in relation to the artist. The play is a daydream of frustrated power and neglected fame: "I dreamed about him, dreamed I had him in the witness box, a masterly cross-examination . . . and I *flung at* him—'And what did you do in the Great War?' 'I wrote *Ulysses*,' he said. 'What did you do?'
    Bloody nerve."
    As presumptuous nobody, Carr has made himself and Joyce chief reflectors. Tzara and Lenin are simply further duplications of the essential opposition of like principles. Both revolutionaries, Lenin and Tzara are antagonists, one an artist of the real believing entirely in world reality, the other a realist of art believing not at all in meaningful world reality. Lenin has been the "creator" of the "Bolshevik orthodoxy"; Tzara's art "has no meaning. It is without meaning as Nature is." Carr comes to find an antagonist in Lenin, deciding in Act II that he must block Lenin's plans. First having argued against Cecily's socialist view of art, Carr begins to consider that he might have made himself important, "might have stopped the whole Bolshevik thing in its tracks," and finally decides that Lenin "must be stopped." Intellectual and moral chameleon, Carr seeks in Act II power and fame in the real world. His dream is that he has become a counter-revolutionary, reflecting Lenin. But as art and life are reflectors,

Carr requires an artist antagonist as well as a world-conqueror antagonist. Predominantly in Act I, but throughout the play, Carr has cast Joyce as his chief antagonist and fellow artist. Carr's own pride in having played the lead role in Wilde's play—"not Ernest, the other one"—qualifies him as artist. But in his presentation of the action, as Old Carr, he characterizes his dream play as literary memoirs, autobiography, tribute. Appropriating a title from Nadezhda Krupskaya—*Memoirs of Lenin*—he begins his imaginative recollection as "Memories of James Joyce." Variations on a title range from "Through the Courts With James Joyce" through "The Ups and Downs of Consular Life in Zurich During the Great War: A Sketch" to, focusing on his political counterpart, "Lenin As I Knew Him."

As artist presenting his version of reality, Carr produces this doubling of reality in the major action and characters and in glimpsed reflections. Tzara's mention of "good old Arp" raises the question of doubling, when Joyce asks, "In what way is the first name of your friend Arp singular?" This comic exchange depends upon the doubling of relationships between word and referent as well as between multiple meanings of words. Its vehicle is the pun. The pun, like irony, calls meaning into question, thereby posing the corollary question, "How does the word imitate its referent?" Joyce's term "singular" means "extraordinary" or "noteworthy." Tzara understands Joyce's meaning, but converts the straight-man's question to paranomasia. Arp's first name is singular "in that it is duplicate." It turns out that in the process of Joyce's scholastic questioning Arp becomes seen as doubled, as "Hans Arp. Jean Arp," but only "linguistically," each name "being a translation of the other." In Arp's case, the ground of doubling is the real, since "he is a native of Alsace, of French background, and a German citizen by virtue of the conquest of 1870." Verbal play manifests the principle of similarity and difference that is essential to the mirror. This incidental joke turns on that principle and opens the question of relationships between reality and language as well as the question of language itself. And again Stoppard's reflexiveness of language is a reminder of Joyce's and Wilde's verbal play. The prologue presents Joyce, Tzara, and Lenin identifying themselves by their own words. Joyce, for instance, dictates to Gwen, "Deshill holles Eamus." Wilde calls reality into question by challenging language. His aphorisms subvert complacently accepted truths. Cecily's diary is "simply a very young girl's record of her own thoughts and impressions, and consequently meant for publication." Cecily remarks to Algernon that is always painful to part from a new acquaintance, though "the absence of old friends one can endure with equanimity." Chasuble calls attention to the way words mean by explaining, "I spoke metaphorically." And finally values are referred to verbal skill: "In matters of grave importance, style, not sincerity is the vital thing." Stoppard's language elaborates this Wildean principle with the exuberance of Joycean word-play. Carr's comment that he feels better after a glass of hock provokes Tzara to question whether he might have felt better regardless. Carr responds, "post hock, propter hock." Like Wilde, Stoppard questions the relationship between words and reality. Carr thinks that the newspapers would not have called "the British to arms without a proper regard for succinct alliteration." Carr, of course, is a literalist, arguing to Tzara that "if there is any point in using language at all it is that a word is taken to stand for a particular fact or idea and not for other facts or ideas." Joyce, according to Tzara, "sorts language into hands of contract bridge." Stoppard's transformations of language are, like Joyce's, ruthless. Foreign languages seem at times little less alien than the English of Stoppard's text. The tendency toward dada courts absolute destruction. But Stoppard's language produces, rather than meaninglessness, a playful opening up of the question of meaning. Reader or auditor is engaged as interpreter and even translator, as are the characters in the play. They cause one another difficulties with interpretation. Person and place can be confused:

> CARR: I expect you'll be missing Sofia.
> TZARA: You mean Gwendolyn.
> CARR (frowns; clears): Bucharest.

But the reader or audience is left with this confusion when in the end Cecily tells Carr that "Sophia married that artist." Can we conclude anything about the *real* identities of women named "Gwendolyn" and "Sophia" in this sort of *mimesis*? Is this another instance of doubling identities?

At any rate, Stoppard utilizes from historical data the doubling of disguise, in Lenin's scheme to return to Russia. Lenin requires for his trip the identification papers of "two Swedes who resemble Zinoviev and me, but since we cannot speak Swedish they must be deaf mutes. I enclose our photographs for this purpose." Tzara's response is predictably incredulous: "Two . . . Swedish . . . deaf . . . mutes . . . ???" Lenin himself, of course, provides the verbal doubling in his two names, Lenin and, "as he was known on his library ticket, Vladimir Ilyich Ulyanov."

This doubling of name, character, and image does not produce Plato's clear, hierarchical structure of greater and lesser realities. From the ideal to the actual to the mirror image are for Plato steps downward on the scale of reality. Stoppard's reflected images raise questions of where reality lies. Lenin's view of the two Gorki's—man and artist—is comfortable. He likes them both. But his view of Mayakovsky is somewhat troubled. He cannot understand why the young people in the communes read Mayakovsky, who "used to shout his fractured lines in a yellow blazer with blue roses painted on his cheeks." Evidently the futurist Mayakovsky Lenin knows is not the reformed Mayakovsky the young people read. Multiple images of character cast identity into doubt. Henry Carr even mistakes himself for someone else, commenting on the "trousers, etcetera, purchased by me for my performance as Henry—or rather—*god dammit!*—the other one." The premise underlying Carr's error seems to be that the actor loses his own identity in playing a role. Theories of acting such as Stanislavski's generate problems in striving for "identification" of subjectivities, as opposed, for instance, to Brechtian "alienated" acting. One theory confuses reflector and reflected while the other keeps clear distinctions and distance. Carr's confusion demonstrates Ben Jonson's theory that "we do play others until we forget ourselves." Carr's mistaking of Jack and Algernon, extrapolated from the disguises and mistaken identities of Wilde's play, is repeated in his confusion of Algernon and himself. His continual resorting to the expression "the other one" reveals his own unstable identity as well as his uncertainty about objective reality.

And the play's confused and confusing versions of reality are the result of the same mimetic principle. As actor imitates character, play imitates action. As Carr refers himself to Algernon, *Travesties* refers itself to *The Importance of Being Earnest*. A reflection of Wilde's play, *Travesties* engages the audience in a referential dialectic. Carr's story "occasionally jumps the rails and has to be restarted at the point where it goes wild." (Stoppard at a later point more clearly exploits the pun on "wild," " 'Drive 'em Wilde' " of course being more likely to strike reader than auditor. The point of return in Act I is Bennett's (alias Lane's) line to Carr (alias Algy): "I have put the newspapers and telegrams on the sideboard, sir." Although the line is not actually Lane's, its function is. The servant in the play reflects social stratification in the play's world. And Carr reflects the values of the world of which Wilde's play is a reflection. As Bennett reports properly on the revolution and the war from the manservant's proper conservatism, the effete gentleman Carr mildly objects, "I'm not sure that I'm much interested in your views, Bennett." These echoes of Algy in Carr are incremental. Carr says to Bennett, "If the servant classes are going to ape the fashions of society, the end can only be ruin and decay." Later to Tzara (Jack) he says, "If society is going to ape the fashions of philosophy, the end can only be ruin and decay." Carr's impetus is toward losing himself in Wilde's play. Of Bennett he says, "I have always found that irony among the lower orders is the first sign of an awakening social consciousness." But these inexact allusions become near the end of Act I Algy's line verbatim, Carr reading from the text of *Earnest*: "Really, if the lower classes don't set us a good example what on earth is the use of them? They seem as a class to have absolutely no sense of moral responsibility."

This doubling of Wilde's play in Stoppard's appears as travesty, and travesty is by nature a particular kind of imitation. A term loosely used, "travesty" may be in a class with burlesque or parody. But the term usually implies that the travesty is doing some violence to the object imitated. That is certainly what Carr means when he complains about the judge's decision on his and Joyce's suit and counter-suit. Carr has lost—"in other words, a travesty of justice." In Carr's mind the end of law is justice, good and true, and a legal proceeding that fails to effect its end is perverse. There is an element of perversity in the travesty, as there is in all art. But as in all art the imitation is not merely destructive, but rather reconstructive. Even when the work of art struggles against form, as in William Carlos Williams' *Paterson*, it is generating its own unique structures. Stoppard's play struggles against the simple dualism implicit in the term "travesty." The plural form *Travesties* implies the openness and multiplicity of a mimetic art freed from the Platonic dualism. Carr's complaint is about a real action in a real world, a particular action based in a repeatable form. Betraying the formal source in law, the particular action becomes travesty. This principle might pertain in the simple repetitions of life, but when art becomes implicated it tends to deny a central vantage for absolute ethical determinations. Stoppard's many-levelled travesty mingles life and art as reciprocally reflective.

If I seem so far to have ignored important distinctions between real characters and events and fictional ones, the result is purposeful. *Travesties* turns upon the central question of degrees of unreality. To that extent an anti-Aristotelean play, it exploits improbability rather than probability. The improbability of history itself places Joyce, Lenin, and Tzara in Zurich with Carr—not as Carr "remembers" them, but there at roughly the same time during the war. But the chief reflective agent in the play, *Earnest*, is improbably the genesis of improbability. Joyce and Carr *were* doing Wilde's play. History is built on the improbabilities of art. Thus the improbabilities of Wilde's play become the overt plot of Stoppard's: the name Jack hits on, Ernest, turning out to be actually his father's name; the recently acquired teacher of Cecily, Miss Prism, turning out to be responsible for Jack's loss of identity. Stoppard's travesty of Wilde's play reveals how *Earnest* is a travesty of life. The happy romantic and social outcome of Wilde's play, the paired couples' being economically matched, becomes a travesty of Gilbert and Sullivan in Stoppard's "discovery" scene. Wilde's play gleefully affirms order and control in the face of the crumbling of values and social structures of *fin de siècle* England. Social order is reaffirmed in the precisely controlled design of Wilde's improbable action.

Life and art, in the dance of travesty, can rapidly change places. Lenin provides Stoppard with a powerful structure of reality in a play that fundamentally parodies a work of art. The second act of *Travesties* begins with Cecily's lecture on Lenin delivered directly to the audience. And Act II develops on the counterpoint of Carr's fiction and Cecily's truth. The presentation of Lenin and Nadya is usually verbatim from primary historical sources. But truth breaking in does not deny the reality of art. On the contrary, Lenin shows a sensitivity to art that must be denied and in the denial brings him near to tragic stature. He denies part of his own nature through commitment. Though he does not "know of anything greater" than Beethoven's Appassionata Sonata, it makes him "want to say nice stupid things and pat the heads of those people who while living in this vile hell can create such beauty. . . . One's duty is infernally hard." Reality is the ultimate object of travesty's imitation, but the travesty calls reality itself into question. Stoppard's play travesties Wilde's, which travesties life. It travesties history as well, which seems to travesty its own principles of cause and effect, of probability.

But *Travesties* refers itself as well to other multiple reflections of life and art. Its primary technical analogue is Joyce's *Ulysses*, appropriately, since envy of that work is the source of Carr's story. And *Ulysses*, like Stoppard's play, travesties life and art. It is a travesty of Homer's *Odyssey*, which in its very artistic control is a travesty of life. But it is also a travesty of life, a day in Dublin. It even converts a real character, Carr, to a minor comedic role. And *Travesties* saves Carr from that ignominy, not in refurbishing his image but in casting him in the role of protagonist. As Joyce says in *Travesties*, if there is "any meaning" in life and art, "it is in what survives as art . . . yes even in the celebration of nonentities." Joyce is here expounding his theory of art to Tzara, but his comment is reflexive. It applies to the "nonentity" Carr as well as to Joyce's own Leopold Bloom. Carr has in a sense been damned to hell by Joyce and translated by Stoppard. Stoppard's play, celebrating the nonentity, displays Carr's creation of an imaginative structure out of history, and as distortion of history it is travesty.

But I have said that travesty may be less destructive than the term implies. Carr, thinking of a simple life reality, finds no difficulty in affirming ethical views, against miscarriages of justice, against Lenin's revolution.

But given the open reflexiveness of reciprocal life and art, a deforming art is always re-forming, and what appears to be merely satiric may be in fact commemorative. Joyce, in his apologia to Tzara, argues that Homer pre-served the Trojan War, which as mere life was, in time, turning itself into dust. And as the *Odyssey* commemorated Odysseus, he says, "I wish my Dublin Odyssey will *double* that immortality" (my italics). *Travesties*, in turn, redoubles the immortalities of *Earnest, Ulysses,* Carr, Joyce, Tzara, Lenin, the great wars of Troy, and the world. The work of art makes permanence out of time's annihilations.

Zurich is, more than setting for the action, symbol of art's trans-forming power. It has become, as Joyce explains, "the theatrical centre of Europe" because of the war. Being a neutral place, it is "the continuation of the war by other means." That is, it is the transformation of world war into the war of art, into which England enters to "show the Swiss who leads the world in dramatic art." Zurich and the artist are antithetical to war. "Neutrality," uninvolvement, is the artist's placidity in the face of life commitments. Carr argues to Tzara that the life of battle in "a foreign field" is "unmatched by anything in the whole history of human carnage." But "to be an artist *at all* is like living in Switzerland during a world war." The artist's withdrawal is to Carr reprehensible, but "to be an artist *in Zurich, in 1917,* implies a degree of self-absorption that would have glazed over the eyes of Narcissus." Ironically, in presenting his own dramatic version of reality, Carr the artist argues for involvement and against art. His allusion to Narcissus suggests an absolute power in the mirror, reflector absorbing reflected object, artist lost in the labyrinth of his art. The work of art achieves permanence and stillness, but at the expense of life. Switzerland is "in a state of rest . . . the still centre of the wheel of war." The static reflector Carr envisions is the opposite of the "doubled immortality" of Joyce's fiction. Carr's art-reality distinction is in the tradition of mimetic theory that reduces imitation and object to a theoretical pair of objects, isolated from other subjects and objects, lifted out of time. Carr ends, of course, with that duality levelled to reciprocal meaninglessness. His defense of life has lost itself in a life-art equation. He may indeed have become Narcissus. The play ends with his philosophizing, "I learned three things in Zurich during the war. I wrote them down. Firstly, you're either a revolutionary or you're not, and if you're not you might as well be an artist as anything else. Secondly, if you can't be an artist, you might as well be a revolutionary . . .

I forget the third thing."

It is precisely the forgotten third thing that could have set Carr free from the thought of the either-or, art-life, the polarities that have lost meaningful distinction for him.

Joyce's mimetic theory opens up manifold reflexiveness. Instead of a Zurich as still center of life's motion, Stoppard's Joycean doubling becomes multiple, open-ended reflection: "In Zurich in Spring in wartime a gentleman is hard put to find a vacant seat for the spurious spies peeping at police spies spying on spies eyeing counter-spies." This image of manifold world reflections is repeated in artists' reflecting one another. "What," Joyce asks, "reduced to their simplest reciprocal form, were Tzara's thoughts about Ball's thoughts about Tzara, and Tzara's thoughts about Ball's thoughts about Tzara's thoughts about Ball?"

Those reflections become at large in the play Lenin's, Tzara's, Joyce's, and Carr's thoughts about one another and about the fundamental reflections of life and art. Consequently the play becomes multiple reflections on dramatic theory and practice. The simple mimetic theory of Carr becomes in Lenin a functionalist view of art, Plato's Replublic transformed into the Marxist state. Tzara complicates the relationship between life and art. Dada is anti-art because life is chance. "Everything is Chance, even design." Even the word "dada" Tzara discovered "by accident." Thus the dadaist poem is truly a de-construction of all art that presumes freedom and power and ordering capability in the artist. It is an essentially negative activity, travesty in the sense Carr intends when he uses the word. According to Tzara we need, not "geniuses," but "vandals . . . desecrators . . . simple-minded demolition men." Shakespeare's eighteenth sonnet is cut into "wild and whirling words" that are recombined at random. A meaningless world frees art of the responsibility to reflect it truly or to serve it profitably. Tzara's world is fecal, and his art is excremental in response. Man is a coffee mill—"Eat—grind—shit"—and art has become the same— "paint—*eat*—sculpt—grind—write—*shit*." "Making poetry," Tzara observes, "should be as natural as making water"; "all literature is obscene"; "art for art's sake—I defecate." Carr warns him that his trick of "multi-colored micturition" will become no trick at all if he "dances attendance on Marxism. . . . They'll have you pissing blood."

At first glance Stoppard's art appears to be Tzara's deconstruction of life and art. Lenin and Nadya are cut up and scattered indiscriminately among other real and unreal characters. But Stoppard's play grows out of an opposing principle. History has produced out of the whirl of time an improbable combination in Zurich, what looks like design in life. And the playwright works that improbability, seemingly chance, into baroque form. Stoppard's deconstruction transforms satire into tribute. Carr's ambivalence toward Joyce becomes reconciled in Carr's own drama, in that the play demonstrates Joyce's aesthetic. In its manifold reflections the play gathers history and art into an artifice of permanence.

One aspect of the play takes on the appearance of pastoral elegy, thus drawing elegy into relationships with the many travestied forms. Not only does Old Carr play with possible titles that would make Joyce the hero of the play. Even in complaining of their litigation, he is conscious of the dead Joyce, "him dead in the cemetery up the hill." The living poet's tribute to the dead poet is as in the elegy a preservation, a lifting up. Carr's pettiness and envy not only cast Carr and Joyce in reflective roles as artists, but also draw the "real" playwright Stoppard into reflective relationship with the dead novelist. And as in pastoral elegy the preservation is doubled. Elegist in denying time, death, and decay translates lost fellow poet into the design of the poem. But he himself, reflecting the dead artist, will become like him too in death. In that doubling, the artist in the act of pastoral affirmation preserves himself as well as his double, in his own work of art, from death. And Carr knows from the beginning that Joyce has been that kind of artist: "To be in his presence was to be aware of an amazing intellect bent on shaping itself into the permanent form of its own monument—the book the world now knows as *Ulysses.*" In turn, Stoppard in his travesty of *Ulysses* becomes that intellect shaping itself in its own monument, mirroring itself among the multiple reflections of its *mimesis.*

III

The doublings and redoublings of *Travesties* appear, then, as manifold interrelationships. The mirroring of the stage produces not merely reflections but the structures of those relationships, permanence and flux, sameness and difference, familiarity and newness, presence and absence, subjectivity and objectivity, past and present. Travesty as a deconstructive art is finally positive, reconstructive. The mirroring necessarily involves subjectivities, interpenetrations of subjects, as well as objectivities. The metaphorical structure of reflection engages us in understanding the very structures of relationships, mimetic art being, as Aristotle says, a development of our instinct to learn through imitation. We are given back, in the imitative event, ourselves as well as the structures of our relationships with others. And we are cut loose from the event, realizing temporal mobility in the play of imagination. The mirror of stage does not singly imitate some object, but primarily puts us in play in a complex of referential structures. It does not merely show us an image of the world, but, like the mirror essential to our seeing ourselves, puts *us* into that play of relationships.

JUNE M. SCHLUETEZ

Moon and Birdboot, Rosencrantz and Guildenstern

Along with Harold Pinter, Tom Stoppard is probably the most important playwright on the contemporary British scene. His plays, like those of Pinter, are informed with a tragicomic sense of the absurd and the contingent nature of man's existence. A frequently recurring character in Stoppard's plays is the marginal man, the character standing on the fringe of the central action, tentatively placing first one foot and then the other into the arena of activity. Speaking of Stoppard's first and best-known play, *Rosencrantz and Guildenstern Are Dead* (1966), C. W. E. Bigsby characterizes Stoppard's vision of man:

> Man, in other words, is a minor character in a drama which he cannot understand, dependent for recognition on people who do not even control their own fate and forces which may not even exist.

Man's confrontation with his world is a recurring theme in Stoppard's plays. Whether rendered in the form of two minor characters from a Shakespearean play assuming heroic status (*Rosencrantz and Guildenstern Are Dead*), a professor of moral philosophy discoursing on God while his ex-showgirl wife plays surrealistic games (*Jumpers*, 1972), or a pseudohistorical meeting in a Zurich library of three radically different revolutionaries, Lenin, Joyce, and Tristan Tzara (*Travesties*, 1974), the theme of man's relationship to reality—his insignificance, exile, and search for self—is manifest.

From *Metafictional Characters in Modern Drama*. Copyright © 1977, 1979 by Columbia University Press.

As important as Stoppard's philosophical explorations, however, is his preoccupation with his own art. Stoppard's plays are nonrealistic in form, undisguisedly theatrical, and supremely self-conscious. Indeed, the playwright has succeeded admirably in uniting the innovative form of his plays with their philosophical content, making his ventures into the nature of reality—and illusion—inquiries into the very rationale for art. One of Stoppard's less well-known plays, The Real Inspector Hound, which premiered in London in 1968, is a particularly fine example of how a playwright integrates these concerns through the use of a metafictional character.

Stoppard's characters acquire metafictional status by virtue of play within play. In the case of The Real Inspector Hound, this "play" is formalized into a structural demand. The characters, who are made to function within two structural units, acquire one identity in the frame play—their "real" identities—and quite another in the inner play—their fictive identities. But the distinction between the identities, and, indeed, between the plays, remains less than absolute. As the characters move across the boundary that separates the outer play from the inner one, the line which separates their identities as critics and members of an audience from their identities as actors and participants in the "whodunit" play becomes increasingly fluid, as does the line which separates the reality of their world as audience and the fiction of the world of Muldoon Manor. In creating first a rigid structural line of demarcation and then violating that line through his protagonists' entrance into the inner play, Stoppard is able to use the play-within-a-play not simply in the traditional way, for enhancing reality, but rather to suggest the nature of role playing and the power of illusion over reality.

The setting for The Real Inspector Hound is an unusually clever one. Besides the seating area for audience and the playing area for actors, there is a third locale in Stoppard's theater: rows of seats—or the impression of such seats—face the audience, with the stage between the real audience and the fictive one. Moon and Birdboot, Stoppard's fictive critics, position themselves in the front row of these seats among the fictive audience. Through this setting, Stoppard is honoring (if only playfully) the classical concept of art imitating nature—the audience is face to face not only with a stage, but with itself. And he is also suggesting, paradoxically, the mirror as a symbol of illusion.

Our initial response to Moon and Birdboot (before the play-within-a-play begins) is amused self-recognition. We watch Moon mimic typical preplay audience gestures: staring blankly ahead, turning his head from side to side as though waiting for someone, and flipping through the pages of his program. When Birdboot joins him, we recognize their conversation as being singularly like our own: they discuss personal matters and professional matters, all on the superficial level permitted by the limited time allowed for preplay patter. The verisimilitude is convincing and works in a conventional way to create a sense of identification between the audience and the critics, but it is in the relationship of Moon and Birdboot to the play-within-a-play that their "reality" is established.

When the play-within-a-play begins, the way in which we view Moon and Birdboot instantly changes. While their identities to this point are those of actors in a mimetic play, when Mrs. Drudge walks on the stage between the critics and audience and begins the Muldoon Manor play, Moon and Birdboot are no longer simply fictive characters. In the presence of Mrs. Drudge, we find ourselves making a distinction between the status of the housekeeper and that of the critics, and as she and the inhabitants of Muldoon Manor take us deeper into the fictionalized world of the play-within-a-play, we increasingly tend to view the frame play, which consists of the conversations of Moon and Birdboot, as an extension of our own reality rather than as play (a process which is once removed from the very experience inherent in the audience/play relationship and to which we are being simultaneously subjected). In fact, we allow Moon and Birdboot virtually to lose their fictionalized status by repeatedly looking to them for their reactions.

As the play-within-a-play continues, we listen to the personal and critical remarks of Moon and Birdboot which Stoppard has cleverly used to intercut and punctuate the acts of the Muldoon Manor play, forcing us to maintain consciously a clear mental line between the world of Muldoon Manor and the "real" world of the critics. Ironically, Stoppard makes no attempt to disguise the fact that Moon and Birdboot are indeed participants in a play; the critics readily admit that the play *has* started *before* anyone has appeared on the Muldoon Manor set. But this, of course, is Stoppard's way of enjoying a private joke, knowing as he does that within moments Mrs. Drudge, clearly a fictional character, will appear to authenticate the critics' reality.

The clear mental line we have established, however, is only temporarily secure. Through the creation of two separate plays, Stoppard manipulates his audience into a compartmentalizing of characters; once the dichotomy of play world and "nonplay" world is established, he proceeds to upset any certainty with respect to those worlds by integrating the plays. Any clear sense we may have had of what is "real" and what is "fictive" is almost irrecoverably disturbed when Moon and Birdboot step forward into Mrs. Muldoon's drawing room and become double characters.

There is a comment made by Moon—almost in passing—between Acts I and II of the "whodunit" play, which at that point seems inappropriate: he says the play is about "the nature of identity." The less than subtle exposition of that play (itself a parody of countless detective tales in which several characters establish their motives for wishing the victim dead) has given Moon little cause to make such a statement, even allowing for his pretentions to intellectualism. Stoppard, however, has every reason to make the remark, and, as an authorial statement, the remark refers not simply to the Muldoon Manor play, but to the entire play. Through the physical interaction between the "real" characters of the outer play and the fictive characters of the inner play, Stoppard is indeed setting up a commentary on the nature of identity.

Part of the conversation of Moon and Birdboot before the beginning of the inner play concerns Birdboot's previous evening's activities. He had spent the evening with an actress who is—not coincidentally—to appear in the play the critics are there to see. Our placement of that circumstance is, naturally enough, removed from the theater; we accept the meeting as having been part of the nonplay world of Birdboot. Similarly, when Birdboot reacts to the beauty of the actress playing Cynthia Muldoon, we place that circumstance as clearly part of that same world. We do not yet make the connection between the events of the nonplay world and the events of the play world. It is only in retrospect, as the play and its surprises unfold, that the exact parallel in the situations of Birdboot and the fictive Simon Gascoyne emerge: just as Birdboot spent the evening with the actress playing Felicity and is now ready to abandon her for the actress playing Cynthia, so did Simon spend the evening with Felicity and is now ready to abandon her for Cynthia.

But more than mimesis is occurring.

The double characters which Moon and Birdboot are to become are anticipated by the dichotomy embodied in this parallel, i.e., that every character has both a real and a fictive identity, the fictive identity being manifested through roles. In much the same way as Pirandello's father and daughter reenact the brothel scene in Six Characters and then watch the actors reenact their reenactment, Stoppard here creates a "real" situation and then assigns actors to play out that situation. We as audience have no difficulty in seeing Birdboot's situation as "real" and Simon Gascoyne's as fictive—until Birdboot unwittingly becomes involved in the fictive action, at which point the role and the "real" merge, seemingly inextricably.

When the Muldoon Manor telephone rings between acts with a call from Birdboot's wife, the critic relinquishes his seat and steps onto the stage. And when Felicity's tennis ball flies through the open window, followed by Felicity, Birdboot becomes—through the unwitting assumption of that role—Simon Gascoyne. The adjustment is no easier for an audience to make than it is for Birdboot. We find ourselves first attempting to reject Birdboot as Simon and to make an adjustment in our perception of Felicity, relinquishing our concept of her as a character in a play and accepting her instead as the woman with whom Birdboot spent last evening. But such a perception cannot sustain itself when Felicity persists in repeating the lines earlier spoken by her to Simon. The fictive Felicity, in control of our perceptions, draws us back, along with Birdboot, into the fictive world. Despite his unwillingness to assume the role and our insistence on still seeing him as critic, Birdboot has become the incarnation of his role, a role which was earlier represented by a fictive character. As critic and Simon Gascoyne, Birdboot has become a double character.

Moon, as yet still a spectator, sees the extent of Birdboot's involvement and attempts to persuade his partner to return to his seat. He is unable, however, to prevent the inevitable consequences of the Muldoon Manor plot: since Birdboot is now Simon, he must be killed. As Moon rushes onstage to retrieve Birdboot, a shot rings out, and Birdboot falls dead. But like his partner before him, by stepping into the Muldoon Manor drawing room, Moon relinquishes more than just his seat; the moment he intrudes upon the fictive world, his identity loses its singularity. With Cynthia's entrance, Moon finds himself caught in a situation just as inescapable as Birdboot's: he has become "Inspector Hound." And, as was the case with his partner, the consequences of that role are inevitable: script has become destiny, and Moon is powerless to prevent the accusation of murder or his ensuing death.

The Real Inspector Hound is, indeed, about "the nature of identity," its central concern being that of a functional or role-playing self. The plight of the critics is reminiscent of our own acquiescence to the demands of social convention, which constantly force us to assume a fictive identity and may result in the essential self's becoming indistinguishable from the role. The remark of the jealous Moon with respect to Higgs, the critic for whom he will always be a stand-in, is an appropriate comment on the double self which develops in the play: "my presence defines his absence, his absence confirms my presence, his presence precludes mine." Moon and Higgs are actually present simultaneously (the dead body turns out to be Higgs), but not in their roles as critics. And the two identities which Moon and Birdboot each possesses exist simultaneously, but when the fictive side of those identities is in operation, the real side cannot be acknowledged. Like actors who assume the part imposed upon them, the individual, by assuming social roles, is sacrificing his essential self.

The final irony of Stoppard's play is that Moon's understudy, Puckeridge, is the mastermind of the confusion. Just as Moon had dreamed of killing Higgs, envisioning a world in which actors are slaughtered by their understudies, magicians sawn in half by glamour girls, and superiors destroyed by their subordinates, so Puckeridge dreamed of an identity independent of Moon, for whom he was an understudy. But Puckeridge realized his dream. In a dramatic insistence upon defining his own identity, Puckeridge arranges—through the very medium which he, Moon, and Higgs criticize—the murder of his superiors.

The end of the play sees a mass interchange of identities: Birdboot's body replaces that of Simon Gascoyne, Moon's replaces that of the murder victim (who is actually Higgs); the actors who played Simon Gascoyne and Inspector Hound step outside the Muldoon Manor drawing room to occupy the seats formerly occupied by Birdboot and Moon and begin making critical remarks about the whodunit play. Now Moon's earlier remark that the play has started and that this is just a pause becomes meaningful. The play is an endless cycle in which two actors—who are, after all, fictive—begin as observers and assume roles within the play they are watching until the line between their reality and the fiction no longer exists. Just as the whodunit play had earlier served to authenticate the critics' reality, now it serves to betray it. Once the fictionalized reality of Moon and Birdboot has become pure fiction, the play, despite its cyclic nature, must end. The audience cannot view the next cycle, since it cannot now accept the two men in the critics' seats as real, and the play depends completely upon that acceptance. In order for the play to continue there must be a new audience, and the line between reality and fiction must again be established.

But Stoppard's play is not only about identity, it is about art as well. The dichotomy between the real and the fictive self which his metafictional characters embody extends as well to the relationship between art and reality.

Stoppard's use of the play-within-a-play structure is in one respect like Shakespeare's use of the device in *Hamlet:* the inner play does indeed fulfill the purpose of art, which is to hold a mirror up to nature. The experience of Birdboot (who is audience) is faithfully duplicated in the inner play. But Stoppard originally told us that his mirror image was "impossible," and his fidelity to the mimetic theory ends with this token honoring.

In fact, art emerges in *The Real Inspector Hound* as a force capable of controlling reality. The inner play in *Hamlet* is able to affect reality only to the extent of the recognition of its audience (Claudius) of the similarity between fiction and reality. Stoppard sets up the play-within-a-play structure so that the distinction between reality and illusion is established, but the distinction is made only so that it might be destroyed. By the end of *The Real Inspector Hound*, the inner play breaks through the boundary separating it from the outer play and encompasses the outer play. In mimetic art, illusion may, in a sense, be said to be giving up its identity, trying to pass for reality. In Stoppard's art, illusion is autonomous. When the inner play breaks through its boundary, illusion imposes itself upon reality, in essence destroying the right of reality to be separately defined. And, as we have seen, the power of illusion is complete: the frame play can no longer be accepted as "reality"; the critics can now be nothing but fictionalized characters. Nor does the power of illusion stop once it has destroyed the reality of the outer play. It extends to our own reality, which is reflected in the reality of the critics, destroying that as well. And if the mirror which reflected our reality is illusion, then perhaps reality is illusion after all.

In Stoppard's earlier play, *Rosencrantz and Guildenstern Are Dead*, a similar set of first marginally involved and then seriously involved characters exists. Every bit as unperceptive as their counterparts in *Inspector Hound*, Rosencrantz and Guildenstern become victims of the play, which defines and controls them. Though philosophically consistent and structurally similar, however, the two plays are hardly carbon copies.

Rosencrantz and Guildenstern Are Dead was first performed as part of the "fringe" of the Edinburgh Festival in 1966. Its first professional performance was in London at the Old Vic, where it opened in 1967; its New York première took place six months later. Reviews were enthusiastic though mixed, John Simon calling the play a "conception of genius" reduced to a "tour de force." As virtually all reviewers noticed, *Rosencrantz and Guildenstern* was clearly derivative, constructed of passages of poetry from Shakespeare (*Hamlet*) and rather loud echoes of Pirandello (*Six Characters*) and Beckett (*Waiting for Godot*). Despite being what Robert Brustein called a "theatrical parasite," however, the play possesses indisputable originality, particularly in the way in which Rosencrantz and Guildenstern achieve their own unique status as metafictional characters.

Though levity is characteristic of most of Stoppard's plays, as we have seen in *The Real Inspector Hound*, that lightness is frequently a surface quality under which more serious concerns lie. Surely this is the case with *Rosencrantz and Guildenstern*, which may be every bit as sober a play philosophically as Beckett's *Waiting for Godot*. In fact, like Didi and Gogo, Rosencrantz and Guildenstern experience the desperation of knowing they must amuse themselves continually in order to pass the time. Like the tramps, the two involve themselves in verbal games and vaudeville routines, and indulge in a kind of self-congratulation for their efforts. A decade and a half removed from their tramp predecessors, however, Rosencrantz and Guildenstern occupy a world in which the questions have changed to premises. The arbitrary quality of the universe which puzzles Vladimir to frustration is a donnée of Rosencrantz and Guildenstern's world, in which even the laws of chance no longer exist: the two flip a coin ninety-two times and watch it turn up heads each time, the unbewildered Rosencrantz experiencing only embarrassment at having won all of Guildenstern's coins. Far from searching for significance in the macrocosm, Rosencrantz and Guildenstern care only about affirming the significance of their own little lives. As Rosencrantz says, "We don't question, we don't doubt. We perform." It is the fact of this performance which is at the heart of Stoppard's investigation into the play's more serious concerns.

Structurally, Stoppard uses a variation of the play-within-a-play to create his characters' metafictional status. The outer play is the ordinary world of Rosencrantz and Guildenstern, a world characterized by coin flipping, game playing, and philosophical discussions on the nature of death. The inner play is *Hamlet*, or scenes from *Hamlet*, which the audience immediately recognizes as it witnesses the meeting between Ophelia and Hamlet, which begins the inner action. Our experience with metafictional characters in a play-within-a-play structure tells us to view the coin flippers, the occupants of the frame play, as "real" and Hamlet's spy friends, the occupants of the inner play, as fictive. But the fact that these characters have an existence which precedes the Stoppard play alters this. Surely Rosencrantz and Guildenstern, though speaking in a modern tongue inappropriate to their Elizabethan garb, can be none other than Shakespeare's ill-fated pair. The fact is that the characters' dramatic existence does not begin with Act I of the Stoppard play; the characters have an inseparable preexistence which significantly affects our response. Though we are aware of the duality, we cannot with comfort divide the metafictional characters into the fictive and the real, for we cannot consider the coin flippers "real" without being haunted by their preexistence. Even before Hamlet appears, then, we are thinking of Rosencrantz and Guildenstern in relation to him, and even before the two become reintegrated into the *Hamlet* play, we are aware of their fate, for our knowledge of Shakespeare, as well as the title of the play, tells us that Rosencrantz and Guildenstern are dead.

Whether we view the inner play or the outer play as Rosencrantz and Guildenstern's real world, however, is not so important as the fact which Stoppard reveals in endowing his characters with literary preexistence. Rosencrantz and Guildenstern may well exemplify Sartre's existential premise, but for them the essence which precedes existence is itself fictive, reducing (or elevating) the status of these two to pure fiction. Indeed, the theatrical metaphor which sustains itself throughout the play underscores the playwright's vision of life as essentially dramatic and of living as nothing more than playing a role. When in the outer play, Stoppard's characters exist through self-created dramas, which increase in emotional intensity as the repartee reaches its climax. Once they are reminded of *Hamlet*, they dramatize their meeting with the young prince as it occurred in Shakespeare, but before it occurs in the inner play, and dramatize their meeting with the English king, which occurred only by implication in *Hamlet*. These dramatic presentations, however, are invariably inadequate, for while they characterize the dramatic quality of Rosencrantz and Guildenstern's lives, they are only a prelude to the more fulfilling roles for which the Shakespeare play predestines them. It is only when Rosencrantz and Guildenstern step fully into the *Hamlet* play and resume their roles without resistance that they realize their sole raison d'être is those roles.

While Rosencrantz and Guildenstern may be unaware of the power of play, there is one character in the play who is supremely aware of it, and that is the Player, head of the travelling tragedians who act out *The Murder of Gonzago*. Strongly reminiscent of Pirandello's *Six Characters*, these actors never change out of their costumes, are always in character, always *on*, roaming the countryside in search of an audience. As the Player explains, "We're actors. . . . We pledged our identities, secure in the conventions of our trade, that someone would be watching." As purely fictional characters, defined by their roles, they are distinguished from Rosencrantz and Guildenstern by their knowledge that they exist only within a script. When Guildenstern naively asks the Player who decides who dies in their tragedies, the surprised Player replies, "*Decides?* It is *written*." And it is Rosencrantz's turn to be surprised when the Player tells him what happens to old actors: "Nothing. They're still acting."

Despite the presence of the players, Rosencrantz and Guildenstern do not fully understand what is happening, nor why, yet by the end of the play they have reconciled themselves to their fate and, indeed, even affirmed it. Befuddlement characterizes the two from the moment they replace the figures in the dumb show who wear their costumes through the moment they read the letter condemning them to sudden death. Rosencrantz, in fact, is even a bit scared and, watching the early stages of the *Hamlet* play, tries to convince Guildenstern that they should leave. Guildenstern, appearing to be the more aware of the two, seems to realize that even though their roles in the *Hamlet* play are minor ones, their dramatic existence—indeed, their *existence*—depends on them, and he convinces Rosencrantz that they must remain. Once their fate is sealed, Rosencrantz too stops resisting, even acknowledging, "To tell you the truth, I'm relieved." But concession is not comprehension, and Guildenstern, baffled even at the moment of death, asks:

> But why? Was it all for this? Who are we that so much should converge on our little deaths? (*In anguish to the Player:*) who are *we*?

And the Player replies, "You are Rosencrantz and Guildenstern. That's enough." That there is no other life for Rosencrantz and Guildenstern outside of the Shakespeare play, outside of their roles, is affirmed by Stoppard's final tableau, in which the bodies of Rosencrantz and Guildenstern become the subject of the ceremony afforded Hamlet in Olivier's film version, receiving all the circumstance due dead heroes. For Rosencrantz and Guildenstern are indeed heroes, having fulfilled (though less than nobly) their obligation in life and in the play, which is to perform.

What Rosencrantz and Guildenstern never realize is that they are part of a larger action than that of their own little lives. The two may go to their deaths without resistance, but they never comprehend what it means to be part of a greater plan. From his limited perspective, Guildenstern blames their fate on the boat:

> Where we went wrong was getting on a boat. We can move, of course, change direction, rattle about, but our movement is contained within a larger one that carries us along as inexorably as the wind and the current. . . .

Though he doesn't know it, Guildenstern's boat has metaphorical import, offering a wry comment on modern man's faith in free will and a bold statement on the nature of art. The confinement of which Guildenstern speaks suggests the limitations of both the individual in life and the character in drama, both of whom are free, "within limits, of course." The inexorability describes the demands imposed both upon man by virtue of the inevitability of death and upon the dramatic character by virtue of the script. Indeed, the preoccupation with death is quite obvious in the play, in which Guildenstern observes the "curious scientific phenomenon . . . that the fingernails grow after death, as does the beard"; in which Rosencrantz wonders whether Guildenstern ever thinks of himself as "actually *dead,* lying in a box with a lid on it"; and in which Rosencrantz asks:

> Whatever became of the moment when one first knew about death? There must have been one, a moment, in childhood when it first occurred to you that you don't go on for ever.

The irony of their intellectual speculations is that they are just that, re-flecting neither frustration nor perspicacity, and never acknowledging that Rosencrantz and Guildenstern are themselves not far from annihilation. Even more ironic is their failure to realize that each footstep into the arena of the *Hamlet* action, however tentative and however necessary, is another submission to the destiny of the script, which prescribes both their reason for being and their certain demise.

In their confusion and fear, Rosencrantz and Guildenstern never suspect that they may fare better as fictional characters than as real ones, for once they enter the *Hamlet* play they become part of an ordered universe which could not permit a coin to turn up heads ninety-two times. As the head of the players explains, ". . . there's a design at work in all art. . . . Events must play themselves out to aesthetic, moral and logical conclusion." Furthermore, in the world of play, the dead actor can rise again for an encore. As preoccupied with *ars moriendi* as Rosencrantz and Guildenstern are with the fact of death, the Player boasts that "it's what the actors do best. . . . They can die heroically, comically, ironically, slowly, suddenly, disgustingly, charmingly, or from a great height . . . [and] they kill beau-tifully." Not so committed to art as the Player, Guildenstern disparages such death, calling it cheap and unconvincing. Yet the Player tells the story of a real onstage death that simply didn't persuade the audience of its reality. And he later proves that Guildenstern's defense of real death is empty, for Guildenstern cannot tell the difference between reality and illusion when he stabs the Player. Apparently mortally wounded, the Player falls to the floor and expires, only to be applauded by his cohorts as he rises again.

The subjects of role and art are frequent ones in Stoppard's writing, and much of what he offers here anticipates the philosophy and technique of *The Real Inspector Hound.* In *Rosencrantz and Guildenstern Are Dead,* however, the play-within-a-play structure produces a somewhat different effect. In *The Real Inspector Hound* Stoppard toys with the concept of the mimetic quality of art, creating situations in the frame play and the inner play which are strikingly similar. In *Rosencrantz and Guildenstern Are Dead,* mimesis, like the ill-fated pair, is dead. The dumb show may preserve its sanctity, but the inner play proper neither reflects nor distorts the reality of the outer play, for Rosencrantz and Guildenstern prove to have no existence outside *Hamlet*. Their entire time in the outer play is overshadowed by our knowledge that they are Shakespeare's, and not Stoppard's, characters; like modern man alienated from an orderly world, their "real" lives only serve to anticipate their immortal roles. Where in *The Real Inspector Hound* the Muldoon Manor play succeeds in encompassing the outer play, in *Rosencrantz and Guildenstern Are Dead, Hamlet* absorbs its frame completely, rendering the protagonists without their *Hamlet* roles nonentities. In both plays, whether the characters' fates are determined by the slick whodunit play or the Shakespearean masterpiece, the power of Stoppard's art is supreme.

JOHN WILLIAM COOKE

Perception and Form in *"Travesties"*

What is pure art according to the modern idea?
It is the creation of an evocative magic,
containing at once the object and the subject,
the world external to the artist
and the artist himself.

— CHARLES BAUDELAIRE

He thought he saw an Argument
That proved he was the Pope:
He looked again, and found it was
A Bar of Mottled Soap.
"A fact so dread," he faintly said,
"Extinguishes all hope!"

—LEWIS CARROLL

Early in Tom Stoppard's novel, *Lord Malquist and Mr Moon*, a character comments, "I look around me and I recoil from such disorder. We live amidst absurdity, so close to it that it escapes our notice. . . . Since we cannot hope for order let us withdraw with style from the chaos." Stoppard likes chaos simply because the mind

From *Modern Drama* 4, vol. 24 (December 1981). Copyright © 1981 by University of Toronto.

hates it, will not stand for it, can only hope in the best of worlds to "withdraw with style" from it. *Travesties* is Stoppard's theater of chaos: snatches of songs, dialogue in limericks, patches of Shakespeare and Joyce, laborious reenactments of Lenin's speeches, crackbrained soliloquies from a senile old man, Zurich during World War I, all shoehorned into a simulacrum of *The Importance of Being Earnest*. Our problem is that we are attracted to this chaos; we cannot withdraw from it any more than we can withdraw from life's seeming randomness. We cope by trying to whip chaos into shape, make it "understandable." One critic exemplifies this urge by stating, with apparent security, that the theme of *Travesties* is "uncertainty and confusion," but that is like saying the theme of *Macbeth* is "murder." "Uncertainty and confusion" is not the theme but rather the raw material from which the story draws its energy. The taming of this sort of chaos demands that we alter our critical perspective; we cannot pick through the mess searching (as did the critic above) for Stoppard's theme, his statement "about the world." Further, we must not think Stoppard's sleight-of-word simply masks "the . . . expression of his deepest concerns." Stoppard is hiding nothing; the mask is the face. His language simply reflects the process evident throughout *Travesties*: the process by which we come to "understand," and hence control, the apparent absurdity of the world around us.

Though this process finds its fullest expression in *Travesties*, this synopsis of a scene from an earlier play, *After Magritte*, provides a rich illustration of the relation between perception and understanding:

> a one-legged blind man with a white beard, who may in fact have been a handicapped football player with shaving cream on his face, has been seen hopping, or perhaps playing hop-scotch, along an English street, wearing striped pajamas, convict garb, or possibly a West Bromwich Albion football jersey, waving with one arm a white stick, a crutch, or a furled parasol while carrying under the other what may have been a football, a wine-skin, an alligator handbag, or a tortoise.

The first step toward understanding is the apparently simple but ever-confounding activity of sense perception. It is through perception, naturally, that we can assume the existence of things, but here more things exist than actually appeared. Each witness saw the same object yet went home believing he saw a different thing: a handicapped football player, a convict with a handbag, or a pajama-clad gentleman with a tortoise. We "understand" both art and life, Stoppard feels, through the process by which percept becomes concept, sense data become reality, randomness becomes truth. "Illusion vs. reality" is not the issue here, however, for in *Travesties* illusion and reality are not opposed. They cannot, and should not, be distinguished. The process of making meaning—be it telling a story, writing *Ulysses*, or composing socialist history—is the central focus of Stoppard's play.

Consequently, it seems ultimately fruitless to analyze *Travesties*, certainly to evaluate it, in terms of Stoppard's ability to make comments "about the world." Least of all is *Travesties* a history play, in which we must judge Tzara against Joyce, or Lenin against (egad!) Carr. Nor is the play primarily "about" the role and status of the artist in modern society. Rather, I think we must look at each level of this play—character, manifest content (art and history), and the language and structure of the play itself—as overlays, creating themselves through the same epistemological process.

Of course, on one level *Travesties* is a debate about art and history, in which each character takes a predictable stance. Traditionalist Henry Carr believes, "An artist is someone who is gifted in some way that enables him to do something more or less well which can only be done badly or not at all by someone who is not thus gifted," while Tzara argues quite the opposite: "nowadays, an artist is someone who makes art mean the thing he does." Joyce contends that "An artist is the magician put among men to gratify—capriciously—their urge for immortality." Consequently, art functions in quite different ways: for Carr, it must "beautify existence"; for Tzara, art's purpose is "scandal, provocation, and moral outrage." Cecily speaks for Lenin when she states, "The sole duty and justification for art is social criticism." (Later, however, we learn of his preference for Pushkin over Mayakovsky.)

As is evident in the debate between Carr and Tzara on the origins of World War I, attitudes toward history diverge as well. Carr believes "the war . . . had causes. . . . Something about brave little Belgium . . ."; he also considers the war a natural response to "feelings of *patriotism, duty,* to my love of freedom, my hatred of tyranny." Tzara argues that "it is the duty of the artist to jeer and howl and belch at the delusion that infinite generations of real effects can be inferred from the gross expression of apparent cause." The debate degenerates into the meaningless repetition of "dada" on one side against Carr's equally meaningless tautology on the other: "we're here because we're here because we're here," etc. "As an artist," Joyce comments, "naturally I attach no importance to the swings and roundabout of political history." (We need not comment extensively on Lenin's ideas about history and causality, which encumber the second act.)

This level of argument, though it energizes the play, fails to touch its soul. On this point one may momentarily, I think, rely on intuition:

these grandiose pronouncements about duty and patriotism, art and artist, history and life emanate from a stage world that is nothing if not chaotic. Macbeth's "tale told by an idiot" has nothing on the whopper Old Carr spins in *his* two hours' traffic of the stage. To understand *Travesties* we have to look at the chaos.

Stoppard's strong sense of spectacle illustrates the essential activity through which we come to "make sense" of things. The first scene reveals Tzara writing in the library; he then "*takes up the scissors and cuts the paper, word by word, into his hat.*" He proceeds to dump the scraps out and arrange them in "*random lines.*" Order (the written poem) becomes chaos (random scraps of paper). We might see this simply as evidence of Tzara's own eccentric art, but soon we find Joyce also "*searching his pockets for tiny scraps of paper*" on which are written short phrases he may wish to use in *Ulysses:* " 'Morose delectation . . . Aquinas tunbelly . . . Frate porcospino . . .'," among others. Immediately thereafter, Joyce "*encounters a further scrap of paper . . . LENIN has inadvertently dropped it.*" This is a Leninesque scrap, " 'G.E.C. (U.S.A.) 250 million marks, 28,000 workers . . . profit 254,000,000 marks . . .'," which *he* may wish to use in composing his *Imperialism: The Last Stage of Capitalism.* Rather than drawing distinctions among Lenin, Joyce, and Tzara, Stoppard emphasizes their similarities: they are all makers, composing their works from facts out of context, apparent scraps. Whether the products are novels, histories, or dadaist poems, the process is the same.

Consequently, it is difficult to distinguish history from art. Joyce wonders what we would think of the Trojan War had it not become a subject for art. "A forgotten expedition prompted by Greek merchants looking for new markets," Joyce answers; "A minor redistribution of broken pots." Whatever the historian and the artist "make" of the Trojan War, the objective "facts" are the same random scraps: broken pots. Since *Travesties* conforms directly to *The Importance of Being Earnest* in both plot and characterization, Oscar Wilde's comment seems more than casually related: "The ancient historians gave us delightful fiction in the form of fact; the modern novelist presents us with dull facts under the guise of fiction."

Lenin, Joyce, and Tzara make meanings by giving form and context to the broken pots of life. Carr recalls Joyce as an "amazing intellect bent on *shaping* itself into the permanent *form* of its own monument—the book the world now knows as *Ulysses*" (my emphases). He notes Lenin, too, "*reshaping* the civilized world into a federation of standing committees of workers' deputies." What more disparate scraps can one propose for any work—historical or literary— than Homer's *Odyssey* and the Dublin Street

Directory for 1904? Even Tzara, the enemy of "reason, logic, causality, coherence, tradition, proportion, sense and consequence," tacitly admits to the inevitability of design: his poetry, he states, "comes from the well-spring where my atoms are uniquely organized."

Here Stoppard pinpoints the primacy of form not only *in* his own work, but also, in this particular case, as a theme in the work. Form—arrangement, order, context—creates meaning. Nowhere is this more apparent than in Stoppard's language. One is appalled at the mileage he gets out of the convenient utterance "dada." Naturally, it "means" the art movement and thus becomes the source of some brutal puns ("my art belongs to Dada 'cos Dada 'e treats me so—well"); as well, Nadya nods "da, da" (yes, yes) in agreement with Lenin, and Carr uses it while impersonating Tristan in order to woo Cecily: "my brother has been a great disappointment to me, and to Dada. His mother isn't exactly mad about him either." Again, it arises as a cute, lyrical endearment:

> TZARA: Have you ever seen my magazine "Dada," darling?
> GWEN: Never, da-da-darling!

While we may wince at such facility, Stoppard sneaks in a serious point: that an utterance gains meaning *only* within context, and can, therefore, explode into several meanings. A more complex example is evident in the opening scene, when Tzara reads off his "random" arrangement of words:

> Ill raced alas whispers kill later nut east,
> noon avuncular ill day Clara!

A well-tuned ear, familiar with French, also hears this:

> Il reste à la Suisse parce qu'il est un artiste.
> "Nous n'avons que l'art," il déclara.

This translates roughly: "He lives in Switzerland because he is an artist. 'We have only art,' he declared." Of course, one is impressed by such gymnastics, if also put off by the literariness, but for our purposes the remarkable feature is the implied relation among verbal utterance, the existence of "meaning," and the reality of the objects signified. Like "dada," the utterance above has several realities. One one level, Tzara's "poem" exemplifies his art: as an assertion of effect without cause, its "meaning" is "meaninglessness," or to use Tzara's phrase, "It is without meaning as Nature is." On a second level, the statement comments upon the artist's presence in Zurich in 1917. Each level has an equal and distinct existence, though dependent upon the same utterance, and those existences themselves depend upon the formal rules of syntax and the referential impact provided by their contexts within the story. Thus, apparent "scraps" of language gain not only meaning, but multiple meanings. In a playful but nonetheless poignant manner, Stoppard illustrates that nothing expressed through any formal arrangement can fail to signify, to "mean."

We have just noted how single utterances may explode into several meanings, have several "existences." The language of *Travesties* also implodes, allowing several distinct utterances to signify the same object. For example, Joyce is referred to also as "Janice," "Diedre," "Phyllis," and "Bridget"; Rumania, as Bulgaria; Serbia, as Belgium; *Ulysses*, as "Elasticated Bloomers"; and Hans Arp, as Jean Arp. In discussing the Limmat River, Carr provides a useful illustration: he first describes it as "swiftly-gliding snot-green," and a few moments later it is "sadly-sliding chagrined." The fact of a river called Limmat seems secondary to its quite distinct existences in Carr's mind. As we noted earlier in the passage from *After Magritte*, one "fact" may have several existences because it must be perceived. The transformation from percept to concept demands verbal expression, and, most important, that expression attains an existence separate from fact. Because of their inevitable dependence on form, these words evoke a reality of their own. The river is, in essence, a scrap, a fact which has no meaning, and hence no existence separate from its expression in words. It exists (that is, has meaning) when signified through a conceptual arrangement, just as " 'Entweder transubstantiality' " has no meaning (or existence) until hungry Joyce scholars unearth it in *Ulysses*. As Wilde notes, the "Truth is entirely . . . a matter of style," which is to say, truth, or reality, is a matter of patterning perceptual possibilities.

Jackson Cope explains this phenomenon epistemologically:

> Works repeatedly draw attention to the nucleus of the artistic transaction, the place where process and product turn inside out to offer a style of illusion opposed to that which we customarily understand when we speak of the illusion of reality created in mimetic art. Rather, continuously interchanging function, process and product fuse to create an effect stylistically analogous to the simple optical illusion, which demands as much from the process of the seeing eye as from the patterns of the object itself, with its spurious, ironic claim to a formal existence independent of that eye.

The dependence of the existence of things upon perception implies, as Ortega y Gasset states, "that the individual point of view is the only point of view from which one is able to look at this world in its truth." We create our own reality distinct from the tangible, here-and-now world. The objective world only provides the scraps from which we fashion reality by creating concepts from sense data. We need not discuss here the "truth value" of art to state simply that the works of Joyce, Lenin, and Tzara do posit a reality of their own, and that that reality begins with poems snipped in pieces, broken pots, fragments of language, and scraps of economic data.

But what of our absent-minded friend Carr? He is, I think, as much of a "maker" of history and art as the others. An exchange with Tzara makes this clear:

> CARR: Don't you see my dear Tristan you are simply asking me to accept that the word Art means whatever you wish it to mean; but I do not accept it.
>
> TZARA: Why not? You do exactly the same thing with words like *patriotism*, *duty*, *love*, *freedom*, king and country, brave little Belgium, saucy little Serbia—

World War I, like the Limmat River, the Trojan War, and the man named Arp, has several "realities"; Carr's romantic "dawn breaking over no-man's land. . . . The trenches stirring to life" is hardly Tzara's "capitalism with the gloves off." Carr and Tzara may as well be speaking of two distinct entities; in neither case do the objective events of the war signify anything until Carr and Tzara "shape" them into a definition.

In light of Cope's emphasis upon the reality of individual perspective, we may see Carr in an even more distinctive position: he is (to use a chapter title from *Lord Malquist and Mr Moon*) the "spectator as hero." Hannah Arendt aptly defines the importance of spectators:

> Without spectators, the world would be imperfect: the participant, absorbed as he is in particular things and pressed by urgent business, cannot see how all the particular things in the world and all the particular deeds in the realm of human affairs fit together and produce a harmony, which itself is not given to sense perception; and this invisible in the visible would remain forever unknown if there were no spectator to look out for it, admire it, straighten out the stories, and put them into words.

Obviously, Old Carr fails to personify the ideal spectator described above; he has not quite been able to "straighten out the stories" to anyone's satisfaction but his own. The entire play, in fact—with the exception of Old Carr's actual appearances on stage—is his "fiction." Carr's failure to reproduce exactly the Zurich of his younger days links him rather more closely to Stoppard's point that art and history are both creative endeavors, the products of "makers." Carr's account is, like *The Odyssey*, "delightful fiction in the form of fact"—art as history. What makes the play fiction (and what makes much of it so damn funny) is the old man's erratic memory, which allows the events of 1917—which Carr recalls "as though it were yesteryear"—to "fit together" with only the slightest concession to actual experience. Mnemosyne *is*, after all, the mother of the Muses. On the level at which *Travesties* is Carr's "play" about himself, memory is the dominant, revitalizing agent.

Memory, even Carr's memory, is never random; it attempts to unify even the most disjointed events of the past. Indeed, given Old Carr's more coherent descriptions, Zurich sounds like the scrapheap of wartime Europe: "Refugees, spies, exiles, painters, poets, writers, radicals" and "riff-raff of all kinds." This randomness, in addition to Carr's faulty memory and his dubious allegiance to truth, accounts for the "derailments"; those moments in which the tale becomes even too high fantastical for its teller. Interest in the derailments goes beyond "the cheap comedy of senile confusion"; we must also note that each "derailment" ends rather quickly through an act of Carr's will, thus indicating his attempt to present a unified if not altogether objective account of his past.

Carr's memory does, in essence, function like art in that both are ideal and formal reconstructions of sensual experience outside of time. As Arendt states, memory "has to do with things that are absent, that have disappeared from my senses. . . . While thinking . . . I am surrounded not by sense-objects but by images that are invisible to everybody else" (II, 126). *Travesties* is, then, an optical illusion in that Stoppard makes Carr's memory present to us. He does so to reinforce our sense of Carr as a "maker," unifying random and historically unconnected sense experiences into the form of a play. " 'Unity'," states Ronald Peacock, "is not a sensuous experience, but an idea about it; it is an interpretation. . . . The understanding of unity cannot be other than a product of thought working with the materials of memory."

CHARACTER AS PERCEPTUAL PROCESS

Does God ever judge us by appearances? I suspect that he does.
(W.H. Auden)

I have thus far sought to illustrate that: (1) *Travesties* is about "makers" and how understanding is predicated upon the act of perceiving random data and converting that data into form; (2) the very existence of things in *Travesties* depends upon this primary act of individual perception; and (3) individual perception is not only a theme in the play, but also an activity which occurs in it, and therefore, each element of the play, and thus the play itself, depends upon this same process.

The most important aspect of this process is Stoppard's emphasis upon the distance between facts (a river, pots, the incidents in Zurich during the war) and the "idea" of them, and upon the consequence of this idea—the form into which the data are placed—attaining an existence, a "reality" all its own. This factor is, I think, the source of the title: Old Carr's "play" about Zurich in 1917 is a "travesty" of what actually occurred during that period, regardless of his insistence on the truth of his story:

> CARR: Oh, Cecily. I wish I'd known then that you'd turn out to be a pedant! . . . Wasn't this—Didn't do that—1916—1917—*What of it?* I was here. They were here. They went on. I went on. We all went on.

Here, of course, I am using the common definition of "travesty" as a "burlesque or ludicrous treatment of a serious work," but the origins of the word point to yet another significant dimension of the play. In earlier usage, "travesty" meant " 'to disguise . . . , or take on another man's habit'," or "an alteration of dress or appearance" (*OED*). Clearly, clothing is a major issue in *Travesties,* and in the following pages I wish to explain how this overcoding of apparel illustrates yet another means by which perception of random sense data (articles of apparel) becomes the concept of a "character."

Before I examine Stoppard's particular use of character in *Travesties,* a brief theoretical outline may be helpful. As it refers to an individual, "character" is a relatively recent term. It came into English via French and Latin from a Greek word meaning to engrave, and its root meaning until recently has held closely to the idea of something engraved or distinctively marked. "Character," then, basically signifies that which we know by certain distinguishing marks and connotes, therefore, something set, immutable, much in the same way that "person" derives from the name for the Greek mask, that emblem of the self frozen into an attitude.

Yet when we seek to "characterize" a person, we encounter not one distinguishing mark but many "marks," or individuating traits, each signifying only isolated aspects of that person's existence. Thus, a conversion must take place, an act unifying many apparently random traits. Character is thus the transformation of an individual's verbal and gestic activity into what Bernard Beckerman calls a "summarized perception." Most important, it is a "theoretical construct," and like art, history, thought itself, a thing which occurs out of time, distinct from the perception of the activity. Character, as Beckerman defines it, "is the impression left by the actions of the dramatis personae." Thus, though character has an existence of its own (a unified concept called Othello or Hedda), that existence is separate from our experience at any given moment in the presence of that individual. Character is a convenient fiction.

So far this analysis is true for any fiction; however, *Travesties* employs these notions not only as an inevitable mode of perception in the play but also as a theme in it. "Character" becomes yet another travesty. We can best understand the notion of "character-as-travesty" by returning momentarily to the idea that the internal action of *Travesties* is Carr's "play" about himself. Reflecting Carr's double role as both player and play-maker, the work demands actually two stage spaces, two separate worlds: the first, inhabited by Old Carr, remains unlocalized, unfixed in time and space; the second, Carr's memory of Zurich in 1917, is grounded in both. Old Carr (and Old Cecily) are what we might call "objective" characters, since the actors actually impersonate figures living in a simulacrum of the objective world. The characters of the internal world—Joyce, Lenin, Tzara, et al.— attain a more complex referential capability. They are totally fictionalized, "subjective" characters, dramatic agents representing forces of Old Carr's memory. Their own existence is strictly theatrical; we can "summarize perceptions" of them, but in doing so we acquire knowledge not of them but of what Carr thinks about them. In *Travesties,* no matter how actors embody these roles, they are denied the possibility of choice, those possibilities being the power of our storyteller, Old Carr. Of course, we inevitably *do* think of these figures as historical characters, because we rely not simply on Carr's memory but also on our own. Like Carr, we too have "intentions" about Lenin, Joyce, and Tzara, hardly more or less fictionalized than Carr's.

Stoppard's use of character allows him to play the same percept-to-concept-to-reality games he employs with other aspects of the play. Character becomes another elaborate visual pun. Like the utterance "dada," the "fact" of "James Joyce" has no meaning yet attains several meanings during the run of the play: he is the ill-dressed "Mr. Joyce, Irish writer, mainly of limericks"; he is the composer of *Ulysses;* he is *our notion* of Joyce; and last, he is the character somehow inextricably intertwined in the plot of *The Importance of Being Earnest,* "playing the part" (by now a rather confused notion) of Lady Bracknell.

Whether our concepts (or Carr's, for that matter) derive from art or historical fact makes no difference; history and art once again fuse. Thus, as products of the perceptual process working through memory, history and art continue to be both an element in the play and a theme of it. (To test the impact of historical fact on the play: what would happen to our responses if Old Carr had recalled obscure individuals rather than prominent figures?) Joyce, Lenin, and Tzara have thus already been "theatricalized" by our vision of history. In explaining his decision not to stop Lenin from leaving Zurich, Carr gives us a sense of character made after the fact: "don't forget, *he wasn't Lenin then! I mean who was he?*"

Carr is theatricalized also, and not only by the fact that through memory he re-represents himself. Theatricalization of character in *Travesties* is not limited to what intentionalities (Carr's, Stoppard's, ours) exist outside the characters. They tend also to theatricalize themselves, and it is in this area that the foregrounding of clothing is significant. Costume first delineates the stage spaces: Old Carr's robe and hat reflect an indefinite neutrality; when he transforms into a young man, both he and Tzara are the epitome of sartorial correctness, "*straight out of* The Importance of Being Earnest." Costume and dress creep into the dialogue of *Travesties* in often surprising ways. Carr indeed seems constantly engaged in the discussion of his apparel; in an indicative scene, Joyce convinces Carr to play Algernon by describing the handsome wardrobe required for the part. Carr attacks Joyce on what must be for Carr a matter reflecting highest principles: "*why for God's sake cannot you contrive just once to wear the jacket that is suggested by your trousers??*"

But beneath this droll vanity lies a link between the individual point of view and "objective" reality. References to clothing are often associated with the war. War is "*capitalism with the* gloves *off,*" "infantile sexuality in khaki *trews,*" and "collective unconscious in a tin *hat*" (my emphasis). Carr tells of the moment he first heard about the war: "I was in Savile Row when I heard the news, talking to the head cutter at Drewitt and Madge in a hound's-tooth check slightly flared behind the knee." "I was there," Carr proclaims, "in the mud and blood of a foreign field, unmatched by anything in the whole history of human carnage. Ruined several pairs of trousers." Carr's vanity determines his view of the war; in effect, the war exists for Carr only through what we may call his sartorial perspective. "When I sent round to Hamish and Rudge for their military pattern book," declares Carr, "I was responding to feelings of *patriotism, duty,* to my love of freedom." This infusion of war and wear is best exemplified in the following, knee-weakening verbal somersault. Our hero begins with what appears to be just another romantic description:

> Never in the whole history of human conflict was there anything to match the carnage—God's blood!, the shot and shell!—graveyard stench!— Christ Jesu!—deserted by simpletons, they damn us to hell—ora pro nobis—quick! no, *get me out!*

Immediately following, Carr (or rather Stoppard) uses an almost identical pattern of sounds (much like Tzara's dadaist poem which opens the play) to convey an entirely different meaning:

—I think to match the carnation, oxblood shot-silk cravat, starched, creased just so, asserted by a simple pin, the damask lapels—or a brown, no, biscuit—no—get me out!

This is more than simply an elaborate pun: (1) like Tzara's passage, the verbal "facts" have no meaning in themselves but two meanings when perceived in context; and (2) the meanings themselves reinforce the idea that the reality of events in the objective world (the war) is a creation of the subjective self (clothing). Here Carr's aesthetics *literally* shapes his vision of war.

Stoppard's use of costume further emphasizes the fact that the self, like character, is also created through perceptual patterning: costume is form. As Anne Hollander explains, "for most people nudity provides incomplete versions of themselves. . . . When putting on clothing, one is aware not of adding artificial coverings to a biological shape, but rather of finishing the creation of the natural self." The nude body is out of context, without form, and thus unable to make a "statement." Carr calls modern artists "rival ego-maniacs—formless painters, senseless poets, hatless sculptors—." Being without form, sense, and a hat is, in each case, being equally inscrutable.

We have noted in discussing other aspects of *Travesties* that form asserts an existence of its own, and we perceive the creation of character in the same manner. If form predicates existence, and clothing is form, then the existence of the individual depends upon clothing. Susan Sontag notes,

> Even if one were to define style as the manner of our appearing, this by no means necessarily entails an opposition between a style that one assumes and one's "true" being. In fact, such a disjunction is extremely rare. In almost every case, our manner of appearing *is* our manner of being.

Character, then, is a collection of scraps (clothing) formally arranged, that arrangement reflecting a unified idea separate from the experience in which we perceive those scraps. But the particular stress upon clothing makes us aware that, unlike histories, novels, and dadaist poetry, the patterning involved is largely not verbal but visual, like painting. Consequently, much of our language concerning the nature of our "selves" suggests perception, "self-image" being the best example. Character is thus a concept of our *image* progressing through time. I emphasize this point because it implies a return to Stoppard's concept of the "spectator as hero."

> Nothing and nobody exists on this planet whose very being does not presuppose a *spectator*. In other words, nothing that is, insofar as it appears, exists in the singular; everything that is is meant to be perceived by somebody.

This dependence upon the spectator, our need to think of the self as an image presented to the world, calls forth yet another concept central to *Travesties:* that since the self is inevitably "theatricalized," art and life are indistinguishable. Thus, Carr's slip at the end of Act I—"purchased by me for my performance as Henry—or rather—*god dammit!*—the other one . . ."—is actually no slip at all. To exist, we must have our audience; the creation of self *is* a performance.

Because we perceive character-as-image in the same manner in both life and art, the pattern of imagery which emerges asserts its own existence; reality and truth are no longer operative or valid concepts. One cannot speak of a "true" or a "false" performance. Performance just *is*. Stoppard stresses the fictional as well as the "real" properties of the physical image in his characterization of Lenin. The playwright is quite explicit regarding Lenin's appearance as he begins his speech on artistic freedom: " '*balding, bearded, in the three-piece suit*'," Lenin should look exactly like a "much reproduced photograph" taken in May, 1920. Yet the author also points out parenthetically that is "*is the photo . . . which Stalin had re-touched so as to expunge Kamenev and Trotsky who feature prominently in the original.*" Thus, Lenin's "image," by which we characterize him historically, is like many other elements in *Travesties*, a combination of both fact and fiction which we willingly accept as the "true" Lenin.

I have spoken at length on Stoppard's use of character because, in foregrounding clothing, he identifies the creation of character with the other perceptual processes evident in *Travesties*. Carr, as a creator of the self, is in this manner linked with the other makers who inhabit Stoppard's play. It should also be obvious at this point that Stoppard implicates yet another "maker" of meanings, another creator of forms: the audience itself. If the spectator is hero, we must acknowledge our own heroism. As I noted in my introduction, *Travesties* is nothing but a series of "scraps" of history, songs and limericks, *Earnest, Ulysses, Hamlet, Much Ado, Merry Wives, As You Like It*, all sorts of what Carr calls "belle-litter." Because they either are art forms themselves or refer to "real" things in the objective world, they tantalize us with their reality yet take on new existences within a new form. These scraps breed chaos, but playwright and audience interact to resolve this chaos by perceiving the form which unifies these apparently disparate elements. We undergo the same perceptual processes upon which the play itself is based. Stoppard has created a play which is about what it does.

. . . [The term] "optical allusion" quite accurately suggests the central dynamic behind this play. *Travesties* alludes to historical fact; this is clear from Old Carr's numerous references to his story as "My memoirs."

The allusion/illusion freshman bungle is here really no bungle at all: the allusions to things outside the play are illusions in that Carr's history never existed, yet we have watched it at least in part as if it had. "Optical" here is also a primary element, for we postulate the "reality" of Carr's play because we "see it" on stage. Joyce-the-magician makes this point clear when he produces the carnation from the pole of paper scraps and the rabbit from his hat: seeing *is* believing.

Indeed, through *Travesties*, the playwright reveals a great deal about the imagination. Stoppard attacks the complacency inherent in our reliance on any single perspective, realizing, in Clive James's words, that "no readily appreciable conceptual scheme can possibly be adequate to the complexity of experience." Further, in giving us familiar images in new and different patterns, Stoppard is responding to what Kluckhohn calls "the obsessive, the compulsive tendency which lurks in all organized thought."

> An audience will always refuse the proposition that the people on stage are engaged in activity which is purely random. . . . [If] randomness is deliberately created (a paradox in itself), the spectators will nevertheless attempt to organize that randomness into wholes, themselves creating their own forms from the formlessness.

Travesties is not formless, but in its excess of forms, the play challenges perceivers to become makers themselves, and thereby exalts the efficacy of the imagination while questioning the locus of truth.

WILLIAM E. GRUBER

Artistic Design in "Rosencrantz and Guildenstern Are Dead"

Tom Stoppard's *Rosencrantz and Guild-enstern Are Dead* ought to cause us to acknowledge some inadequacies in the vocabulary we currently use to discuss plays, and the nature of our shortcoming can be demonstrated, I think, with some representative summaries of Stoppard's art. Ruby Cohn, for example, suggests that Stoppard proved "extremely skillful in dovetailing the *Hamlet* scenes into the *Godot* situation"; Ronald Hayman writes that "Stoppard appeared at the right moment with his beautifully engineered device for propelling two attendant lords into the foreground"; Charles Marowitz comments that "Stoppard displays a remarkable skill in juggling the donnees of existential philosophy"; and Thomas Whitaker argues that "the *raisonneur* of this clever pastiche is of course The Player . . . [who] knowingly plays himself."

Such language—"skillful in dovetailing," "beautifully engineered," "clever pastiche"—condemns while it praises, subtly labeling Stoppard's play as a derivative piece of workmanship. We tend to mistrust anything which is not obviously new, not wholly original; yet surely our modern bias here obscures crucial differences between Stoppard's play and, say, the *Hamlet*-collages of Marowitz and Joseph Papp. These latter works may be summarized accurately as examples of skillful joinery. But Stoppard's drama

From *Comparative Drama* 4, vol. 15 (Winter 1981–82). Copyright © 1982 by *Comparative Drama*.

does not simply "fit" together different pieces of theater. His play has no clear theatrical precedent, and a workshop vocabulary proves unable to explain what occurs when the script of *Hamlet* mingles with the script of *Rosencrantz and Guildenstern Are Dead.*

Part of the reason this subject has not been clarified is that it is impossible to assess accurately the extent to which the audience will recognize allusions to *Hamlet.* Even one of Stoppard's stage directions poses insoluble problems: *"Hamlet enters upstage, and pauses, weighing up the pros and cons of making his quietus."* Is this a reference which only readers who are familiar with Hamlet's soliloquy can pick up? Or can the actor who mimes Hamlet's actions somehow call the audience's attention to a specific portion of an unspoken soliloquy? Or, to cite a related problem, what is the audience to make of references to *Hamlet* which occur out of immediate literary context? For example, Guildenstern, on board the ship for England, suddenly speaks portions of Hamlet's "pipe-playing" speech, a speech he had heard (yet can we really assume this?) during an earlier scene from Shakespeare's play which Stoppard does not reproduce. Is it possible that Stoppard here intends to show that Guildenstern ironically is locked into the text of *Hamlet?* But if this is Stoppard's intent, how many viewers, in passing, could make the necessary connections between the two plays? Because of these and other similar instances, it is clear that different kinds of audiences are going to experience significantly different responses to the various allusions to *Hamlet.* Those who read *Rosencrantz and Guildenstern Are Dead* are more acutely aware of the numerous subtle references to *Hamlet;* and, of course, those readers and viewers who are thoroughly familiar with Shakespeare's drama will recognize many more interactions between the two plays than those members of the audience who know *Hamlet* only as a famous old tragedy.

The key to Stoppard's design, however, cannot be found by wrestling with ambiguities such as these, and there is no point in laboring to answer what percentage of what audience catches which *Hamlet* allusion. Instead, it will be more profitable to speculate regarding the general expectations of one who comes to see or to read the play. It would be a mistake to underestimate the pervasive influence of Shakespeare's most famous tragedy, even among those whose interest in the theater is minimal. Our belief that *Hamlet* is *the* central drama of our culture has been growing since late in the eighteenth century, so that the language of the play shapes our idiom, governs the way we think on certain critical matters. Indeed, the play's status is mythic. Stoppard can assume of every member of his audience an almost religious attitude toward *Hamlet,* a belief that this play comes closer than any other to capturing the mystery of human destiny. The audience does not expect *Hamlet* itself, and this is an important distinction. Stoppard's audience is not prepared for any specific response to the *Hamlet* material; and the great secret of his method is that he offers us a wonderfully suggestive way of seeing human action performed simultaneously in several modes.

If one assumes that Stoppard is using *Hamlet* as ancient playwrights used myth—and not for irony or for plot line or for laughs—one sees his play in ways which are wholly invisible to those who mistakenly treat it as a "worm's eye" view of tragedy, or as a witty experiment in Absurdist drama, or as a clever Shakespearean pastiche. From this perspective, I plan to review three noteworthy features of *Rosencrantz and Guildenstern Are Dead*. My aim is to correct a number of misconceptions regarding the play, misconceptions which have persisted for so long that they are in danger of becoming accepted as facts.

The first thing that impresses one about the play is its peculiar "literariness." So marked, in fact, is this quality that no one seems able to avoid mentioning it. Though there has been no agreement as to its effect, it is generally taken to be more-or-less undesirable. Robert Brustein, for example, once called the play a "theatrical parasite"; Normand Berlin has dissected the play into specific borrowings from Shakespeare, Beckett, and Pirandello, concluding that the play exists exclusively on an intellectual level rather than an emotional one; Andrew Kennedy believes that "the real pressure in the play comes from thought about the theater rather than from personal experience"; and almost every other commentary or review of *Rosencrantz and Guildenstern Are Dead* stresses Stoppard's indebtedness to Absurdist dramatists, Beckett in particular. Clearly, *Rosencrantz and Guildenstern Are Dead* is so consciously a distillation of literature and literary method that, to paraphrase Maynard Mack's point about *Hamlet's* mysteriousness, the play's literariness seems to be part of its point. We feel this literariness in numberless ways. We feel it in the particular use of the Shakespearean materials: in the characters, certainly, and in the numerous scenes or part-scenes from *Hamlet*, in the broad sweep of the action, and in the incessant probing of familiar questions as to Hamlet's madness, his motives, his ambitions, fears, loves. And we feel it in a less specific sense, too: partly because of The Player, of course, who points the thought of the play with his frequent discussions of tragedy, of melodrama, and of the significance of playing and acting; but partly, too, because of the general bookish consciousness which seems to be diffused evenly throughout the play, manifest in a score or more of literary or linguistic biases: syllogisms, puns, rhetoricians' games, pointed repetitions, along with a host of allusions to literature and literary topics that at times threaten to make the play into an exclusively literary epistemology, shifting our attention from pictorial to verbal theater.

In this respect, in fact, the play is remarkably exploratory. "Like a Metaphysical poet," Hayman writes, "or a dog with a bone, Stoppard plays untiringly with his central conceit, never putting it down except to pick it up again, his teeth gripping it even more firmly." One feels here enormous pressures of language operating through the characters, pressures which, say, in the work of Ionesco or Beckett, are distinguished only in a negative sense, as they are in the broken discourse of Lucky in *Godot* or in the ludicrous absurdities of *The Bald Soprano*. Here, however, language is not an imperfect instrument, a thing to be scorned. There is so much conscious experimentation with language, it is as if Stoppard were permitting his characters the freedom to strive for the linguistic combination, so to speak, that will unlock their mystery. Ros and Guil often exchange banalities, to be sure; but sometimes, too, their words frame truths, as when they analyze the history of Hamlet's condition (end of Act I), or when they discover (on board ship in Act III) the purpose of their voyage to England.

For these reasons, the dramatic power of *Rosencrantz and Guildenstern Are Dead* involves more than skillful juggling or witty commentary, and Stoppard has done more than to dovetail his story with an older one in the manner, for example, that Eugene O'Neill created *Mourning Becomes Electra*. The staged events of *Rosencrantz and Guildenstern Are Dead* in fact have little in common with the events of *Hamlet*; they are not the same play, but different plays, jostling for the same space. And the outcome of the duel, so to speak, between the respective plots of *Rosencrantz and Guildenstern Are Dead* and *Hamlet* is hardly a foregone conclusion. Stoppard's play is not an "interpretation" of *Hamlet*, if by "interpretation" one refers merely to a modern rendering of a fixed text. The real technical innovation of *Rosencrantz and Guildenstern Are Dead* can be understood only when we see that, for Stoppard, the text of *Hamlet* is potentially invalid, or at least incomplete—something to be tested, explored, rather than accepted without proof, just as a myth may generate endless versions of itself, some contradictory. Hence Stoppard is not using *Hamlet* as a script; rather, the script of *Hamlet* forms part of the material for a discursive experiment, a literary exercise, as it were. In this most superficial sense, Stoppard's play may be considered simply an honest effort to clarify some matters of Hamlet's story that Shakespeare for unknown reasons ignored. Thus Brian Murray commented of the play: "This strikes a blow for everyone who was ever puzzled by a minor Shakespeare part."

In a more profound sense, however, the play does not clarify mysteries, only multiplies them. Yet this does not mean that Stoppard equivocates, teases his audience with a methodical changing of signs. Like its famous Elizabethan predecessor, *Rosencrantz and Guildenstern Are Dead* attempts to close with the fact of meaninglessness, to enfold it with words. Here we touch the core, I think, of the play's literariness, perceive the motive behind its experimentation with a variety of scripts. What, this play asks again and again, is valid dramatic language, and what is its relationship to the modes of human action? Is that relationship heroic? or is it comic, a poignant statement of our own insignificance? Two possible and variant texts, one willed and one predicted, here compete for the same stage in a contest which is mediated by the figure of The Player, who moves easily between the heroics of Hamlet's court and the anterior world of Ros and Guil. It is important when experiencing Stoppard's play to be alive to its rich variety of contrasts. We must wince at the jolt, so to speak, whenever the play shifts from one mode to another, from one cast and its story to its alternate, and back again. Iambics and prose, vigor and lassitude, seriousness and silliness, skill and ineptitude, all coexist, alternately and repeatedly testing the efficacy and theatrical appeal of each. We must not hold up one mode at the expense of the other, but must be sensitive to each of the two as an element in an ongoing dialectic. Moreover, we ought not to see these incompatible elements as an experiment in Absurdist drama, either in philosophy or in form. For the play does not advance a simplistic philosophy by means of its constantly shifting perspectives, but develops a debate: Do we wish our drama in meter, or in prose? Do we prefer silly gaming, or coherent action? Do we, like Ros, want a "good story, with a beginning, middle and end"? Or do we, like Guil, prefer "art to mirror life"? And finally, are these ancient classical directives of any relevance nowadays, times being what they are?

Thus the literariness of Stoppard's play is pervasive, total. Its significance cannot be grasped simply by documenting the numerous specific echoes of earlier plays and playwrights, "intellectualizing" the play and its author, assigning them the appropriate thematic and technical camp, or postcamp. Not a failure of words, which proves the playwright's lack of originality or demonstrates his place in the Absurdist ranks, but a bold assertion of language's worth: for all the theatrical and literary elements, it turns out, are not ends in themselves, but help clearly to frame deeply personal considerations of human action, its motives and limitations and values. From its earliest moments, Stoppard's play reopens a number of very old questions related to the meaning of the simple *event*, questions which *Waiting for Godot* had effectively closed. The play begins by posing such questions: a coin falls "heads" almost ninety times in succession. It must, as Guil says, be "indicative of something besides the redistribution of wealth. List of possible explanations. One: I'm willing it. . . . Two: time has stopped dead. . . . Three: divine intervention. . . . Four: a spectacular vindication of the principle that each individual coin spun individually is as likely to come down heads as tails and therefore should cause no surprise each individual time it does."

Since the operations of their world lie generally beyond their comprehension, it is not surprising that critics, used to modern theater, have found in Ros and Guil's plight yet one more image of humans' bafflement as to their proper roles. Ros and Guil have usually been seen (in Thomas Whitaker's words) as "two characters in search of an *explication de texte,* two muddled players in reluctant pursuit of the roles they already play." It is in this respect, of course, that the play seems most closely to resemble Beckett's *Godot.* For we hear echoes of Vladimir and Estragon in the repetitious emptiness of Ros and Guil's conversations as they, like Beckett's clowns, wait to play their parts: "Where's it going to end?" "That's the question." "It's *all* questions." "Do you think it matters?" "Doesn't it matter to you?" "Why should it matter?" "What does it matter why?" "Doesn't it *matter* why it matters?" "What's the *matter* with you?" "It doesn't matter." "What's the game?" "What are the rules?" Whether or not Ros and Guil's bewilderment suggests the play's essential kinship with the work of Beckett is a matter I would like to take up later. One final point concerning the two courtiers: it is clear that their essence—hence their character—is conceived in terms of emptiness: "*Two Elizabethans* [establishes the opening stage direction] *passing the time in a place without any visible character.*"

Concomitant with this emptiness of act and motive, of course, is a second important feature of *Rosencrantz and Guildenstern Are Dead,* an emphasis on play and playing. Like *Hamlet, Rosencrantz and Guildenstern Are Dead* examines human acts and acting within a variety of contexts ranging from practical to the metaphysical to the theological. Central to Stoppard's play are the figures of Rosencrantz and Guildenstern, two of literature's most unimportant people, mere concessions to the expediencies of plot. Shakespeare jokes about the courtiers' lack of individuality by playing on their metric interchangeability. And Stoppard, as did Shakespeare, first conceives his creations as broadly comic. That there should exist two persons with a corporate identity, as it were, mocks some of the fundamentals of human order both on stage and off. The world may well be a stage; if so, however, the metaphor requires identities to be unique: each must play his part. Hence the concept of identical twins—two actors playing one role—is inherently chaotic, traditionally comic. In fact, we may trace the dramatic lineage of Ros and Guil back much further than Beckett and the music hall, back at least to Roman Comedy, and even further to the primitive notion that there is something downright foolish to two people who compete for a single identity.

But if the actions of Ros and Guil seem foolish and aimless, it is equally true that divine secrets seem to govern their madness. There is no doubt that the various collisions of identity and motive that occur in *Rosencrantz and Guildenstern Are Dead*—taken singly—are humorous. Yet here, as is true of the comic elements that are characteristic of mature Shakespearean tragedy, what is funny and what is serious seem interchangeable— or, rather, seem independent analogues of a grim reality. We realize very soon, for example, that the Fool's witticisms in *Lear* are "no play." Something similar conditions our appreciation of Stoppard's drama: grappling with the concept of death as a state of negative existence, for example, Guildenstern concludes that, "You can't not-be on a boat," a statement which is mocked immediately by Ros's foolish misinterpretation, "I've frequently not been on boats." Yet the courtiers' inept mishandling of language does not long remain a comic malapropism, but bends, to use Robert Frost's image, with a crookedness that is straight. Both twisted syntax and twisted logic are appallingly true: wherever they are—on boats, on the road, within a court—it is the fate of Ros and Guil never to be.

The play returns us, then, to thoroughly familiar territory, to a consideration of some of the fundamental perplexities that gave shape and lasting meaning to *Hamlet*. We of this century do not know with any greater clarity what it might require for a man "to be." Nor are we any closer to the secret which resolves the separate meanings of "play," whereby we fill empty time with arbitrary activity, and "play," that art which defines for us human time endowed with maximum meaning, maximum consequence. Here it has seemed to many that Stoppard's answer lies with The Player: always in character, always in costume, The Player's essence is his abiding changeability. The simple fact of his endurance argues for his wisdom. At the play's end, corpses litter the stage. Yet The Player, like Brecht's Mother Courage, seems infinitely adaptable, infinitely resourceful. Although his numerous "deaths" are impressive and even credible, he inevitably returns to life for his next performance. In a world in which everyone is marked for death, The Player's survival capabilities seem especially significant.

Because of the apparent emphasis Stoppard places on "play," it has been frequently suggested that Stoppard wants us to believe that *mimesis* fosters understanding. In Act I, for example, Ros and Guil deepen their awareness of Hamlet's transformation through an act of role-playing, whereby Ros questions Guil, who pretends to be Hamlet:

ROS. (lugubriously): His body was still warm.
GUIL.: So was hers.
ROS.: Extraordinary.
GUIL.: Indecent.
ROS.: Hasty.
GUIL.: Suspicious.
ROS.: It makes you think.
GUIL.: Don't think I haven't thought of it.

Even more important is their playing in Act III, in which they act out a possible script for their arrival in England. Here Ros, who is taking the part of the King of England, becomes so convinced of the reality of his situation that he tears open their letter of instructions and discovers the order for Hamlet's execution. Suddenly, unexpectedly, Ros and Guil are illuminated by moral crisis; "Their playing," Robert Egan writes, "has made available to them the opportunity to define significant versions of self through a concrete moral decision and a subsequent action, even if a useless action."

It is inevitable, perhaps, in this shadow world made of parts of old plays that one of the largest roles should be that of the Player. And it is also inevitable that in such a shifting and offtimes morally weightless world the advice of The Player should carry the negative equivalent of weight. Regarding the question of how to act in their situation, for example, he advises Guildenstern to "Relax. Respond. That's what people do. You can't go through life questioning your situation at every turn." Or, later, his professional comments seem universally applicable: "We follow directions— there is no *choice* involved. The bad end unhappily, the good unluckily. That is what tragedy means." And, finally, it is The Player who convinces Guil (and us) of the impressive efficacy of mimetic understanding. Indeed, for a time it seems as if *mimesis* represents the only valid mode of knowing: the play's closing scenes forcefully demonstrate that what we considered a "real" stabbing and a "real" death was merely competent acting, merely the fulfillment of the bargain between actor and audience. "You see," The Player explains to the dumbfounded Guildenstern, "it *is* the kind they do believe in—it's what is expected." And the truth of this seems to be rein-forced a few lines later, when we truly witness "real" deaths as merely an actor's casual exit. Ros simply disappears, disappears so quietly that his friend does not notice his passing. And Guil makes death into a game of hide-and-seek: "Now you see me, now you—."

There is a series evident here, of course: Hamlet is to Ros and Guil as Ros and Guil are to Alfred. And naturally this projects an engulfing form, an engulfing dramatist for *Hamlet*, and so for Stoppard's audience. Yet we ought not to presume to have uncovered the message of the play within this problematical series of regressions. The mind wearies of such esoteric speculations; and Stoppard's aim here may well be to cause us eventually to reject any fancies regarding our own wispy theatricality. Indeed, the line of argumentation which makes play the only reality can be pursued too far, resulting at best in empty theatricality, at worst in excessively sophisticated dogma. It is, in Horatio's words, "to consider too curiously." This is not to deny the concept of playing an important place in Stoppard's work. Nevertheless, to make The Player exclusively into a source of affirmation betrays the meaning of the remainder of the characters, ultimately of the entire drama. "Do you know what happens to old actors?" inquires The Player, setting the context for still one more joke about occupations. Ros, here playing the comic-hall straight man, obediently asks "What?" "Nothing," replies The Player, "They're still acting." Here, in a single word, is focussed the whole of the play's chilling analysis of human freedom and providential design. Actors are *nothing*. As The Player admits elsewhere, actors are the opposite of people. It is not a matter of how we take the sense of "nothing"; for in a play whose deepest levels of meaning concern the minimum essentials for human action and human identity, "nothing" can refer only to a waste of being, the squandering of human potential through cowardice. Perhaps the play's literariness may help clarify this crucial point: to be "nothing," in literary terms, has been considered the most terrible fate of all. Recall, for example, the horde of lost souls whirling endlessly outside Dante's Hell, desperately pursuing all banners, any banner that might ultimately give them human shape, human meaning.

As is true of so much of the superficial horseplay in *Rosencrantz and Guildenstern Are Dead*, then, words here turn on their user, twisting themselves into enigmatic truth. The Player, because his role is eternally to be someone else, is thus no one in particular. Free of every human limitation, he exists wholly within the sphere of play. Thus nothing happens to the actor because nothing can: he is wholly amorphous, wholly uncertain, without identity, feeling, or meaning apart from that conferred on him by his audience, without—and this is most important—responsibility for who he is. What The Player espouses is that a person should "act natural." That is, he argues that one should merely respond to circumstances, secure in the belief that in the end all one can do is to follow one's script. This is of course an acceptable concept to propose to explain human activity, but let us acknowledge it for what it is: fatalism. And there is little evidence in this play—less in later plays—that Stoppard holds such a view. The point is this: in this play, as in most of the important tragic statements of Western theater, there is no single perspective that hits the mark.

We are left, then, with a third problem, possibly the most intriguing: what sort of play is *Rosencrantz and Guildenstern Are Dead?* To call the play a burlesque or a parody betrays one's insensitivity to its rich and manifold significances; and "tragicomedy" is a term grown so vague as to be almost without meaning. Clearly, Stoppard has surrealist longings in him (*After Magritte; Travesties; Artist Descending a Staircase*), but *Rosencrantz and Guildenstern Are Dead,* despite its veneer of gimmickry, proves instead the lasting power of straightforward theater. There is a small measure of truth in Brustein's term for the play—"theatrical parasite"—for it is obvious that Stoppard needs *Hamlet* if his play is to exist at all. Stoppard's play seems to vibrate because of the older classic, as a second tuning fork resonates by means of one already in motion.

Nevertheless, the tone of the modern play is distinct. Properly speaking, Stoppard has not composed a "play within a play," nor has he written a lesser action which mirrors a larger. The old text and the new text are not simply "joined"; they exist as a colloidal suspension, as it were, rather than as a permanent chemical solution. Or, to change metaphors to illustrate an important point more clearly, the texts of Hamlet's play and Ros and Guil's play form two separate spheres of human activity which, like two heavenly bodies, impinge upon each other because of their respective gravitational fields. The history of Rosencrantz and Guildenstern swings into line the scattered chunks of *Hamlet;* and the courtiers' story in turn is warped by the immense pull of Hamlet's world. Even though we cannot see much of that world, we may deduce its fullness. Though it exists largely offstage, or on another stage, we nevertheless sense that world's glitter, its nobility, and its grandeur, and we feel its awesome power.

This is not to imply that the sum of the two texts results in determinism, or that we leave the theater pitying Ros and Guil for being victimized. To the contrary: Helene Keysson-Franke speculates that the juxtaposition of *Hamlet* scenes and invented scenes "creates a sense of the possibility of freedom and the tension of the improbability of escape." Such is Stoppard's economy of technique that he chills us with Fate's whisper without a single line of exposition, without an elaborate setting of mood or of theme. Immediately the play begins our attention is mesmerized, as the two courtiers spin their recordbreaking succession of coins. The atmosphere is charged with dramatic potential, tense with impending crisis.

The coin which falls "heads" scores of times in succession defines what has been called a "boundary situation"; the technique is notably Shakespearean, reminding one of the tense, foreboding beginnings invoked by the witches of *Macbeth*, or, of course, by the ghost of *Hamlet*. Ros and Guil's playing is not the aimless play of Beckett's tramps, with which it has been compared, but a play obviously freighted with imminent peril. We are impressed not by the absurdity of their situation, but by its terrible sense; one senses the chilling presence of *Hamlet*, waiting menacingly in the wings.

But *Hamlet*, as is true of all myths, is what is predicted, not what is ordained. The two courtiers are not sniveling, powerless victims of time and circumstance, and their story does not illustrate the baffling absurdity or the blind fatality that has sometimes been said to arrange their lives. This is the conclusion which many who comment upon the play have reached, guided, in part, by the anguish of Guil: "No—it is not enough. To be told so little—to such an end—and still, finally, to be denied an explanation—." We are wrong here to view events wholly through the eyes of the characters, and our pity for them must be conditioned with a little judgment. It is necessary to recognize that the Ros and Guil whom we see in the final scene are in no important way different from the Ros and Guil of the opening scene, and that such implied insensitivity to their world— puny though that world may be—bespeaks a deeper, mortal insensitivity to humanity and to themselves. Facing death, speaking his final lines of the play, the burden incumbent upon him to touch the shape of his life and so give it meaning, Ros one last time chooses to evade responsibility: "I don't care. I've had enough. To tell you the truth, I'm relieved." Nor is the more speculative Guil alive to his context: "Our names shouted in a certain dawn," he ponders; ". . . a message . . . a summons. . . . There must have been a moment, at the beginning, where we could have said— no. But somehow we missed it."

The context of men's action remains forever a mystery. It was a mystery for Hamlet, it is a mystery for Ros and Guil, it is a mystery for us. Yet between the two plays there exists an important difference in the quality of the characters' responses to what must remain forever hidden from their sight. We do not here—as we did in the closing scenes of *Hamlet*—discover new men. Hamlet, it is true, submits to his world with weary resignation. But Hamlet acknowledges human limitations without lapsing wholly into despair. The difference is between Hamlet, who accepts an ambiguous world while yet believing in the need for human exertion at critical junctures in time, and Ros and Guil, who quail before their world's haunting mysteries, wishing never to have played the game at all. Guil despairs, groping for his freedom "at the beginning," when he might—so he reasons—have refused to participate. He wishes—there is no other way to put it—to avoid human responsibility. Thus his undeniably moving cry must be understood in the light of our clearer knowledge that his real opportunity came not at the beginning, but near the end of the play, when he accidentally discovered that his mission was to betray Hamlet. He misunderstands, in other words, the nature of his freedom, misunderstands as well the meaning of his choice. Too, we must not overlook the fact that Guil's misreading of his life provokes one final confusion of names: unaware that Ros has silently departed—died—Guil asks, "Rosen—? Guil?" In a play in which the floating identities of the two central characters has steadily deepened in seriousness, this final misunderstanding is especially important. Guil's fate is never to know who he is. Ultimately, as Robert Egan has pointed out, "Guildenstern does die the death he has opted for."

To insist on Ros and Guil's freedom, and therefore on their responsibility, may seem wrongheaded, particularly because one is reluctant to condemn them for being confused by a script which they have not read. The courtiers are baffled by onstage events; hence it is not surprising that critics and playgoers have been tempted to draw parallels between this play and *Waiting for Godot.* Yet in truth the dramaturgy of Stoppard does not simply grow out of the theater of Beckett. True, Stoppard employs elements of that theater; but the effect of this is to call the validity of Absurdist theater into question. Stoppard uses Absurdist techniques, as he uses the *Hamlet* material, to frame questions concerning the efficacy and significance of these diverse ways of understanding human action.

Evidence for this may be found by examining Stoppard's handling of the *Hamlet* material, and by noting how this handling varies over the course of the three-act structure of *Rosencrantz and Guildenstern Are Dead.* Act I first poses the dilemma, defining, as it were, the conflict of the play as a struggle between two plots, between the story an individual (here, two individuals) wills for himself and the story the myth tells about him. Here the two texts seem most at odds, for *Hamlet* intervenes in two large chunks, each time unexpectedly, almost forcing its way on stage. In the second Act, however, the compositional pattern shifts: here Shakespeare's text intrudes more frequently, and in shorter bits, as if the completed play were being broken down and assimilated by—or accommodated to—the play in the making. In this second Act we feel the maximum presence of *Hamlet,* the increased pull of the myth. Structure here may be clarified by reference to classical terminology: in this Act we witness the *epitasis,* the complication or the tying of the knot. Between the growing design of *Hamlet* and the intertextual freedom of Ros and Guil's discussions there develops maximum tension, maximum interplay between what Keysson-Franke calls "the possibility of freedom and the improbability of escape." Then, in the final Act, the process whereby *Hamlet* is accommodated to *Rosencrantz and Guildenstern Are Dead* seems completed. Here is staged the famous sea voyage of Hamlet, for which no dramatic precedent exists. No lines from Shakespeare's play can here intrude, for none is available. In *Hamlet*, we learn of the events of the voyage only in retrospect, during a subsequent conversation between Horatio and Hamlet. So, even though those of us who know the play remember what happened at sea, we know nothing of the causes of that action. Even knowledgeable playgoers, then, assume that the events at sea had resulted from chance, or, as Hamlet later suggests, from heaven's ordinance. This is an important point: most of Act III of *Rosencrantz and Guildenstern Are Dead* exists between the lines, as it were, of *Hamlet*, in what has always represented an undefined, unwritten zone. Stoppard here invites his characters to invent their history according to their will. He offers them alternatives, if not absolute choice. This is confirmed by the courtiers' imaginings concerning their arrival in England. Ros mourns:

> I have no image. I try to picture us arriving, a little harbour perhaps . . . roads . . . inhabitants to point the way . . . horses on the road . . . riding for a day or a fortnight and then a palace and the English king. . . . That would be the logical kind of thing. . . . But my mind remains a blank. No we're slipping off the map.

The passage chill us, and invites us to recall that for Rosencrantz and Guildenstern there will be no future. Yet does it not invite us equally to reflect upon the courtiers' imaginative shortcomings, their own sinful—not too strong a word—despair? Indeed, soon afterwards they are graced with the opportunity to devise their own script, but they fail to do so because they cannot transcend their own banality, cannot for one moment rise out of their slough. Upon reading the letter which discloses the King's intent to have Hamlet executed, Guil lapses into an empiricism so bland, so callous as to lack utterly moral context:

> Assume, if you like, that they're going to kill him. Well, he is a man, he is mortal, death comes to us all, etcetera, and consequently he would have died anyway, sooner or later. Or to look at it from the social point of view—he's just one man among many, the loss would be well within reason and convenience. And then again, what is so terrible about death? As Socrates so philosophically put it, since we don't know what death is, it is illogical to fear it. It might be . . . very nice. Certainly it is a release

from the burden of life, and, for the godly, a haven and a reward. Or to look at it another way—we are little men, we don't know the ins and outs of the matter, there are wheels within wheels, etcetera—it would be presumptuous of us to interfere with the designs or fate of even of kings. All in all, I think we'd be well advised to leave well alone. Tie up the letter—there—neatly—like that.—They won't notice the broken seal, assuming you were in character.

Only by considering Guil's comments in full can we appreciate their slowly deepening repulsiveness. They are spoken, recall, while our hearts are yet moved by Ros' intuitive reaction to the letter ordering Hamlet's death: "We're his *friends*." As Guil speaks, the stage grows quiet, empty: we feel the crisis, feel the awful pressure of a thing about to be done, feel that (in Brutus' words) "between the acting of a dreadful thing and the first motion, all the interim is like a hideous dream." Given the opportunity for meaningful action, Guil (and thus, by way of tacit compliance, Ros) refuses to act. Given suddenly—one is tempted to say beneficently—ample room and time to define their selves, the courtiers cannot swell to fit their new roles. For a moment, *Hamlet* is swept away, suspended powerless; for a brief interim we sense that the fate of the prince and his play rests in Ros and Guil's hands. That interim is theirs alone; it does not belong to *Hamlet*. And they refuse to act. To choose not to choose, of course, is a manner of choosing. Ros and Guil fill their moment of time, their *season*, with emptiness—until the text of Shakespeare's *Hamlet* rushes back to fill the vacuum. Scarcely has Ros concluded, "We're on top of it now," than Shakespeare's text looms to meet them.

In this light, then, Guil's desperate attempt to slay The Player who brings the courtiers the news of their deaths seems triply ironic. Guil is wrong about death, in that it *can* be counterfeited by a successful actor. And he is wrong about the shape of his life, too, and about the meaning of human action. No one—not Fate, not Shakespeare, and not Tom Stoppard—"had it in for them." Where Guil and Ros erred was not in getting on a boat; they failed when they chose freely to be cowards, chose freely, that is, to be themselves. Stoppard stresses their cowardice, not their ignorance, and his irony here flatly contradicts those who see Ros and Guil as powerless victims. And Guil is wrong, finally, in his desperate attempt to murder The Player. Guil seems here to hope to win dramatic stature by an act of violence, to gain identity from a conventionally heroic act of will. In fact, Stoppard seems to be saying, such conventional heroism is not necessary; all that was required of Guil was the destruction of a single letter.

Thus it is inevitable that the stage lights dim on Ros and Guil's play and shine in the end on *Hamlet*: "immediately," Stoppard directs, "the whole stage is lit up, revealing, upstage, arranged in the approximate positions last held by the dead tragedians, the tableau of court and corpses which is the last scene of *Hamlet*." The text of Shakespeare's play suddenly appears to overwhelm its modern analogue, as the old play and the new play here converge in a genuine *coup de théâtre*. Yet the point here is more than mere theatrics, more, too, than weary fatalism or anguish at the absurdity of human life. The sudden sweeping reduction of Ros and Guil completes Stoppard's play at the same time it affirms unconditionally the morality of Shakespeare's. On this crucial point, Stoppard is unequivocal: in rehearsals, and in all published editions of the play after the first, Stoppard excised a bit of action which brought his drama full circle, so that it ended with someone banging on a shutter, shouting two names. Stoppard's alteration moves his play away from the cultivated theatricality and ambiguity one finds often in Absurdist drama; and we are left with the clear knowledge that Ros and Guil, despite their being given an entire play of their own, have not advanced beyond the interchangeable, nondescript pair who took the boards more than three hundred years ago. Just as he disappears from view, Guil quips, "Well, we'll know better next time." But the evidence from *two* plays, now, suggests that they won't. Oddly, Stoppard is here not following Shakespeare's script so much as he is redefining and reasserting its tragic validity: *Rosencrantz and Guildenstern Are Dead* proves that Shakespeare had it right after all. For this reason, Ros and Guil are not permitted to "die" on stage; they merely disappear from view. Is this not one final demonstration of Stoppard's consistent dramatic technique?—for he merely whisks the courtiers off the stage, lest their corpses—visible proof that they had lived—convince an audience of their dramatic substance.

Wheels within wheels: *Rosencrantz and Guildenstern Are Dead* is deeply ironic, yet the irony is not at all the mocking, ambivalent irony we have come to expect of the modern theater. To be sure, to rank the orders of reality in this haunting play is to invert *mimesis*, for here the admitted fiction—the world of *Hamlet*—possesses most substance. It turns out, in fact, that even The Player is more real, that is, of more worth, than Ros and Guil. But this does not mean that The Player—whose essence is his artifice—forms the play's thematic center. Like *Hamlet*, *Rosencrantz and Guildenstern Are Dead* brings into conjunction a number of states of being, examines from a variety of perspectives some modes of human action. What the play *means*, it means largely by virtue of these numerous contrasts and resulting tensions. No one perspective is so broad as to embrace the whole;

each, by itself, is faulty, both intellectually and morally. Nevertheless, together they assert a view of human activity that stresses men's ultimate responsibility—whether prince or actor or lackey—for what they do, and so for who they are.

It is simply incorrect, for this reason, to call *Rosencrantz and Guildenstern Are Dead* an example of Absurdist drama, even to call it "post-Absurdist" drama (in all but the literal sense). In the first place, we do not find here a "sense of metaphysical anguish at the absurdity of the human condition," a theme which Martin Esslin long ago defined as central to Absurdist playwrights. Certainly, Ros and Guil die without knowing what their lives were all about. But the whole point of the *Hamlet* material is to define for the audience—if not for Ros and Guil—a knowable logic that shapes men's fortunes, even as it permits them a part in the process. We must distinguish here the difference between two varieties of offstage material, such as one finds, say, in *Waiting for Godot* or in *The Birthday Party*, on the one hand, and in *Oedipus Rex* and in *Rosencrantz and Guildenstern Are Dead*, on the other. In the former plays, the offstage material functions exclusively to deepen the audience's awareness of human ignorance; it is mockingly obscure, purposely baffling to characters and to spectators. But in the latter plays, the offstage material functions both as mystery *and* as myth, the myth with its powerful implications of logic, design, even—in the right circumstances—knowability.

In other ways, too, *Rosencrantz and Guildenstern Are Dead* rejects much of the Absurdist canon. It is not "anti-literary"; it does not "abandon rational devices and discursive thought," but instead depends upon them; and finally, it does not lament the loss of opportunities for meaning, even for heroism, because Ros and Guil enjoy, albeit briefly, such potential. This play, as has been said of Stoppard's *The Real Inspector Hound*, is "comfortingly classical." It testifies to the informing aesthetic power even today of a tragic dramatic form far older than the Elizabethan play which inspired it. *Rosencrantz and Guildenstern Are Dead* offers its audience the vision of two characters caught in the agony of moral choice. At a moment when they least expect it, and in a place they had never forseen, they must decide the shape of their lives. To be sure, the information upon which they must base their decision comes to them in the form of riddles, half-truths, things only partly-known; but when has it ever been otherwise? Like other tragic protagonists before them, Ros and Guil must choose, and they choose in error. Leading up to and away from this moral crisis which forms the dramatic center of his play, Stoppard constructs a linear plot, set in time, and moved by a group (or, if you will, two groups) of characters who are consistent in both motive and response. Behind the play stands an ancient way of ordering experience, a way which is both mythic and ritualistic. And for this theme, Stoppard (with the aid of *Hamlet*) offers a version of justice: all the characters get what they deserve. So simple, so moving, so regrettable, but, finally, so consoling: what, in the end, could be more like classical tragedy than that?

JIM HUNTER

"Night and Day"

By the time *Travesties* had been staged Stoppard was evidently conscious that the theatre of frenzied activity has its limitations. "I'd like to write a quiet play," he told Ronald Hayman in 1974, and again in 1976, after watching J. B. Priestley's *The Linden Tree* on television: "It would be rather nice to write about a professor or a doctor with a grey-haired wife and a problem child, and the maid comes in with the muffin dish and they talk about the weather a bit."

That sounds not only like quietness but also like realism, a mode hardly previously employed by Stoppard away from television, *Enter a Free Man* being a fairly half-hearted use of it. A quiet, realist play which would nevertheless use the full imagination of Stoppard is something to dream of: perhaps a true succession to Chekhov at last. Meanwhile, it looks as if *Night and Day* is the play that grew out of the yearnings expressed to Hayman. Quite apart from being fed up with the "paintbox" of *Jumpers* and *Travesties*, Stoppard the professional, the craftsman, the writer "for hire," probably wanted to show that he could do a realist play every bit as well as his more eccentric pieces.

In important respects the play departs from realism. First, though, we can recognize how accomplished the realist writing is. The characterization is nothing extraordinary, but it is clear and convincing; as with many masters of realism, it is most questionable when most interesting—here, in the character of Jacob Milne, the young and not yet hard-boiled journalist who has struck lucky. We are not quite sure what to make of

From *Tom Stoppard's Plays*. Copyright © 1982 by Jim Hunter. Faber and Faber Ltd.

Milne; but then neither are the other characters. (It is a constant problem for the realist dramatist, as for the novelist: anyone unusual enough to be worth writing about may risk not being immediately credible. Most of us, after all, have our doubts about Hedda Gabler.) After the many caricatures of earlier Stoppard plays we can appreciate his care *not* to caricature such an obvious potential target as Geoffrey Carson, who is "placed" but still respected, or as Dick Wagner, who is certainly a hard-boiled journalist but very much a distinct individual too. . . .

The shock opening of very loud noise and apparent slaughter impresses on our minds and senses the violence which is not far away and which is discussed at intervals throughout the action. The jeep with three people in it anticipates what is to happen outside Malakuangazi. But what follows is, relatively, a quiet play; and its most imaginative scene is very quiet indeed.

It can be said, in fact, to move from one stillness to the next. Some early examples: Guthrie who "doesn't move at all" as he lets the nightmare drain away from him; Ruth who "remains perfectly still" after Guthrie mentions Wagner's name; Wagner and Guthrie watching Milne; Wagner holding Milne's gaze and his further stricken pause. This is the technique of psychological realism: puppets are not interesting in stillness, and—quite reasonably and satisfactorily—most of Stoppard's plays are peopled by puppets. George and Dotty, and up to a point Ros and Guil, are the only earlier Stoppard characters with the depth to live through stage pauses like these; the others have to talk to react.

Long before *Night and Day* was written, Clive James wrote that Stoppard leaves "weighty" dramatists behind "not because he can't do what they can do, but because he can do what they can do so easily." Certainly the conventional realist writing in *Night and Day* is highly skilled. (*Professional Foul* the previous year had already demonstrated, of course, Stoppard's delicacy in television realism.) [Early on] Ruth is badly upset by the news that Wagner is coming. "RUTH: He told you to meet him *at my house?*" The tone alerts Guthrie, and the audience; and the "my" is a give-away, as Guthrie indicates ("Well, he didn't mention *you*")—prompting the first "Help" from Ruth's thoughts. "The boy," Guthrie goes on, "said to sit in the garden till Wagner comes." Ruth is lost for words for a moment, then struggles to establish a conversation. After two pauses, her edginess, and Guthrie's pushiness (we remember that he was badly rattled by his nightmare and woke to find himself at a disadvantage in Ruth's presence, so he has plenty of self-esteem to regain) break out in this exchange:

RUTH: By the way, we don't call them boy any more. The idea is, if we don't call them boy they won't chop us with their machetes. (*Brief smile.*) Small point.

(GUTHRIE *holds his arm out, palm to the ground.*)

GUTHRIE: Boy about this high, fair hair, your mouth, knows about cameras, has a Kodak himself; said I could wait in the garden.

(RUTH *acknowledges her mistake, but* GUTHRIE *pushes it.*)

His name's Alastair.

(*He has pushed it too far and she snaps at him.*)

RUTH: I know his bloody name.

This is worlds away from the double-acts of *Jumpers* or the operatic duets of *Travesties;* but it is superbly done, creating that feeling of naturally growing encounter, which realism achieves at its best. The play sustains this poise.

Its effectiveness is founded, as much as that of the earlier plays, in theatrical method. Take, for example, the basic element mentioned above, the audience tingling with special knowledge. We share throughout the play Wagner and Ruth's knowledge of their encounter in London; [at one point] we share Wagner and Guthrie's knowledge of Milne's front-page success (and the stage-direction describes them as "*like people watching a play*"), and later we enjoy Milne's unawareness that he is talking to the man he's talking about, and Milne's naïve association, a little later, of Guthrie with Alastair's camera. A version of this element is watching one character playing another like a hooked fish, while others (and the audience) are in the know: Wagner begins to play Ruth ("Do you know London, Ruth?"); she takes over and between them they are teasing first Carson, then Guthrie—who takes his big spill at "When were you last there?/RUTH: Friday./GUTHRIE: (*Pause*) I think I'll just sit and drink my beer." Mageeba's playing of Wagner is on a grander and fiercer scale: long before the climax Ruth's thoughts are crying "Run" to Wagner and telling us that Mageeba is going to have Wagner on a plate for his supper.

Again, in the traditional "well-made play" it is an allowed convention that one or two characters may enter at peculiarly appropriate moments, and Stoppard employs this once for comic effect (Milne's first entry) and once to sustain maximum theatrical urgency (Guthrie's return as Mageeba finishes his onslaught on Wagner).

On first view, the play seems to do what it sets out to do neatly and modestly—the faintest hint of Arthur Miller in Ruth's *arioso* is a warning of how the argument could go if pushed harder. If the play has disappointed Stoppard's admirers, it is because what it sets out to do still seems to them restricted. A critique of the Press, nicely balanced between affection, respect, and outrage, is offered, and our attention is mildly engaged by the abortive relationships of Wagner and Ruth and of Ruth and Milne. This is not enough to make us feel, for example, like recommending it to friends or going to see it again ourselves. The limitation seems partly traceable to the realist, single-view, fourth-wall method. "You get into trouble with my plays," Stoppard told Ronald Hayman in 1976, "if you think that there's a static viewpoint on events. There is no observer. There is no safe point around which everything takes its proper place, so that you see things flat and see how they react to each other."

Of the main action of *Night and Day* this seems untrue.

But the play is not so simple. Disconcertingly, but often funnily, Stoppard intrudes into the dialogue the private exclamations of one, but only one character. Why Ruth? Well, she is in the falsest position. "I'm in the wrong movie, I think. I should be in *Ruth Carson, Speakeasy Queen*." This to her *husband*, whose response is "I really don't know what you're talking about half the time./RUTH: And that's the half I do out loud./ CARSON: (*Confirmation*) There you are."

Her audible thoughts achieve different and equally useful effects at different times—Stoppard's thriftiness at work. By them Ruth can clearly communicate her own momentary panics; she can also voice, poignantly, to her husband the confession she is unlikely ever to make; and once Mageeba is on stage she can alert the audience, by her unspoken but audible warnings to Wagner.

All this gives piquancy to the realist action, but hardly affects it. Something more fundamental happens at the start of Act Two. The "true" action of the Act begins when Ruth asks Carson for a cigarette. [Prior to this point the Act is] a sad fantasy by the lonely Ruth waiting for Milne's return—while he in fact lies dead in a jeep jolting its way back from Malakuangazi. This is why her understudy is asked to walk off naked into the darkness after Milne; and in passing we should note a delicate touch which this enables for the actor playing Carson, who "stands thoughtfully watching as 'Ruth' moves into the dark." The gentle implication is that Carson has at least some understanding of Ruth's fantasy life, and particularly perhaps of her feelings for Milne. It is a small touch, Stoppardian in its humane appreciation of an aspect of marriage.

The fantasy scene is perplexing for the audience, because as it occurs it is likely to be taken as "real," in spite of the clues: ("RUTH:" No. Fresh start. Had a good trip?" . . . "You say something"). Stoppard attempts to get away with two different layers of theatrical irony at the same time: a realistic Ruth–Milne conversation when the man is actually absent; and even within *this* conversation the former distinction between Ruth's words and "Ruth" 's thoughts. "Ruth" is allowed to explain it later:

> I talk to myself in the middle of a conversation. In fact I talk to myself in the middle of an *imaginary* conversation, which is itself a refuge from some other conversation altogether, frequently imaginary. I hope you don't mind me telling you all this.

The "you" is herself. . . .

It is risky; it is not entirely absorbed into the play as a whole; yet it is also the best of the play. Without it, the emphasis would be firmly and unambiguously on Wagner, the need for a scoop, and the ironies of his various professional fouls; a play about newspapermen, with a woman thrown in for diversity. Milne would not appear at all in Act Two, and his death, though still upsetting, would carry less pain, as would Ruth's feelings for him. *With* the fantasy scene, the play is at least as much about Ruth as it is about newspapermen (Bigsby sees this as a weakness, but many successful plays do handle multiple topics); and it takes a look at questions of private morality, to balance the debate about the morality of "junk journalism."

Let me develop this last point: we are still talking about "staging," because it is the fantasy scene which really creates the inter-relationship of two moral areas in the play. The title *Night and Day* is loosely used to suggest similar dualism. Milne in Act One describes himself as a young reporter feeling "part of a privileged group, inside society and yet outside it, with a licence to scourge it and a duty to defend it, night and day." Guthrie's final speech sees information as "light." "It's worse in places where everybody is kept in the dark." In the fantasy scene Ruth presses Milne to describe his "lewd thoughts" (her phrase) about her: "Was it dark or daylight? . . . In the jeep? (*Pause*) It was in the jeep. / (MILNE: (*sharply*) No it wasn't."

(We are to discover later that at this moment he is lying shot to pieces in the jeep.) He continues, after a pause: "It was in a parallel world. No day or night, no responsibilities, no friction, almost no gravity./RUTH: I know it."

Doesn't she just? A moment later she tries to take up Milne's "parallel world" idea, but in a cheaper, less creditable way: "hotel rooms shouldn't count as infidelity. They constitute a separate moral universe."

The audience gets a laugh. But we know that this isn't true about hotel rooms. We also know—or rather, we are to discover—that we are in the "parallel world" of fantasy throughout this scene. All the moral debate is Ruth's. Milne here is her imaginative extension of him, and one of his attractions is his honour. (It recalls momentarily Angelo lusting for Isabella.) Her fantasy makes him hard to get—though more likely to yield, by a shrewd psychological intricacy, when she admits that it would be *wrong*. ("Be a bastard. Behave badly./MILNE: That's better.") Ruth here almost acts as her own confessor, to whom the fleshly sin would be all too human, but the attempt to deny that it was wrong would be satanic.

What is heavily on Ruth's mind here and throughout the play, of course, is her "slip" with Wagner a few days earlier in London. If we are to believe her—and it makes sense—this is the first time she has been unfaithful to Geoffrey Carson. The coincidence of Wagner's turning up at her house on another continent shakes her fundamentally: it reminds her that hotel rooms are *not* in a different universe; and she fears that Wagner "thinks I hop into bed with strange men because I hopped into bed with a strange man." (The real point is that she fears it may be true.) To Wagner himself she says:

> I let you take me to dinner because there was no danger of going to bed with you. And then because there was no danger of going to bed with you a second time, I went to bed with you. A lady, if surprised by melancholy, might go to bed with a chap, once; or a thousand times if consumed by passion. But twice, Wagner, *twice* . . . a lady might think she'd been taken for a tart.

As it seems the priest of her conscience has told her, the adultery will be a great deal easier the second time, and the vehemence with which she resists the idea of being thought a tart, together with the slippery escape clause ("or a thousand times if . . .") suggests that she is in fact well on the road downhill. As she herself says to herself in Milne's presence a few moments later, "Watch yourself, Tallulah."

Even a very sympathetic priest would suggest that it was experience with Wagner, unsatisfactory though that was, which has now opened to Ruth the fantasy of possibly sleeping with Milne. The fluttering uncertainty of her own sense of moral identity comes through in the fantasy scene, even to an audience not yet aware that it is fantasy. When we are fully aware—as in reading the text afterwards—the scene seems wonderfully subtle and regrettably short; perhaps its subtlest point—and a very Stop-pardian one—is Ruth's consciousness of the meaning of her own name. That Jacob Milne, the young Grimsby reporter, should quote Milton is a shade unlikely (but he is, as we have said, an unusual man, as Stoppard himself was an unusual cub reporter before him); but that Ruth should project the quotation on to him, in her fantasy, is entirely believable and very poignant. She knows, and is weighed down with the knowledge, that her name means "that which is lacking in ruthlessness. . . . Compassion—contrition." Terribly, she plays upon it a moment later: "What's PCR?/ Post-coital remorse. Post-coital ruth."

This woman needs no priest to sharpen her moral sensibility; what she needs acutely is some firm but generous sustaining person, probably male, to help her through the next hours and days as the woman of honour she still wants to be. Her husband is cheerfully baffled by her and in any case preoccupied with matters of war and peace (it recalls George's trying to get Bertrand Russell "away from the day-to-day parochialism of international politics"). With Wagner she ends the play: we know that he will sleep with her this once more and then will ditch her, and we recall "but twice, Wagner, *twice* . . . a lady might think she'd been taken for a tart."

Wagner, who doesn't miss much and has shreds of honour of his own, is far from throwing himself at her at the end and explicitly reminds her that she "didn't want to be a tart." But Milne's death has demoralized her: the lady will be a tramp (though *Wagner* doesn't hear her sing this) and perhaps the kindest thing he can do as the play ends is exhaust her physically—"I want," she tells him, "to be hammered out, disjointed, folded up and put away like linen in a drawer."

I wrote of being fully aware when reading the text afterwards, and the charge of "literariness" in Stoppard may again be made, this time where the characterization is realistic and moving. I don't think the full subtlety of the fantasy scene, and its place in the play, do come across on first seeing; but then the same is true of some of the finest effects of major dramatists, and when we return to the plays on stage they are *dramatic* effects. *Night and Day* is about Ruth, and about "ruth" or the lack of it: it is the play in which Guthrie refers to the Vietnam war as having killed forty-five "people" (he means pressmen), in which Carson can say "We're Geoff and Ruth to everyone round here. Isn't that right, Francis?" and *expect* the reply "Yes sir, Mr Carson," and in which Wagner can scheme relentlessly to get his story with absolute indifference to Guthrie, Milne, or—it goes without saying—the people of Kambawe. Of course there is no attempt at an over-near parallel between the ruthlessness of journalists or politicians and the moral lapses of Ruth; but they fit well in the same play and it feels like the same universe. Two scenes bring them most delicately together—the "real" scene between Milne and Ruth, late in Act One, at the end of which "MILNE goes into the lighted house. RUTH stays in the dark," and the fantasy scene at the start of Act Two, "in a parallel world."

Perhaps the shift between the two remains uneasy, and perhaps indeed Stoppard may eventually be criticized for not carrying the moral issues further (a death is, in one sense, an easy solution); but this still seems to me one of his most thoughtful pieces of theatre yet.

THOMAS R. WHITAKER

Language, Lunacy and Light

Reacting against the "theatricality" of *Jumpers* and *Travesties*, Stoppard said in 1974 to Ronald Hayman: "What I'd like to write now is something that takes place in a whitewashed room with no music and no jumping about, but which is a literary piece—so that the energy can go into the literary side of what I do." But two years later he was questioning the "literary" as much as the "theatrical." He had now "done a little joke play rather quickly" for Ed Berman and "a piece to go with an orchestra" for André Previn, was currently working on a screenplay of Nabokov's *Despair* for Rainer Fassbinder, and expressed to Hayman his great admiration for J. B. Priestley's "sheer craftsmanship." Watching *The Linden Tree* on television, he found himself wanting to write a conservative play about a middle-class family. "I felt I was sick of flashy mind-projections speaking in long, articulate, witty sentences about the great abstractions." Having promised Michael Codron a play, he thought of it as "a chance to write my West End play, to write *The Linden Tree* or the *Rattigan Version.*"

It is easy to understand Stoppard's feeling that he had reached the end of one line of development, that he could not improve on *Travesties* if he were "to write that kind of play in that kind of idiom." It is harder to believe that his talents could ever be fully engaged by an array of more limited challenges, or to see why he would want to imitate Priestley or Terence Rattigan as he had once imitated Bolt and Miller. In 1973 he had told Janet Watts, however, that he "would like ultimately before being carried out feet first to have done a bit of absolutely everything." And in "Ambushes for the Audience" he had warned: "I'm a professional writer—

I'm for hire if you like—as well as being someone who pursues his own path in his writing." Since *Travesties* he has also been increasingly concerned about the denial of civil liberties in Eastern Europe. In 1975, as a member of the Committee Against Psychiatric Abuse, an arm of Amnesty International, he marched in protest against the treatment of Soviet dissidents. In 1976 he met Victor Fainberg, who had been exiled from the USSR after five years in prison-hospitals for having protested the invasion of Czechoslovakia. In February 1977, as a member of the International Committee for the Support of the Principles of Charter 77, he wrote to *The Times* about the harassment of Vaclav Havel by the Czech government. During the same month, he visited Moscow and Leningrad, reporting on the visit in *The Sunday Times*. Then in July he went to Czechoslovakia, where he met Vaclav Havel and Pavel Kohout and gained a first-hand acquaintance with their political situation, which he described in *The New York Review of Books*. During the same period, Stoppard's various dramatic projects began to reflect these concerns.

Reviewers have written with approval or dismay of a newly "serious" Stoppard, who has diluted or sacrificed his distinctive qualities in pursuit of simpler styles and more narrowly political themes. It is true that in his recent work the structures are less elaborate, the implications less rich, and the sallies of wit no longer so incessant. But Stoppard was never an absurdist or a mere showman, and his basic assumptions remain the same. Even when seeming ambivalent on almost every issue, Stoppard's work has always implied a firm belief in freedom of expression. Now, in meeting his commitments to Berman, Previn, and Codron, and in urging the cause of free speech, he has made yet more explicit his faith that collaborative play, as it explores our slippery language and potentially murderous lunacy, can both lighten and enlighten our condition.

First performed in April 1975, as a lunch-hour production at Inter-Action's Almost Free Theatre (and later moved to the Arts Theatre for a long run), the one-act combination of *Dirty Linen* and *New-Found-Land* was commissioned by the expatriate director, Ed Berman, for a series ("The American Connection") to celebrate his British naturalisation during that American Bicentennial year. *Dirty Linen* treats as farce a situation that arises easily enough in London or Washington when our political, sexual, and journalistic games collide. The political game, as played here by members of a Select Committee on Moral Standards in Public Life, meeting in the tower of Big Ben, requires the continual pretence that one is engaged in a complex task of national importance. ". . . I think it is fair to say," says McTeazle as he instructs the Committee's new secretary:

that this Committee owes its existence to the determination of the Prime Minister to keep his House in order, whatever the cost in public ridicule, whatever the consequences to people in high places, and to the fact that the newspapers got wind of what was going on.

What is going on is the sexual game played by these same MPs, which seems to require their going to bed as often as possible with a certain "Mystery Woman." "This Committee," McTeazle continues:

> was set up at the time when the good name of no fewer than 21 Members of Parliament was said to have been compromised. Since then rumour has fed on rumour and we face the possibility that a sexual swath has passed through Westminster claiming the reputations of, to put no finger point upon it, 119 members. Someone is going through the ranks like a lawn-mower in knickers.

But that "someone" (as we immediately guess, and as McTeazle already knows) is none other than the shapely, commonsensical, but nympho-maniacal secretary that he is now addressing, Maddie Gotobed. The journalistic game, of course, requires that all such dirty linen be exposed, ostensibly for the public good but really for the competitive advantage of individual journalists. "They're not writing it for the people," says Maddie, "they're writing it for the writers writing it on the other papers. . . . The *pictures* are for the people."

But anyone who enjoys this farce can hardly condescend to "the people," and Stoppard's theatre game therefore insists that the pictures are also for *us*. Whenever an MP is transfixed by a pin-up photo of Maddie in a tabloid, the action freezes and a bright flash catches her on stage in a provocative pose. Other sight-gags involve the members' accidental exposure of their own dirty linen (knickers and briefs pop up everywhere) and their progressive stripping of Maddie herself. Their approval of a windily defensive report is resisted for some time by a late arrival, the proper Mr. French. But when they adjourn for ten minutes for a voting call from the floor of the House, the nearly stripped Maddie asks his help: "Could you show me the ladies cloakroom." And after the adjournment (during which we watch *New-Found-Land* take place in the same committee room), French has reversed himself. Explaining that Maddie has "poured out her heart" to him, he offers a substitute report embodying the position that she had earlier urged on the Committee. "All you need," she had said, "is one paragraph saying that MPs have got just as much right to enjoy themselves in their own way as anyone else, and Fleet Street can take a running jump." French's own language, of course, is loftier: "this principle is not to be sacrificed to that Fleet-Street stalking-horse masquerading as a sacred cow labelled 'The People's Right to Know'." But after the vote he wipes his brow with the knickers that, in the play's opening moment, we had watched Maddie put on. And Big Ben, which has been punctuating their lunacy with its deafening vibrations, strikes the quarter hour.

Visually and topically, this play may be the "undergraduate satire" that one New York reviewer, Martin Gottfried, declared it. (Another reviewer, Walter Kerr, thought it "slovenly" and "altogether intolerable.") Stoppard himself was rather deprecatory: "My director thinks he's got a profound comment on British society," he told Robert Semple. "What he really has is a knickers farce." As French's strained rhetoric suggests, however, Stoppard's theatre game has also a more serious (through not at all solemn) interest. It uses low farce as a field within which to explore our chronic intoxication with language. The opening dialogue signals that intention: McTeazle and Cocklebury-Smythe speak for quite some time without using a word of English, being content to toss off French, Latin, and Italian clichés. We then follow an astonishing sequence of linguistic leaps, slithers, switch-backs, and catalogues. The MPs complicate their usual triple-lingo (bureaucratic obfuscation, high-flying rhetoric, and street talk) with punning innuendoes ("the papers naturally resort to sticking their noses into upper reaches of top drawers looking for hankie panties, etcetera"), Freudian slips ("why don't you have a quick poke, peek, in the Members' Bra—or the cafeteria"), and anxiously romantic admonitions to Maddie that, when interrupted, slide smoothly in and out of an allusion to Dickens or a definition of "quorum." As the chairman says when defending the football jargon Maddie has introduced: "The terminology of committee practice is in a constant state of organic change, Mr French. If you can't keep up you'll be of no use to us." Varied by rapid-fire parliamentary formalities and slow-motion dictation of angry debate, the dialogue skips onward through impertinent retorts ("What is that?" "Pair of briefs." "What are they doing there?" "It's a brief case"), pertinent misunderstandings ("Do you use Greggs or do you favour the Pitman method?" "I'm on the pill"), and tongue-twisting anti-mnemonic refrains ("Never at Claridges, Coq d'Or, Crockford's with Cockie. Never at Claridges, Coq d'Or, Crockford's with Cockie") to Maddie's potentially endless confessional chant:

> . . . I was at the Poule au Pot and the Coq au Vin and the Côte d'Azur and the Foo Luk Fok and the Grosvenor House and Luigi's and Lacy's and the Light of India with Johnny and Jackie and Jerry and Joseph and Jimmy, and in the Berkeley, Biancis, Blooms, and Muldoons with Micky and Michael and Mike and Michelle. . . .

We seem by now such stuff as language is made of—and *New-Found-Land* cuts in to make just that point. Two Home Office types, one very old and deaf and the other very young, enter the room to consider an application for citizenship, the visual and verbal language of which—an American, a beard, a farm in Kentish Town, £10·50 a week, interests in publishing, buses, theatre—suggests to the elder nothing but disadvantages: ". . . are we supposed to tell the Minister that he's just the sort of chap the country needs?" Indeed, each official is turned on only by his own style of language. The elder has told with relish but imperfect comprehension a tedious an-ecdote from his childhood about meeting Lloyd George (who, we gather, must have been playing his own sexual game); and the younger now delivers, as his partner dozes off, an even lengthier bravura celebration of a trans-American train-trip (in verbiage that sounds as if Thomas Wolfe had been hired to write a travel brochure). When *Dirty Linen* resumes, we are prepared to admit that national styles, like those of occupations and individuals, are mainly composed of pretentious nonsense and inadvertent self-disclosure. And yet, when the Home Secretary whips out his pen to sign Ed Berman's application after all ("One more American can't make any difference"), we wish the new Britisher well. The light shed by this playful linguistic lunacy has been more than adequate to the occasion.

Every Good Boy Deserves Favour leads us into a much subtler pattern of lunacy, not only amusing but also ominous and poignant. The title, a mnemonic aid used in teaching children the lines in the treble staff, here expands in meaning to evoke a society based on a rigid notion of harmonious order, its systems of miseducation and injustice, and its attempts to use paternal responsibility as a weapon against conscientious dissent. Not a "play" but a "piece for actors and orchestra," with music by André Previn, *EGBDF* was first performed at the Royal Shakespeare Company under Trevor Nunn's direction and the 100-piece London Symphony Orchestra conducted by Previn. Recast, and with a 32-piece orchestra, it has an extended run at the Mermaid Theatre. In the summer of 1979 Stoppard himself followed Nunn's production concept in directing it, with an 81-piece orchestra conducted by David Gilbert, at the Metropolitan Opera in New York.

Despite the verbal playfulness in its title and its form, *EGBDF* contains only one insistent punster, an exuberant, sardonic, and sometimes aggressively paranoid triangle-player named Alexander Ivanov, who con-ducts an imaginary orchestra in the mental hospital to which he has been confined. (John Wood played this role with dazzling virtuosity in the first performance.) Ivanov's lunacy does not obscure from us his talents: his inventive language is pure Stoppard, and his orchestra, which we can usually hear, plays music worthy of Previn. In accord, no doubt, with bureaucratic logic, the Colonel in charge of what is really a hospital-prison has also assigned to Ivanov's cell another inmate bearing the same name. Called Alexander in the script, though not on stage, the second Alexander Ivanov seems the psychological and stylistic opposite of the first. (Ian McKellen played the role with moving restraint in the first performance, and Eli Wallach brought to it a more obstinate passion in New York.) A laconic man of plain sense, firm will, and quiet irony, he tells how he was imprisoned here for doing something "really crazy": he had said, truly enough, that a friend of his had been put in prison for saying that sane people are being put in mental hospitals. He now refuses to eat, tells his story with an algebraic reticence, and composes affectionate letters in doggerel verse to his little son, Sacha. That son, the third Alexander Ivanov in the insistently triangular pattern of this piece, is a rather stubborn but vulnerable child who refuses to accept the skewed logic and ethics that ostensibly justify his father's imprisonment, and who also plays both triangle and drum with wilful passion in his school's percussion band.

The three Ivanovs are counterpointed against three functionaries who render the lunatic style of a system that not only denies human freedom but also distorts art and thought. The Doctor is an anxious conformist, skilled in psychoanalytic put-downs, who plays the violin in a real orchestra. The Teacher is an authoritarian who responds to the definitions in Sacha's geometry book with her own self-contradictory definitions of "antisocial malcontents," and who also directs the percussion band. And the Colonel in charge of this hell of repressed creativity and suppressed language is a semanticist and Doctor of Philology whose reputed "genius" is hard to distinguish from stupidity.

As Stoppard has said in a note to the published script, his portrayal of a rigidly orchestrated society draws on the experiences of Victor Fainberg and Vladimir Bukovsky. Alexander's account of his treatment in the Leningrad Special Psychiatric Hospital is taken from Fainberg's article in *Index Against Censorship*, "and there are other borrowings from life, such as the doctor's comment, 'Your opinions are your symptoms'." This Russian perversion of psychiatry has also been described in *A Question of Madness* by Zhores Medvedev, a scientist who had been diagnosed as having "incipient schizophrenia" with "paranoid delusions of reforming society." Such coercive defining of abnormality, however, is not just a Russian temptation. *EGBDF* makes that point obliquely through the first Ivanov, who, in a mad-scene somewhat reminiscent of *King Lear*, becomes a hyperbolic image of the repressive mania of which we are all capable. Earlier scenes have shown how language, music, logic, geometry, politics, and ethics are all distorted by the Doctor's and the Teacher's authoritarian sanity, which Sacha has parodied in his own rebellious definitions: "A triangle is the shortest distance between three points," and "A plane area bordered by high walls is a prison not a hospital." Now sitting in the Doctor's chair, Ivanov terrifies Sacha with raving axioms that travesty Euclid, the Declaration of Independence, and Matthew 19:24 ("Everyone is equal to the triangle," "It is easier for a sick man to play the triangle than for a camel to play the triangle"), and that build to this screaming climax: "What is the Golden Rule? . . . A line *must be drawn!*" (The geometrical wit of Ivanov's summation brightly transforms such middle-class wisdom as that of Shaw's Johnny Tarleton in *Misalliance*: "You can draw a line and make other chaps toe it. That's what I call morality.")

Perhaps the ultimate question implicit in *EGBDF* is simply this: On what authority do we decide not to treat our neighbour with love or respect but to define him as "mentally ill" and lock him up in a plane area bordered by high walls? A good many social scientists, of course, have recently explored that question—among them Erving Goffman (in *Asylums*), Thomas Szasz (in *The Myth of Mental Illness* and other works), and Michel Foucault (in *Madness and Civilization*). But since Pirandello, many playwrights have also explored it; and *EGBDF* brings especially to mind Pinter's *The Birthday Party* (with its pseudo-psychiatric interrogation of Stanley), Orton's *What the Butler Saw* (with its vision of a mental institution run by the stark raving sane), and N. F. Simpson's *One Way Pendulum* (in which a strangely withdrawn young musician conducts his weighing machines in the "Hallelujah Chorus"). But Stoppard himself has always been fascinated by the languages of withdrawal, hysteria, and rebellion. And the "insane" Alexander Ivanovs belong to that line of antithetical twins (the jailor and prisoner of *The Gamblers*, Lord Malquist and Mr Moon, Guildenstern and Rosencrantz, Archie Jumper and George Moore, Tzara and Lenin) through whom he has long been defining and redefining his bipolar world: flashy wit and plodding earnestness, narcissism and sympathy, art and politics.

The semi-musical form of *EGBDF* emerges from problems playfully invited and solved. Previn had first suggested that Stoppard write a narration around which he could build an orchestral piece. Stoppard responded almost at once with the more original and more genuinely collaborative notion of a piece for actors and orchestra. The risks were obvious: a symphony orchestra on stage might easily overpower the actors, the music might dilute or impede the action, and the total effect might seem unwieldy or pretentious. For the most part, those risks have been avoided or turned to advantage. The orchestra here seems a virtuoso actor: it delights the audience with its mimed passages, its various responses to its lunatic conductor, and its parody of the Doctor's movements; it plays a threatening nightmare when Alexander sleeps and a bit of Tschaikovsky's "1812 Overture" when he confronts Ivanov over Tolstoy's *War and Peace;* it suggests through pastiche of Prokofiev and Shostakovitch the controlling Soviet ethos; and it becomes the percussion band in which Sacha bangs away without regard for the written notes. Conversely, the actors often seem individual instruments: they enter into dialogues with the orchestra and antiphonal "duologues" with each other, and Alexander's longest speech is scored and lit as a solo. Though Previn's somewhat cinematic and perhaps "overscored" music does tend to blur chronology and suspend the action, those effects are appropriate in the limbo of an asylum or prison. And though the slender dramatic line may hold its own rather precariously against a full symphony orchestra on stage, that effect too is thematic. As a massive visible and audible environment, the orchestra renders the inner and outer forces that have already dominated four characters and threaten to overwhelm the other two. At the Metropolitan Opera the orchestra nearly filled a bank of red-carpeted elevations that led up to a red-draped back wall. Within that ominously formal and often darkened space were the three small and separately lit playing areas—the prisoners' cell (in front of the podium), the Doctor's office (on a platform behind the string bases), and the school-room (on a platform behind the violins)—and through it Sacha finally wandered in search of his father.

Stoppard's stylistic counterpoint interweaves the uneasily comic theme of the paranoid Ivanov, the heroic theme of the firmly resistant Alexander, and the poignant theme of the vulnerable Sacha, developing them through many symmetries, contrasts, and incremental repetitions. Encounters between Sacha and the Teacher, Ivanov and the Doctor, and Alexander and the Doctor stress both analogies and differences among the three patterns of resistance to authority. These dovetail with scenes relating Ivanov to Alexander, Alexander to Sacha, and then Sacha to Ivanov, which render conflicts or misunderstandings among the resisters themselves. After Sacha's terrifying encounter with Ivanov, the sequence climaxes in the "duologue" between Alexander's doggerel letters and Sacha's sung pleas that his father give up his hunger strike, lie to the authorities, and live.

Because Alexander's resistance cannot be broken even by that appeal and the authorities cannot allow him to die, a "logical impasse" occurs, which requires of the Colonel (and the playwright) a surprising strategy.

In a grandiose sky-blue uniform, the Colonel makes a long and impressive entrance accompanied by full organ music. Brushing interruptions aside, he asks each Alexander Ivanov a question appropriate to the other. Because Ivanov does not think sane people are put in mental hospitals and Alexander has no orchestra, both can be released at once. Some critics have questioned the realism of this sly bureaucratic confusion; but the style of the Colonel's entrance has already declared him a *deus ex machina;* and his decision, like the release of MacHeath in the "rewritten" ending of Gay's *The Beggar's Opera,* is also the author's own ironic acknowledgement of our desires. Stoppard's ambiguous finale expands this irony in another mode. After the Teacher, the Doctor, and Ivanov have joined the orchestra, Sacha meets his father downstage and then runs ahead of him through the orchestra up a central aisle—and (in the Stoppard-Nunn production) toward a shaft of light. Reaching the top, he sings again, as if Alexander had not yet been released: "Papa, don't be crazy! Everything can be all right!" Alexander calls to him; and the boy repeats his optimistic refrain, which echoes a sentence earlier used by both Alexander and the Teacher. Beneath his innocence and insistence, we feel a darkness that *Every Good Boy Deserves Favour* does not pretend to dispel.

Though simple in outline, *EGBDF* is remarkably complex in its inner form. Reviewing the New York production, Mel Gussow complained that the metaphor of the "dissident" as a "discordant note" in society works for the theatrical but not the musical part of the evening. "What if all the triangles, piccolos, cellos, and kettle drums went blissfully in their own direction without benefit of score or conductor? The result would not be dissidence or dissonance but cacaphony." But nowhere has the piece suggested through its carefully limited analogy any endorsement of such rigid and extreme alternatives. It has clearly differentiated Ivanov's unwilled rebellion, which produces music audible only to himself and us, from Sacha's wilful tantrums, which do indeed produce cacaphony, and both from Alexander's sober ethical commitment, which is quite consistent with a freely collaborative social order. Nor is music here essentially tyrannical. *EGBDF* recognises, of course, that any constructive or healing order can be perverted and misused by those who anxiously shout that "a line *must be drawn!*" But its own playful and collaborative harmonies—both theatrical and musical—illuminate for us the social lunacy that turns music (or language, or psychiatry, or geometry, or the Gospel) into a tyranny from which a conscientious man can only dissent.

Professional Foul, a television play of September 1977, dramatises a similar political situation in a much more conventional form. But it brings to that popular medium a subtle exploration of a problem posed in *Jumpers*: How can we justify ethical action in a time distrustful of all claims in behalf of absolute values and sceptical of language itself? Anderson, a distinguished but diffident Cambridge professor, is attending a philosophical congress in Prague, where he is slated to give a paper on "Ethical Fictions as Ethical Foundations." He has less interest in the paper, however, than in his slightly "naughty" plan to take in the World Cup qualifying football match between England and Czechoslovakia. He is approached by a former student, Pavel Hollar, now barred from Czech academic life, who has just completed his doctoral thesis on the source of the collective ethic in the individual ethic. Hollar partly justifies his argument that individuals have inherent rights by observing the behaviour of his own son, Sacha. (The position is less naïve than it might seem: the psychologist Jerome Kagan now argues in his recent book, *The Second Year*, that nineteenth-century thinkers were correct in holding that the child has an innate sense of morality.) When Hollar asks Anderson to smuggle the thesis back to England, Anderson refuses: "I mean it would be bad manners, wouldn't it?" He also rejects, as inconsistent with Hollar's own ethics, a suggestion that Hollar might hide the thesis somewhere in his luggage.

The next afternoon, intending to return the thesis on his way to the game, Anderson finds that Hollar has been arrested and that police are searching the Hollar apartment. Detained during the search, which ostensibly turns up some illegal dollars, Anderson can only listen to the game on the radio. That night he meets with Mrs. Hollar and Sacha in a park. Serving as his mother's translator and also as a moral agent in his own right, Sacha warns Anderson that Hollar has really been arrested for signing Charter 77 and that Anderson himself will surely be searched at the airport. When Anderson returns to the hotel he finds that another philosopher, McKendrick—who has seemed more interested in women and jazz than in his professed Marxism, and whose own paper argues that ethical principles reverse themselves at the "catastrophe point"—has become drunk and is self-righteously attacking an English football player for having committed a deliberate or "professional" foul that afternoon in the hope of preventing a Czech goal. These events lead Anderson to reverse his own position. He had previously remonstrated with McKendrick: "What need have you of moral courage when your principles reverse themselves so conveniently?" But now he answers his own question by committing one act that is unmannerly and another that is both illegal and unethical. He writes a new paper on the conflict between individual and community rights, in effect a critique of totalitarianism, and insists on presenting it to his session. (The chairman finally silences him by faking a fire alarm.) He also hides Hollar's thesis in McKendrick's luggage, unbeknownst to McKendrick himself, and so smuggles it out of the country. On discovering that he has been so used, McKendrick is predictably outraged; but Anderson disarmingly grants that his colleague might be right: "Ethics is a very complicated business." In fact, Anderson has committed his own "professional foul" for the sake of freedom.

His new position, which requires him to break lesser rules for the sake of an ultimate concern, contrasts not only with McKendrick's self-indulgence and self-righteousness but also with the absolute ethics and the naiveté of young Chetwyn, a neo-Thomist who has been active on behalf of persecuted professors and is now caught when trying to carry out some letters to Amnesty International and the United Nations. A fourth philosopher, an American named Stone who pedantically argues for an un-ambiguous "logical language" but is quite unaware of his own verbal ambiguity and non-verbal rudeness, seems absurdly remote from any ethical discourse or action. Commenting reluctantly on Stone's paper, Anderson observes that "language is not the only level of human communication, and perhaps not the most important level. Whereof we cannot speak, thereof we are by no means silent." That witty reversal of a famous sentence near the end of Wittgenstein's *Tractatus Logico-Philosophicus* points to An-derson's new ethical ground. His own paper argues (against linguistic phi-losophy, and with Hollar's help) that we have an obligation to regard our ethical fictions as if they were true, and that the fiction of "natural justice" is "an attempt to define a sense of rightness which is not simply derived from some other utterance elsewhere." Playing his new role with moral courage and finesse, Anderson justifies the light of his conscience with an axiom that , strange as it may seem, underlies all of Stoppard's own linguistic jugglery: "There is a sense of right and wrong which precedes utterance."

HERSH ZEIFMAN

Comedy of Ambush:
"The Real Thing"

When the curtain rises on *The Real Thing*, Tom Stoppard's most recent comedy, we see a solitary figure, Max, seated in his living-room; "[h]e *is using a pack of playing cards to build a pyramidical, tiered viaduct on the coffee table in front of him.*" Suddenly we hear the off-stage front door being opened; Max calls out "Don't slam—," but before he can finish his sentence, the door slams and his viaduct of cards collapses. The door-slammer is his wife, Charlotte, who pops briefly into the room before returning to the hall to remove her topcoat. Charlotte has just come back from a business trip to Switzerland—or so she claims; the problem is that, during her absence, Max has ransacked her private belongings and discovered her passport in her recipe drawer:

> CHARLOTTE: . . . You go through my things when I'm away? (*Pause. Puzzled.*) Why?
> MAX: I liked it when I found nothing. You should have just put it [your passport] in your handbag. We'd still be an ideal couple. So to speak.
> CHARLOTTE: Wouldn't you have checked to see if it had been stamped?
> MAX: That's a very good point. I notice that you never went to Amsterdam when you went to Amsterdam. I must say I take my hat off to you, coming home with Rembrandt place mats for your mother. It's those little touches that lift adultery out of the moral arena and make it a matter of style.

Without her passport, Charlotte has obviously not been abroad; where *has* she been, then, and, more important, with whom? Charlotte refuses to

From *Modern Drama* 2, vol. 26 (June 1983): 139–48. Copyright © 1983 by University of Toronto.

answer, and the scene draws to a close with her picking up her suitcase and walking out. Abandoned, Max reaches down to open the present she had brought him from her supposed trip to Switzerland. When he sees what it is, he begins to laugh: it is "*a miniature Alp in a glass bowl. He gives the bowl a shake and creates a snowstorm within it.*" End of Scene One.

Despite Dotty's putative affair with Archie in *Jumpers*, despite Ruth's acknowledged infidelity with Wagner in *Night and Day*, Stoppard has never before written a play focusing primarily on middle-class adultery. Yet if the theme of his new comedy seems at first glance somewhat startling and unexpected, the style is reassuringly Stoppardian. The entire panoply of Stoppard's trade-mark comic devices is abundantly present in the scene: witty puns, elegant jokes, comic misunderstanding. Here is Max, for example, launching into a long, funny, seemingly irrelevant encomium on the superiority of Swiss watches:

> And they've done it without going digital, that's what I admire so much. They know it's all a snare and a delusion. I can remember digitals when they first came out. You had to give your wrist a vigorous shake like bringing down a thermometer, and the only place you could buy one was Tokyo. But it looked all over for the fifteen-jewelled movement. Men ran through the market place shouting, "The cog is dead." But still the Swiss didn't panic. In fact, they made a few digitals themselves, as a feint to draw the Japanese further into the mire, and got on with numbering the bank accounts. And now you see how the Japs are desperately putting hands on their digital watches. It's yodelling in the dark. They can yodel till the cows come home. The days of the digitals are numbered.

The scene is, moreover, cunningly patterned and allusive, another Stoppardian signature. Stoppard opens his play by deliberately echoing the close of Ibsen's *A Doll's House*, the most reverberating door-slam in all of drama. Charlotte's entrance on this fateful day, like Nora's exist, thus symbolizes the shattering of a marriage; the structure of Max and Charlotte's life together falls apart in front of our eyes, as surely as Max's house of cards collapses.

Scene Two takes us to a different living-room, a messier one. As the scene opens, Henry is discovered searching his shelves of records for a particular piece of music; Charlotte enters, wearing Henry's dressing-gown. Is Henry Charlotte's lover, then, the man with whom she has betrayed Max? He appears to be, and yet there are too many jarring details which puzzle us. To cite just one example: Max eventually turns up and, though there is some awawkwardness, there is not the kind of sexual tension we expect in a confrontation between cuckolded husband and gloating or embarrassed lover. What is going on here? Gradually we learn the truth. Henry is a playwright—a playwright with a reputation for being witty, clever, "intellectual," much like Stoppard—and he is not Charlotte's lover, but her husband. Charlotte and Max are actors; the scene with which the play opened was not "real life," but a scene from Henry's current play, *House of Cards,* in which Charlotte and Max are starring. The "real" situation of Stoppard's play is thus very different from what we at first assumed: the focus is still on love and marriage and adultery, but Charlotte and Max are *not* the main characters. It is Henry who is the "real" adulterer here; as the scene progresses, we discover that he is having an affair with Annie, an actress married to Max. But is their love "the real thing"? What *is* "the real thing" when it comes to love?

The rest of the play attempts to answer these questions—or rather, as is typical of Stoppard's plays, it bounces the questions around in a kind of endless debate, with no single "answer" shown to be indisputably right. Different characters hold different views on love, *embody* different views. For Henry's teen-age daughter, Debbie, for example, love has nothing to do with sexual fidelity: "Exclusive rights isn't love," she pontificates, "it's colonization." Henry's reply is instructive: "Christ Almighty. Another *ersatz* masterpiece. Like Michelangelo working in polystyrene." The *ersatz,* the fake, the artificial, versus "the real thing": this is Stoppard's primary concern in the play, specifically in relation to the theme of love. But if love holds centre-stage here, there are numerous side-acts which prompt the same sort of questioning and which parallel and enrich the central theme: "real" music versus sham, for instance; "real" sex versus mere biology; the "real" self versus various masks; the "real" motivations behind political commitment; and, most significant of all, "real" writing versus trash.

In a sense, all of Stoppard's major plays are about defining "the real thing"; the only element that varies from play to play is the nature of the particular "reality" under debate: philosophy, art, political freedom, the press. What remains constant is the debate formula itself, and the method of dramatizing it. Stoppard involves his audience in that debate not just intellectually, but viscerally. Thus the very structure of his newest play—not simply its thematic content—dramatizes the difficulty inherent in determining precisely what "the real thing" is; once again, the *form* of a Stoppard play mirrors its theme. We might consider, for example, the Pirandellian opening of *The Real Thing.* For the entire first scene, we think we know exactly where we are: the play will be about the effect of Charlotte's adultery on her marriage to Max. Half-way through the second scene, however, the ground shifts beneath our feet; what we *thought* we were seeing in the first scene turns out to be an "illusion," a scene from Henry's play. Stoppard is deliberately shaking his audience up, like Max's miniature Alp in a snowstorm. When the snow settles, we discover we have been tricked; just when we think we have latched on to "the real thing," the reality alters. We have, in effect, been ambushed; and that is precisely Stoppard's aim. "I tend to write," he once noted, "through a series of small, large and microscopic ambushes—which might consist of a body falling out of a cupboard, or simply an unexpected word in a sentence"—or, as in the present case, an opening scene which, structurally, brings into immediate question the whole thematic concept of what is "real" and what is not.

This kind of ambush in Stoppard's plays is fundamentally comic— an audience laughs when it discovers it has been tricked, laughs at the sheer audacity of the trick. But it is also disconcerting: it is so easy to be tricked, so difficult to know precisely what is "real." Stoppard uses this kind of structural dislocation repeatedly in *The Real Thing*. In Act Two, for example, Annie asks Henry to help rewrite a television play in which she is thinking of appearing; the play is autobiographical, written by a friend of hers, a Scots soldier named Brodie, currently in jail for committing criminal acts during an antinuclear protest. Henry is unsympathetic both to Brodie's politics and to his play-writing. In Henry's opinion, Brodie's play is execrably written, and he proceeds to quote a few lines to make his point. In the passage he quotes, Brodie, entering a train compartment while en route to the protest, encounters a young woman, Mary, reading a book (it is the part of Mary which Annie considers playing):

HENRY . . . (*Reading*): "Excuse me, is this seat taken?"
"No."
"Mind if I sit down? [. . .] Do you know what time this train is due to arrive in London?"
"At about half-past one, I believe, if it is on time."
"You put me in mind of Mussolini, Mary. People used to say about Mussolini, he may be a Fascist, but at least the trains run on time."

Despite the play's stilted language, Annie disagrees violently with Henry's contemptuous dismissal of Brodie's work, and the scene ends with the two of them having a blazing row before finally making up.

We then shift immediately into the following scene:

ANNIE *is sitting by the window of a moving train. She is immersed in a paperback book.*
BILLY *walks into view and pauses, looking at her for a moment. She is unaware of his presence.* [. . .] *He speaks with a Scottish accent.*

BILLY: Excuse me, is this seat taken?
(ANNIE *hardly raises her eyes.*)
ANNIE: No.
(BILLY *sits down by the window opposite her.* [. . .] *She doesn't look up from her book.* [. . .])
BILLY: You'd think with all these Fascists the trains would be on time.
(ANNIE *looks up at him and jumps a mile. She gives a little squeal.*)
ANNIE: Jesus, you gave me a shock.
(*She looks at him, pleased and amused.*)
You fool.
(BILLY *drops the accent.*)
BILLY: Hello.

Stoppard is teasing us mercilessly here. When the scene begins, we *think* what we are watching is a scene from a play—Brodie's play, from which Henry has just finished reading. We have been fooled once before, after all, and are not about to make the same mistake twice. In fact, we make the *opposite* mistake; it turns out that the scene is *not* part of Brodie's play, it is "really" happening. Annie is on her way to Glasgow to rehearse a new play; Billy is an actor travelling to Glasgow for the same production. Billy, we discover, has also read Brodie's play; when he sees Annie in the train compartment, immersed in her book, he is unable to resist taking advantage of the situation by putting on a Scots accent and lapsing into the appropriate lines from the parallel moment in Brodie's play. This scene *reverses* the Pirandellian trick of the opening scene, but the point, of course, is the same: what appears to be "the real thing" may be an illusion, and vice versa.

The comic ambush of such Pirandellian playing with reality sets us up for the image of theatre as *illusion* which runs through Stoppard's entire play. Dramatists write constantly about love, but can its "real" essence ever accurately be captured on-stage? Henry is doubtful, at least as far as his own play-writing is concerned:

> I don't know how to write love. I try to write it properly, and it just comes out embarrassing. It's either childish or it's rude. [. . .] Perhaps I should write it completely artificial. Blank verse. Poetic imagery. [. . .] I don't know. Loving and being loved is unliterary. It's happiness expressed in banality and lust.

Does this mean, then, that all drama dealing with love is, by definition, artificial, not "the real thing"? Stoppard explores this issue through a further series of comic ambushes, deliberately juxtaposing the "real-life" love scenes between Henry and Annie, now divorced from their respective mates and married to each other (or, at any rate, living with each other), with love scenes from specific plays. Thus, in Act One, Annie launches into a passionate scene from Strindberg's *Miss Julie*, a play that she is about to perform and whose lines she is shown trying to memorize. And in Act Two, Annie is seen rehearsing a production of Ford's *'Tis Pity She's a Whore*, with Billy playing Giovanni opposite her Annabella.

In both instances, the particular play being cannibalized by Stoppard is left deliberately unidentified—somewhat in the manner of Christopher Hampton's *The Philanthropist*, which never actually names the Molière play to which it is so pointedly indebted. The closest Hampton comes is having one of his characters describe a recent visit to La Comédie Française:

> BRAHAM: . . . Last time I went, I had this enormous American lady sitting next to me, and just as the lights went down, mark you, and they were banging that thing on the stage, she leant across and said, "excuse me, I haven't had time to read my programme, would you mind telling me what the play is about, because I just can't understand a word they're saying." So I said, "Well, madam, it's about a man who hates humanity so much that he would undoubtedly refuse to explain the plot of a world-famous play to an ignorant tourist."
> ARAMINTA: You didn't really?
> BRAHAM: She thanked me. Profusely.
> ARAMINTA: Which play was it?
> BRAHAM (*coldly*): Three guesses.

Stoppard is being equally sly. Thus *Miss Julie*, for example, is never explicitly identified as such in *The Real Thing*; and our initial allusion to *'Tis Pity* is a teasingly oblique passage in which Henry, reminding Annie that she cannot possibly do Brodie's play because of a conflicting theatrical engagement in Scotland, amusingly confuses one famous play about incest with another:

> HENRY: Anyway, I thought you were committing incest in Glasgow.
> ANNIE: I haven't said I'll do it.
> HENRY: I think you should. It's classy stuff, Webster. I love all that Jacobean sex and violence.
> ANNIE: It's Ford, not Webster. It's Elizabethan not Jacobean.

The fact that these plays are unnamed does not mean, however, that the audience is being deliberately tricked in quite the same way as in the Pirandellian opening, for in these instances we are never in any doubt that what we are witnessing is indeed a play-within-a-play. Stoppard's ambush here is of a different kind.

In the first act of *Travesties*, Joyce, echoing Lady Bracknell echoing the "Ithaca" episode of *Ulysses*, catechizes Tzara about the history of Dada:

JOYCE: Did [Hugo] Ball keep a diary?
TZARA: He did.
JOYCE: Was it published?
TZARA: It was.
JOYCE: Is it in the public domain by virtue of the expiration of copyright protection as defined in the Berne convention of 1886?
TZARA: It is not. [. . .]
JOYCE: Quote discriminately from Ball's diary in such a manner as to avoid forfeiting the goodwill of his executors.

With a work like *'Tis Pity*, Stoppard has no such copyright worries, and he is therefore free to reproduce two key love scenes from Ford's play in *The Real Thing*. In Scene Six, Annie and Billy are shown rehearsing the scene in which Ford's lovers first declare their mutual passion; in Scene Eight, they enact the scene in which Annabella and Giovanni have just consummated their love. What is the point of such specifically theatrical interpolations?

In the case of Stoppard's allusions to *'Tis Pity*, both the play itself and the circumstances in which it appears in his text are clearly seen as artificial—not "the real thing." The language Ford's lovers speak is blank verse, a language totally alien to contemporary life; in addition, both Annie and Billy are known to be merely *acting* when they speak those words. Presumably, only the most unsophisticated theatre-goer confuses the identity of actor and role. When Annie kisses Billy, for example, it is *Annabella* kissing *Giovanni*: the gesture has nothing to do with how Annie "really" feels about Billy. By the same token, Annie's playing a "whore" (by which term Ford meant an adulteress—or, to use Angelo's lethally precise term in Shakespeare's *Measure for Measure*, a "fornicatress") obviously does not imply that she herself is a whore. I am belabouring the obvious here because it is precisely the obvious Stoppard is so intent on ambushing. For during the course of their rehearsals in Glasgow, Annie and Billy begin an affair; when they then declare their passion for each other in the words and embraces of Ford's theatrical lovers, who are we watching make love— Annabella and Giovanni, or Annie and Billy? It is *Annie*, as well as *An-nabella*, who is expressing her love here; *Annie*, as well as *Annabella*, who has become a whore. The "artificial" and the "real," theatre and life, have begun to overlap and merge, to bleed into other another: which is "the real thing"?

A similar kind of ambush underlies Stoppard's brief quotations from *Miss Julie*. Again, the theatrical interpolation is introduced in such a way that its artificiality is specifically emphasized. Intent simply on memorizing her lines, Annie "reads" the part of Julie *"without inflection,"* while Henry cues her by reading, equally mechanically, the part of Jean. Strindberg's intensely erotic love scene, in which Jean and Julie flirt passionately with each other (" 'I'm young.' "/" 'And handsome. And conceited! You're probably a regular Don Juan. I'd say you were a ram',") is thus delivered by two "actors" acting dispassionately. Likewise artificial is the dialogue itself: the words are self-consciously "stagy," a fact to which Strindberg (and by extension, of course, Stoppard) explicitly draws our attention. " 'Where did you learn to talk like that?'," the aristocrat Julie inquires of the flowery-tongued valet Jean. " 'Do you spend a lot of time at the theatre?'." And yet, for all their artificiality, Strindberg's words are later "used" by Henry to declare his genuine love for Annie, a love he finds difficult to express in "real life": " 'I'm here . . . I'm young . . . and handsome . . .' Your turn—tell me I'm a Don Juan. Tell me I'm a ram. (*He tries to 'read' his way into an embrace, but she pushes him away*)." Who, ultimately, is speaking here—Jean or Henry? by attempting *"to 'read' his way into an embrace,"* Henry deliberately blurs the boundaries between the "artificial" and the "real," leap-frogging from theatre into life—just as Billy, under the guise ostensibly of "rehearsing" in the scene on the train Giovanni's declaration of love for Annabella, expresses thereby his *own* attraction to Annie.

And if theatre keeps ambushing "real life," so "real life" constantly evokes theatre: Stoppard's play is a two-way mirror. Thus, just after the *Miss Julie* quotations, Henry bravely risks his own "voice" by declaring his love for Annie in a moving, sincere passage seemingly no longer mediated by theatrical borrowing:

> HENRY: . . . I love love. I love having a lover and being one. The insularity of passion. I love it. I love the way it blurs the distinction between all the people who aren't one's lover. Only two kinds of presence in the world. There's you and there's them.
> I love you so.
> ANNIE: I love you so, Hen.
> (*They kiss. The alarm on* HENRY's *wristwatch goes off. They separate.*)

That alarm startles us—not simply because it is an unexpected sound breaking a tender love scene, but because the fact that it breaks the scene emphasizes that what we have been watching is indeed a *scene*: a "theatrical" moment deliberately created and then shattered. The sound of the alarm is like the voice of a director yelling "Cut!" We have heard that sound before—specifically in the opening moments of Genet's *The Maids,* where it similarly destroys the illusion of reality. When *The Maids* begins, we think we are watching a confrontation between Madame and her maid Claire, but the sudden ringing of an alarm clock "wakes us up" to the reality of the situation: what we were watching was, in fact, "real," but a "theatrical" charade in which the maid Solange "played" Claire while the maid Claire "played" Madame. As hard as we try, there appears to be no escape in *The Real Thing* from this dilemma of determining "the real thing": is Henry's "real" love declaration more or less genuine than the "artificial" love scene from *Miss Julie* with which it is so cunningly counterpointed?

The love scenes from Ford and Strindberg thus function, structurally, as deliberately theatrical, "artificial" models against which we are meant to judge the "real" love of Stoppard's central characters. The most important of these theatrical models for Stoppard is *House of Cards,* that witty, intricately patterned play written by Henry ("Henry Ibsen," as his daughter calls him) which we saw dramatized in Scene One. According to Charlotte, Henry's play may be amusing, but it is utterly phoney, too clever by half (and where have we heard that before?); it tells us nothing about how people in love "really" behave. To some extent, Charlotte's complaint expands to indict theatre generally: all plays are artificial, and thus so are the images of love they present:

> CHARLOTTE: . . . Having all the words to come back with just as you need them. That's the difference between plays and real life—thinking time, time to get your bottle back. "Must say, I take my hat off to you, coming home with Rembrandt place mats for your mother." You don't really think that if Henry caught me out with a lover, he'd sit around being witty about place mats? Like hell he would. He'd come apart like a pick-a-sticks. His sentence structure would go to pot, closely followed by his sphincter. You know that, don't you, Henry? Henry? No answer. Are you there, Henry? Say something witty.

Is Charlotte's complaint justified? Stoppard proceeds to test her hypothesis by, in effect, twice replaying that opening scene, wrenching it out of the sphere of obvious theatre into the sphere of supposedly "real life." Thus, in Scene Three, the "real" Max discovers the "real" adultery of his "real" wife. The scene opens with Max sitting alone in his living-room; we hear the off-stage front door being opened, and his wife Annie pops briefly into the room before returning to the hall to remove her topcoat. When she re-enters, Max confronts her with Henry's semen-stained handkerchief which he has found in their car. The Max we see here behaves very differently from the witty, suave Max we saw "acting" in Scene One: he weeps, hurls abuse at Annie, and flings himself on her "*in something like an assault which turns immediately into an embrace.*" In Scene Ten, Stoppard's second replay, the "real" Henry likewise discovers the "real" adultery of his "real" wife. The scene opens with Henry sitting alone in his livingroom; we hear the off-stage front door being opened, and his wife Annie pops briefly into the room before returning to the hall to remove her topcoat. Annie has just arrived on the morning train from Glasgow—or so she claims. Why then was Henry told she had checked out of her hotel when he telephoned the previous evening? Again, Henry's reaction here is far removed from that of his theatrical persona in *House of Cards;* crumbling emotionally in front of our eyes, he indeed "come[s] apart like a pick-a-sticks."

In his plays, Henry knows all the right words to come back with, waxing witty about place mats and digital watches and much else besides. Even outside his plays, Henry's verbal response is sharp and instantaneous when the pain does not threaten him *personally;* he has no trouble writing "dialogue" for Charlotte, for example, when her lover accuses her of infidelity after discovering she had taken her diaphragm with her on a brief out-of-town trip:

> HENRY: What did you say?
> CHARLOTTE: I said, I didn't *take* my diaphragm. It just went with me. So he said, what about the tube of Duragel? I must admit he had me there.
> HENRY: You should have said, "Duragel! No wonder the bristles fell out of my toothbrush."

But when the adultery is "real"—not in a play, and not somebody else's problem—Henry finds himself mute with pain. The theatrical brittleness of Noël Coward-like dialogue so evident in *House of Cards* cracks under the strain of "real life":

> HENRY: . . . I don't believe in behaving well. I don't believe in debonair relationships. "How's your lover today, Amanda?" "In the pink, Charles. How's yours?" I believe in mess, tears, pain, self-abasement, loss of self-respect, nakedness.

As Charlotte predicted, even his sentence structure goes to pot; Annie actually has to correct his grammar. "The real thing" would thus appear to be very different from Henry's theatrical version of it.

It is obvious that both replays are initially set up so that, structurally, each explicitly mirrors the opening scene; it is equally obvious that the reaction of the "real" husband to his wife's betrayal is, in both cases, utterly opposite to the graceful wit under pressure displayed by the theatrical husband in *House of Cards*. The structural similarities would thus appear to be deeply ironic, underscoring the disparity in emotional truth between theatre and life; we finally seem to have discovered "the real thing." But have we? Are those structural similarities there paradoxically to *clarify* the distinction between the artificial and the real, or rather to *cloud* it? Stoppard has one more ambush up his sleeve, for the claims of theatre cannot be so easily dismissed. Thus, in the first replay, Max discovers his wife's infidelity through an incriminatingly dropped handkerchief. At the very heart of this "real" scene, then, we are implicitly reminded of theatre—of a highly theatrical, and therefore artificial, Moor who likewise bemoaned (and in blank verse!) the loss of his wife's handkerchief. Is Max's love, Max's pain, greater than Othello's? Is this discovery scene necessarily more "real" than Shakespeare's theatrical discovery scene? Similarly, while the pain felt by Henry is naked, intense and terribly moving, is it necessarily more "real" than the suffering of his theatrical alter ego in *House of Cards*? In both "real life" and Henry's play, the betrayed husband ransacks his wife's personal belongings; as Annie comments, in a direct echo of the opening scene, "You should have put everything back. Everything would be the way it was." In both "real life" and Henry's play, the accused wife claims no longer to know her husband. And the "real" scene ends with Henry alone on-stage, opening the present his wife has brought him from her adulterous trip to Glasgow: it is a tartan scarf. Unlike his theatrical counterpart, Henry does not laugh. But an audience, however much it genuinely feels for him, might be tempted to: life has a disconcerting habit of imitating theatre. Stoppard has ambushed us once again.

Nor are Max and Henry the only characters who replay variations on that opening scene. At the end of Act One, the "real" Annie is seen "*methodically and unhurriedly*" ransacking Henry's personal belongings, a gesture which closes the act by echoing its beginning: she too mimics the despair and jealousy of the protagonist of the theatrical *House of Cards*. Stoppard, that irrepressible joker, has stacked the deck. Theatre, then, far from being a necessarily artificial distortion of love's complexities, may, in fact, be uniquely capable of most truthfully reflecting them. Like Major Monarch and his wife in Henry James's tale "The Real Thing," a parable of the conflict between art and life from which Stoppard presumably derived both the title and theme of his play, we are foced to bow our heads "in bewilderment to the perverse and cruel law in virtue of which the real thing could be so much less precious than the unreal. . . ." And *is* the supposedly unreal so unreal after all? Stoppard's ambushes never cease: *The Real Thing* keeps circling endlessly back on itself, a play constantly playing with various plays-within-the-play. Dizzy from this series of comic ambushes of our perceptions and preconceptions, we thus find ourselves at the end invariably questioning, among a host of other "realities," the precise nature of love—as Stoppard, of course, intended. Love speaks in many different tongues, with many different accents. Which of them, finally, is "the real thing"?

RICHARD CORBALLIS

"Dirty Linen" and "New-Found-Land"

Dirty Linen was written for Ed Berman's company, Inter-Action, and was performed by them at the Almost Free Theatre in April 1976. It quickly transferred to the Arts Theatre, where it became Stoppard's first big success outside the pale of the subsidized national companies. The commercial quality of the play may owe something to the fact that it was written very quickly. The verbal texture is consequently thinner and the farce broader than in the large-scale plays. To submit this lightweight, frothy piece to rigorous analysis would be to break a butterfly upon a wheel. Still, the point must be briefly made that Dirty Linen exhibits the same juxtaposition of "mystery" and "clockwork" as do the other plays.

As usual Stoppard provides a couple of condensed statements of his principal theme near the beginning of the play. Cocklebury-Smythe's distinction between real peers and artificial ones (Life Peers) anticipates the distinction between real and artificial relationships on which the play as a whole focusses. But a more important indication of things to come is provided by the opening exchange between Cocklebury-Smythe and McTeazle. Although their dress and accents proclaim them to be British, both men speak at first in a strange amalgam of French, Latin, and Spanish. This artificial dialogue is eventually interrupted by a spontaneous ejaculation in good, earthy English from Cocklebury-Smythe: "Bloody awkward though."

From *Stoppard: The Mystery and the Clockwork*. Copyright © 1984 by Richard Corballis. Amber Lane Press/Methuen, Inc.

Immediately, however, he excuses his lapse with a topsy-turvy apology—
"Pardon my French"—and reverts to foreign tags for a few moments more.
This is merely the first of a series of clashes between an artificial, public,
"clockwork" idiom, on the one hand, and a realistic, spontaneous, private
idiom, on the other. Before looking at the clashes, let us examine the two
idioms separately. An example of the former is the Tennysonian Chairman's
Report which the Committee debates in the first part of the play and which,
if Cocklebury-Smythe is correct, has been foisted on Withenshaw, the
Chairman, by the Prime Minister. Another example is the language used
by the newspapers. Stoppard suggests that journalists are capable of a realistic idiom when they are off-duty, "chasing after everything in a skirt,"
and even when they are on-duty, covering football matches. But when it
comes to the matter of immorality among M.P.s they adopt a pompous,
foreign-phrase-ridden idiom. Here, for example, is *The Times* on the subject:

> *Cherchez La Femme Fatale.* It needs no Gibbon come from the grave to
> spell out the danger to good government of a moral vacuum at the centre
> of power. Even so, Rome did not fall in a day, and *mutatis mutandis* it is
> not yet a case of *sauve qui peut* for the government. . . . Admittedly the
> silence hangs heavy in the House, no doubt on the principle of *qui s'excuse
> s'accuse*, but we expect the electorate to take in its stride *cum grano salis*
> stories that upwards of a hundred M.P.s are *in flagrante delicto*, still more
> that the *demi-mondaine* in most cases is a single and presumably exhausted
> Dubarry *de nos jours*.

The Guardian is equally pompous in tone and equally reliant on foreign
phrases. Foreign phrases are lacking in *The Daily Mail*'s coverage of the
matter—Stoppard has to make some concessions to realism—but the pom-
posity is still evident.

The M.P.s themselves use a similar idiom for their public pronouncements. Foreign phrases are rare after the opening exchange between
McTeazle and Cocklebury-Smythe, although the word "quorum" crops up
often enough to remind the audience of this feature of the pattern, and
exchanges like the following (which is a variation on a formula first used
early in *Enter a Free Man*) are so nonsensical that they virtually constitute
a foreign language:

> COCKLEBURY-SMYTHE: It's rather more complicated than that—er—Arab
>   oil and . . .
> CHAMBERLAIN: . . . the Unions.
> COCKLEBURY-SMYTHE: M.P.s don't have the power they used to have, you
>   know.
> MCTEAZLE: Foreign exchange—the Bank of England.

MRS EBURY: The multi-national companies.
MCTEAZLE: Not to mention government by Cabinet.
CHAMBERLAIN: Government by Cabal.
MRS EBURY: Brussels.
COCKLEBURY-SMYTHE: The Whips . . .

The absurdity of this catalogue is accentuated not only by Stoppard's direction that the speeches should overlap each other but also by the fact that it is a response to a perfectly sane and simple, if naively optimistic, remark by Maddie:

Why don't they have a Select Committee to report on what M.P.s have been up to in their *working* hours—that's what people want to know.

Indeed throughout the play Maddie uses a plain, realistic idiom which comes straight from the heart (or thereabouts). Obvious symptoms of her directness are her habit of calling all her male acquaintances by the first names they use in bed rather than by the titles which they use during the day, and her habit of converting voting figures into football scores. (As in *Professional Foul* football becomes a kind of symbol for ordinary down-to-earth activities.)

The two idioms collide spectacularly and hilariously whenever there is intercourse (of one kind, at least) between Maddie and the M.P.s. Right at the beginning of the play McTeazle enquires pompously of Maddie, "Do you use Gregg's or do you favour the Pitman method?"; she replies bluntly, "I'm on the pill." On this occasion there is no response from McTeazle; like so many of Stoppard's "clockwork" characters he is directed to remain expressionless. On other occasions, however, there is evident tension between the M.P.s' bland public image and the private lust which Maddie inspires in them and which is latent in their very names—or in most of them; I confess to some uncertainty about the implications of Withenshaw and Mrs. Ebury. Sometimes this tension is revealed involuntarily, as in this glorious speech of Cocklebury-Smythe's:

McTeazle, why don't you go and see if you can raise those great tits—boobs—those boobies, absolute tits, don't you agree, Malcolm and Douglas . . . , why don't you have a quick poke, peek, in the Members' Bra—or the cafeteria, they're probably guzzling coffee and Swedish panties, Danish . . .

More often the tension between public and private in the speech of the M.P.s is expressed voluntarily, private appeals to Maddie giving way to public statements of various kinds (italicized below) whenever a third person comes into earshot, as in the case of this speech by McTeazle:

Maddien*ing the way one is kept waiting for* ours is a very tricky position, my dear. In normal times one can count on chaps being quite sympathetic to the sight of a Member of Parliament having dinner with a lovely young woman in some out-of-the-way nook—it could be a case of constituency business, they're not necessarily screw-*oo-ooge is, I think you'll find, not in* "*David Copperfield*" *at all, still less in* "*The Old Curiosity Sho*"-cking though it is, the sight of a Member of Parliament having some out-of-the-way nookie with a lovely young woman might well be a case of a genuine love match . . . (Stoppard's emphasis).

Attempts are made in the first part of the play to impose this tension between public and private on Maddie herself as, one by one, her lovers enjoin her to keep quiet about the scenes of their compromising encounters. She struggles desperately to "Forget the Golden Carriage, the Watched Pot and the Coq d'Or . . ." but on her open and ingenuous nature hypocrisy can never stick, and the injunctions to forget succeed only in "achieving the opposite" of the effect intended.

Stoppard is on Maddie's side, of course. The politicians have to be taught to take down the artificial barriers which they have built around their natural instincts. And the newspapers, if not the public at large, have to be taught,

. . . that it is the just and proper expectation of every Member of Parliament, no less than for every citizen of this country, that what they choose to do in their own time, and with whom, is . . . between them and their conscience . . . provided they do not transgress the rights of others or the law of the land . . .

Translated into stylistic terms this means that the formal, public idiom of the newspapers and of the committee members, while it might be appropriate in situations which involve "the rights of others or the law of the land," is quite inappropriate to the entirely private relationships which are at issue in this play.

Once again, then, we find that Stoppard has juxtaposed the real and the abstract and has opted unequivocally for the former. And it is worth noting at this stage how this portrait of the abstract is embellished with references to various literary (and not so literary) works—novels by Dickens, poems by Tennyson, and, of course, the newspapers. These references are really a sort of scaled-down equivalent to the plays-within-the-play in *Rosencrantz and Guildenstern Are Dead*, *The Real Inspector Hound* and *Travesties* and the music-within-the-play in *Every Good Boy Deserves Favour*, and they serve the same purpose of accentuating the artificiality of the attitudes with which they are associated. (Consider, for example,

McTeazle's references to *David Copperfield* and *The Old Curiosity Shop* in the italicized section of the speech quoted above.)

But it is the M.P.s' responses to the pin-up photographs in the popular press that indicate most obviously the artificiality of their attitudes. Each time an M.P. comes upon one of these pictures Stoppard initiates a stage routine which is designed—rather like Rosencrantz and Guildenstern's confrontations with their stage replicas—to sharpen the distinction between Maddie's real, private sexuality and the bogus public version of it. This is what happens:

> *This moment of the man reacting to the pin-up photograph, and the coincidental image of* MADDIE *in a pin-up pose is something which is to be repeated several times, so for brevity's sake it will be hereafter symbolized by the expletive "Strewth!" It must be marked distinctly; a momentary freeze on stage, and probably a flash of light like a camera flash.* MADDIE *should look straight out at the audience for that moment.*

This routine occurs six times in the first part of *Dirty Linen*. On the first four occasions it is a single politician who says, "Strewth!" and he is commenting on the newspaper pin-up. The audience, on the other hand, has its attention firmly fixed on the *real* pin-up—Maddie, in an ever-increasing state of undress. On the fifth occasion the presentation of the tableau is slightly different. Maddie herself displays one of the newspaper pin-ups to the Committee. But still the distinction between the artificial pin-up seen by the Committee and the real pin-up seen by the audience is preserved. This fifth tableau acts as a kind of bridging device between the earlier ones and the all-important final one, where the circumstances are significantly changed. Again it is Maddie who displays the newspaper pin-up from *The Sun* to the Committee but her reasons for doing so are much deeper and more personal than they were on the previous occasion. At first she was simply trying to make a point about newspapers; now she has become incensed at the artificial cant going on around the table, and she wants to expose its hypocrisy. More important, the pin-up in question features Maddie herself so that the distance which has so far been observed between the real pin-up and the artificial one in the newspaper is removed.

It is French who remarks on the identity of the two pin-ups, at the same time reducing Maddie to her bra and panties so that her actual appearance corresponds exactly to her image in *The Sun*. This is appropriate because French is the one member of the Committee who has not so far been seduced by Maddie and who has therefore remained free of the hypocrisy which taints everything said by the others. To date his sincerity has been misdirected; he has been assiduous in his search for evidence relating to misconduct by M.P.s and has thus vindicated Withenshaw's description of him as "a sanctimonious busybody with an Energen roll where his balls ought to be." Nevertheless, once the Energen roll has been rooted out by Maddie during the interval, his openness, redirected, will prove a decisive influence for the good. He is of course a catalytic figure in the sense defined by Birdboot in *The Real Inspector Hound*, but he is one of the few such characters in Stoppard whose function is not subverted.

French's initiative in naming Maddie causes the others to focus directly on her for the first time in the play; the collective "Strewth!" on this occasion is directed at Maddie and not at the newspaper. The sixth tableau is therefore constructed in such a way as to indicate that a collective awakening, initiated by Maddie and French together, is at hand. Moreover, the fact that Maddie is now virtually naked suggests that the naked truth is about to emerge. But before this can happen the Division Bell rings, the cast of *Dirty Linen* troops off and we find ourselves confronted by what the stage direction calls "another play."

Is *New-Found-Land* a wholly separate piece? It has certainly been performed and recorded separately, and the story of its genesis, told here by Hayman, would seem to confirm its autonomy:

> To celebrate his naturalization as a British subject and the 200th anniversary of the American Revolt, Ed Berman commissioned Stoppard to write the first in a series of new plays to be staged at the Almost Free Theatre under the title *The American Connection*. . . . Having started on *Dirty Linen*, Stoppard found that it was developing into something which had no connection either with Ed Berman or with the United States, but which was too good to scrap. The solution was to write a shorter play, *New-Found-Land*, which could be interpolated, like an entr'acte, between the two halves of *Dirty Linen*.

Hayman proceeds to discuss *New-Found-Land* in isolation from *Dirty Linen*. He does acknowledge in passing that the two are "seamed neatly together with small overlaps," but this seems to be a reference to the purely physical links between the plays—their use of the same setting and its associated sound-effects, and the way in which they literally overlap when the cast of *Dirty Linen* returns to the stage and brings the business of *New-Found-Land* to a summary conclusion.

There are, however, important thematic links as well. One that proves ultimately to be something of a red herring is the link between Withenshaw's casual observation that he "once took a train journey right across America" and Arthur's long monologue on the same subject. A more meaningful link is that between the two Frenches—the M.P. in *Dirty Linen* and the First World War general. In his first long speech in *New-Found-Land* Bernard claims that Lloyd George once told him that "French was a booby." The word "booby" has of course already been subjected to sexual innuendo in the early stages of *Dirty Linen,* and so the fact that it is now attached to French's name should tell us, if we have not already guessed, just what French and Maddie are up to in the ladies' cloakroom and while Bernard and Arthur are occupying the stage. And, having recognized this, we are in a position to see that Bernard's entire monologue about winning £5 from Lloyd George is relevant to the themes of *Dirty Linen.* For the speech is a piece of romanticism which glosses over the fact that Bernard's mother was Lloyd George's mistress in much the same way that the politicians and the newspapers gloss over the reality of Maddie's affairs.

Arthur's monologue about America is similarly idealistic and again the idealism is directly relevant to *Dirty Linen.* Ostensibly the speech arises out of an eccentric American's application for British citizenship, which Bernard and Arthur are supposed to be considering. But at a deeper level what Arthur says is again relevant to the French/Maddie liaison by virtue of the quotation with which it opens: "My America!—my new-found-land!" The line is of course lifted from Donne's "Elegy XIX: To His Mistress Going to Bed," though it is perhaps worth remarking that it occurs also in Beckett's *Murphy.* Arthur's extrapolation of an image from a famous poem on this subject can be regarded as a sort of literary counterpart to those suggestive scenes of natural ebb-and-flow-and-ultimate-climax with which the cinema used to titillate us while the hero and heroine were at their business off-screen.

New-Found-Land—note the spelling, which links the play with Donne's poem—thus emerges as a kind of idealized dream-sequence, comparable to Ruth's dream, which occurs at the same point in *Night and Day.* The fact that Bernard goes to sleep once Arthur launches into his monologue reinforces this impression. So does Arthur's topsy-turvy geography. His journey through America can only be a journey of the mind; its landmarks are drawn from myth and literature rather than from reality.

The dreamy idealism of *New-Found-Land* is abruptly shattered when the cast of *Dirty Linen* returns to the stage. Bernard, eager to relate his Lloyd George story to a new audience, produces his £5 note again, only to have it unceremoniously destroyed by Withenshaw, who takes it for one of Maddie's *billets doux.* The Home Secretary undercuts Arthur's romantic vision of America by coming to a completely arbitrary decision about the citizenship issue: "One more American can't make any difference." This minor triumph of realism is proleptic. When the Select Committee resumes its deliberations, French, who has become a "booby" during the interval and can produce a pair of Maddie's knickers to prove it, brings matters abruptly to a head by proposing the adoption of a new Chairman's Report. This new report, which has obviously been dictated to French by Maddie (whereas the original one had been dictated to Withenshaw by the Prime Minister) is couched in the direct, private idiom which she has used throughout the play. Its substance, as I have already noted, is that M.P.s are as free as any other citizen to do what they like in their spare time.

Although French lapses nervously into foreign phrases several times when introducing his proposal and even once after its adoption ("Toujours l'amour"), it is clear that the unanimous vote in its favour ("Arsenal 5— Newcastle nil") represents an unequivocal triumph for reality over the sort of abstract cant which was so prominent in the first part of the play and in *New-Found-Land*. The dumb blonde has prevailed over the clever dicks and it is only fair that now, with the pressure off her, so to speak, she should be allowed to indulge in her one unprompted foreign phrase of the play: "Finita La Commedia." (Her earlier lapse into French is the result of a misunderstanding; she takes Cocklebury-Smythe's introduction of Mr. French as a request that she should speak in French, and so she responds, "Enchantée.") As she delivers her Italian epilogue Big Ben chimes the quarter-hour—the fourth time it has struck in the course of the play, which, taken literally, would mean that the whole of *Dirty Linen-cum-New-Found-Land* should last a little over three-quarters of an hour—impossible. It is all too easy for critics to wax lyrical over the manifest intrusion of so meaty an abstraction as time into a work of literature, and I hope that I am not being over-ingenious when I suggest that the insistence on time passing in this play underlines the insistence on reality at other levels. In *If You're Glad I'll Be Frank* Gladys stresses the distinction between the artificial, mechanical clock and the reality of time:

> It's only the clock that goes tick tock
> and never the time that chimes.
> It's never the time that stops.

Similarly in *Travesties* Stoppard distinguishes between the "cuckoo-clock artificially amplified" that signals Carr's time-slips and the "naturalistic cuckoo-clock . . . seen to strike during the here-and-now scene of Old Carr's monologue."

In *Dirty Linen* the chiming of Big Ben seems related, paradoxically enough, to Gladys's time rather than her clock, to the here-and-now rather than the artifice in *Travesties*. It is in the service of "mystery" rather than "clockwork." Perhaps the point can be made more clearly by reference to another analogous statement about time, in Auden's poem, "As I Walked Out One Evening." (That Stoppard knows the poem intimately is suggested by the fact that in "Ambushes for the Audience" he talks enthusiastically of "Auden's glacier knocking in the cupboard"—an allusion to line 41.)

After Auden's lover has given vent to his Burnsian idealism about true love lasting "Till China and Africa meet,/And the river jumps over the mountain/And the salmon sing in the street"—sentiments echoed early in *The Real Inspector Hound*—the narrator steps in with this grim rejoinder:

> But all the clocks in the city
> Began to whirr and chime:
> "O let not time deceive you,
> You cannot conquer time . . ."

The whirring and chiming of Big Ben in *Dirty Linen* make the same point, which is indirectly related to the much more palatable point that the delightful reality of Maddie's sex-life should remain a private "mystery," or series of mysteries, instead of being subjected to "clockwork" public inquiries.

KEIR ELAM

After Magritte, After Carroll, After Wittgenstein

T he noble tortoise occupies an important place in the history of philosophy, in the history of the moral fable, not to mention, naturally, the history of zoology in its testudinal branch. If it has yet to leave its claw print on the history of theatre (with episodic exceptions such as a couple of passing and not very flattering references in Shakespeare, or a burlesque reduction to its shell in Jonson), this might be put down to the animal's fabled slowness and timidity rather than to any innate lack of theatricality. Indeed there are signs, as we shall see, that the said chelonian beast may finally be clambering its comical reptilian way onto the boards.

Now the peculiar emblematic and pedagogic utility of the tortoise, and of the *testudo* family in general, in its moral-philosophical guise, emerges most unequivocally in the Mock Turtle's impatient reply to Alice's naïve question in Wonderland, namely as to why his old schoolmaster, in reality a turtle, should have been called Tortoise: "We called him Tortoise," snaps the Mock Turtle, "because he taught us. . . . Really, you are very dull!" Well, what, throughout history, has the tortoise, as opposed to his cousin the turtle, really taught us? In one of Aesop's more renowned and retold moral fables, the plodding *khēlonē*, in defeating the athletic but sleeping hare, teaches us allegorically the virtue of steady application. In the equally notorious second paradox of the Greek philosopher Zeno, the similarly

From *Modern Drama* 4, vol. 27 (December 1984). Copyright © 1984 by University of Toronto.

tortoise-paced tortoise, in similarly defeating, given a charitable head start, the even more athletic and this time perfectly wide-awake Achilles, demonstrates instead the logical and mathematical impossibility of the Greek hero's ever reducing the distance between them because of the infinite divisibility of temporal and spatial intervals (Achilles, in order to catch his opponent and thereby avoid eternal humiliation, has to complete an infinite set of arithmetical reductions within a finite time).

The first modern logician to revisit this thorny or horny or shelly problem of the tortoise's Jesse Owens-like invincibility was C.L. Dodgson, the same Lewis Carroll who fathered the Mock Turtle, in his facetious but intriguing dialogue "What the Tortoise said to Achilles," published in the quite unfacetious *Mind* (1895). Carroll's articulate reptile, this time more plausibly overtaken by the Greek warrior, proves that he is at least intellectually quicker by lecturing Achilles on the dangers of deductively overstretching, as Zeno does, the premiss of a syllogism: Zeno, in effect, omitted to take into account the fact that the two competitors were moving at different speeds. Carroll's defeated but philosophical testudinian has in turn won a series of more recent admirers and followers (in an intellectual rather than athletic sense), from epistemological heavyweights like Gilbert Ryle, to paradoxical narrative game-players like Jorge Luis Borges (see the story "Avatars of the Tortoise" in *Labyrinths*), to modishly ludic computer scientists like Douglas R. Hofstadter, to logically and semiologically self-conscious dramatists like—I would argue—Tom Stoppard.

It might be noted that the tortoise, perhaps because of its provocatively enigmatic and unco-operative character, has been traditionally associated with a deviant, paradoxical, and somewhat sadistic mode of logical reasoning. And it is precisely in such a context of an irrational excess of rationality that it makes its first conspicuous appearance on the modern stage, albeit a purely verbal and in the event quite illusory appearance, namely in Stoppard's *After Magritte* (1970). The narrative fulcrum—inasmuch as it has one—of this heady hermeneutical farce is a banal off-stage event barely glimpsed by the play's main characters, the three members of the Harris family, who devote much of the cross-talking dialogue to arguing out their three rival interpretative hypotheses: Thelma Harris interprets the scene as comprising a one-legged footballer in West Bromwich Albion gear his face covered with shaving-cream, hopping down the street, wielding an ivory cane and—the essential detail here—carrying a football under his arm; her mother-in-law perceives instead a gentleman dressed in gaberdine, wearing a surgical mask and dark glasses, waving a cricket-bat and carrying under his arm not a football but a handbag; while Mr. Harris, her son, perceives a one-legged and white-bearded blind man in pyjamas prod-ding before him a white stick and bearing neither football nor handbag but that mad logician's pet of pets, a tortoise. Each interpretation has its own narrative and logical coherence, however improbable the results, with re-spect to the interpreter's original premiss or perception.

Now the play's ambiguous title raises explicitly the question of its debts (of whom, as it were, it takes "after"), or of the direct cultural influences on the verbal and visual follies it pursues with such manic energy and rigour. And it is this question of Stoppard's relationship with the cultural patrimony—specifically the non-*dramatic* patrimony—of our age, his intellectual and intertextual "afterness" or posteriority with respect to those figures whose artistic practice or theoretical models are closest to the principles of his theatrical poetics, that is the main concern of this paper. A question that regards, in effect, Stoppard's engagement with certain of the central aesthetic, philosophical, and especially semiological issues of our time. Above all, this essay has to do with the means by which Stoppard dramatizes and theatricalizes such issues, since it is, in my opinion, his success in finding precise and persuasive theatrical co-ordinates for appar-ently intractable conceptual material that represents this playwright's major contribution to contemporary dramaturgy.

Stoppard's openly acknowledged debt, or indeed homage, to René Magritte in his farce is multiple. The "After" of the title has first a simple chronological sense, since the play's controversial central event is witnessed by the Harrises on their way back from a Magritte exhibition (the implicit suggestion being, naturally, that their very perception of the mysterious figure may have been contaminated by what they saw of Magritte's way of seeing). And second, it has an iconographic sense, by way of a pseudo-painterly quotation (as in "after Leonardo"), in that the play's opening stage configuration appears to be a Magrittean pastiche, both because of its inexplicability as composition or juxtaposition (elderly woman on iron-ing-board, younger woman in ball-gown on all fours, semi-naked man in fisherman's waders fixing the light, with a framed policeman looking in), and, as it were, in its component "lexical items," all objects stolen from Magritte's attic: a tuba, a window with a dark menacing figure outside it, a black bowler hat perched on the old lady's body, a screen that might be a canvas *mise en abîme*, and so on.

But both the apparent surrealist adjacencies and the specifically Magrittean iconographic idiolect here turn out to be species of *trompe-l'oeil*, a visual joke in the spirit of Magritte himself. As the farce frantically unfolds, the inexplicable is explained or at least expounded, while the Magrittean furniture takes its place duly within the dramatic landscape and contemporarily within the logical narrative order of the play. What remains is quite a different mode of "afterness" towards, or intertextual rapport with Magritte, not so much at the level of iconographic quotation as at the level of apparently shared semiotic territory. Here the point of reference is less any single painting or group of paintings by the Belgian artist than his theoretical theses on the complex three-way relations among objects, iconic signs, and linguistic signs in "Les mots et les images," published in *La Révolution Surréaliste* in 1929. Under the evident influence of Saussure, Magritte reflects on the arbitrary and contingent nature of the sign, but extends the Saussurean principle to include not only linguistic but apparently "motivated" iconic signs. Thus, if "an object is not so tied to its name that one cannot find another that suits it better," the word being only too readily and demonstrably detachable from its referential hold on the world, at the same time "any form at all may replace the image of an object" since the seemingly inviolable iconicity of the visual representation is in practice no less subject to cultural determination and to perceptual relativism. It is on the grounds of this shared and reciprocal contingency as mutable cultural units within the same semiotic or semiosic universe that the linguistic sign may substitute the iconic sign within visual discourse and the iconic sign may replace the lexical item within verbal discourse.

Now these, of course, have become (after Magritte chronologically, if not directly after him doctrinally) standard tenets of twentieth-century semiology. But the most radical and interesting move in this *Cratylus* for the surrealist movement brings into play the status of the very referent or represented object itself, which not only inevitably delegates its material presence to the representational powers of the sign but also is subject to the same laws of cultural mediation and epistemic instability. One of Magritte's theses, which expounds the sober Aristotelian principle whereby "everything leads us to believe that there is little relationship between an object and that which represents it," is illustrated, in his best paradoxical fashion, by a spot-the-difference sketch in which the "*objet réel*" and the "*objet représenté*" appear instead perfectly identical—*not* because the icon or image magically or platonically incarnates the so-called real object, but because the real object turns out to be already and only a sign unit on another plane. Or better, the segmentation of the perceived physical universe into discrete and atomic objectual parts is governed by, rather than unilaterally determining of, the play of the sign and the interplay between signs. Object, image, and lexical unit stand—as Charles Sanders Peirce would say—in a multilateral dialectic as "interpretants" one of the other, and there is no way of breaking this interpretational chain or hermeneutic circle so as to arrive finally and reassuringly at the chimeric "*objet réel*." Magritte's perceptual world is presented as a "mosaic" of adjacent and interdefining forms rather than an assembly of fixed and autonomous substances.

The frustrations in store for the epistemological positivist who wishes to put a stop to this giddy prospect of an endless interpretational *regressus* are most pleasingly and teasingly emblematized in what we might term Magritte's second paradox, namely the painting "The Two Mysteries" of 1966, which revisits and reworks his famous "This is not a pipe" joke of 1928. Where the earlier painting simply places in contradictory juxtaposition iconic representation and linguistic predication, the reworked version goes further in putting the earlier work in a frame (or *en abîme*) and displaying outside it what might be taken to be the "*objet réel*," the referent which ought to put a *deus ex machina* or *res extra picturam* end to such paradoxical nonsense. Except, of course, that the second pipe proves to be subject to identical material and conventional conditions as "interpretant" of the first painting, and far from breaking the interpretational chain, threatens merely to set off an unstoppable pipeform series or pipeline.

Stoppard's "afterness" with respect to Magritte has to do chiefly with just such a daunting semiotic regress within which objects, images, and linguistic signs interact and interchange in a vertiginously self-propagating series. In each of the Harrises' conflicting accounts of the bizarre predramatic happening, the originally and Magritteanly perceived objects start off an associative visual-verbal delirium in which every element or "interpretant" confirms the starting image: the tortoise is to the blind man is to the white stick is to the pyjamas as the football is to the West Bromwich player is to the uniform is to the ivory cane. This is Magritte's mosaic universe of contiguous and mutually defining forms, in which all "*objets réels*" are condemned to be at the same time "*objets représentés*." But Stoppard gives the already tortuous hermeneutic chain a further and spectacular twist in the farce's pseudo-dénouement, where it emerges (or where at least we are requested to believe) that the limping, uniformed or pyjamaed, tortoise- or gourd-carrying "*objet réel*" of all this hypothetical ado is the same Inspector Foot ("Foot of the Yard") who has come to investigate the Harrises' curious domestic and extramural behaviour, and moreover that his sleuthish suspicions are aroused by a telephone report of the very scene witnessed by the Harrises, of which he is the unwitting protagonist. How hermeneutically circular can you get? The play's interpreters not only are all victims of the play of the "interpretant," but prove also to be the very objects or referents of their own perceptual hallucinations and associative speculations. So that the play's most tellingly ironical line is perhaps Inspector Foot's feeble alibi for his detectional débâcle: "But bear in mind that my error was merely one of interpretation. . . ."—as if (as the actress said to the bishop) there were anything else in this world.

It is, of course, this element of error in the play, as well as the consequent implicit moral judgement of a kind present in all bourgeois farce, that distinguishes Stoppard's interpretative follies from the irresolvable and amoral ambiguities of Magritte. Stoppard's dramatis personae, far from heroically exemplifying the epistemic dubieties of the surrealist *homo oneiricus*, turn out in the end to be the rather foolish victims of their own logical absolutism—a perspective which brings us back to Carroll's tortoise and his lesson to Achilles. The play's affinities with Carroll and *his* deviant logic are clearly less overt and probably less direct than its verbally and visually declared allegiance towards Inspector Magritte. But there may be, in the opening pseudo-surrealist rebus set, an occult iconographic reference to the Reverend Dodgson and his logical (or as he prefers to call them, "magical") games. [Consider the object in the opening tableau of the play,] described in the stage directions as a light fixture on a counterweight system, the counterbalance specifically consisting of a basket of fruit. One of the play's recurrent visual jokes concerns the miraculous domestic physics whereby this extremely precarious equilibrium is lost and recovered: Harris removes the light bulb, forcing the shade to ascend; he takes an apple out of the basket, causing the shade to redescend; he takes a bite out of the apple, re-establishing the lost balance, etc. Now this device bears a distinct family resemblance—if only, as it were, on the vertical axis—to one of Carroll's more notorious games, the so-called monkey puzzle, which presents a monkey on a rope counterbalanced by a weight, and poses the question as to what happens to the weight when the monkey begins to climb: does it go up or does it go down? The puzzle has engaged serious mathematical minds, and opinions have varied as to the answer (no doubt Carroll's objective was precisely to set his colleagues squabbling, in the spirit of Achilles and the tortoise). In the case of Stoppard's equilibristic engineering, of course, the puzzle posed is more banally pragmatic, not so much a mathematician's "how does it change?" as a prestidigitator's "how does he do it?," so that the result is less a brain-teasing enigma than a crowd-pleasing *coup de théâtre*. But just as Carroll's monkey game deliberately and provocatively tests the limits of conventional logical laws, so Stoppard's basket trick emblematizes the farce's desperate reduction to the absurd of conventional pragmatic reasoning.

There may also be a more or less hidden *verbal* link in the play with the Reverend logician. Carroll's ancient Greek tortoise hazards a passing and anachronistic contrast between the laws of Euclid, not yet formulated, and the game of football, not yet invented, prompting Achilles to point out that in any case a tortoise playing football would be something of an anomaly. Both the specific tortoise-football juxtaposition and the bizarre sporting event impossibly hypothesized by the tortoise are close to the possible but improbable worlds imagined by the members of the Harris family. More substantial, however, is what we might term the common ethical ground on which the two texts move: the cognitive and existential vice explored in the dialogue and ridiculed in the farce is that blinkered deductive reasoning in straight lines that fires Zeno's arrow, in the tortoise's view, and that guides the white stick of Harris's blind man.

Stoppard's second histrionic tortoise has a somewhat more verifiable, if equally mixed, parentage, and a decidedly more concrete stage presence, although it is scarcely for that any the less the subject or object of perils logical and semiological. In *Jumpers* (1972), the domed (or *domused*) quadruped finally overcomes its stage fright, being brought on, in accordance with the best ancient and modern traditions, as an emblem-cum-referent in a heated philosophical debate. Here the dramatist's posteriority is in the first instance of a strictly doctrinal kind. His protagonist, the moral philosopher George Moore—himself cruelly afflicted by a chronic case of secondariness due to the name he is doomed to share with his far more renowned philosophical predecessor—attempts to uphold certain traditional ethical and epistemological values against the nonchalant scepticism of his colleagues. Moore turns polemically in this attempt to Zeno's two paradoxes (the arrow that can never reach the target, Achilles who can never catch the tortoise), in order to prove in a kind of metaphysical cabaret act that the Greek thinker was demonstrably wrong-headed in his paradoxically absolute relativism. Hence the empirically verifiable reachability of tortoises and targets; hence the existence of observable laws, hence the affirmability of physical and moral values, etc., etc.

Moore's immediate problem, however, apart from his evident philosophical mediocrity, is his inability to distinguish the mathematic from the mythopoeic: he manages to confuse Zeno's tortoise with Aesop's, substituting for Achilles a (presumably more accessible) hare. He then succeeds in sparking off a further, and in the event tragic, short circuit between the Aesop fable and the first of Zeno's paradoxes, shooting the supposedly athletic hare with the only too emphatically arriving arrow, thereby indeed proving the Greek philosopher—though not necessarily the Greek fabulist—mistaken on at least one count. And just to complete the physical and metaphysical slaughter, Moore, in a state of shock at the death of his hare, steps onto his tortoise with equally pathetic results. As Lewis Carroll's philosophizing beast complains when Achilles sits on him: "You flatter me—*flatten*, I mean, . . . for you *are* a heavy weight, and *no* mistake!"

What, exactly, has Stoppard's second and hapless pedagogic tortoise taught us? Allegorically, by way of an Aesopian moral fable, the lesson would appear to lie in the vanity of attempting to resolve life's uncertainties—ethical, metaphysical, and personal—by supporting oneself, literally in Moore's case, with reassuringly concrete points of reference, like Dr Johnson kicking his stone. The supporting object, Moore's tortoise, simply gives way under the weight.

But as with the iconic clutter and magical machinery of *After Magritte*, the real point of the play's disastrous didactic demonstration is aesthetic or semiotic, and specifically theatrical—because Moore's abortive argumentational sleight-of-hand, or rather sleight-of-claw-and-paw, in introducing into his demonstration lecture the two emblematic animals is a somewhat vulgar exercise in ostensive exposition, that mode of direct showing rather than telling on which, as Moore and that other moral philosopher, Aristotle, well know, theatrical mimesis (as well as show business in general) is founded. Not by chance Moore is married to a former star of the music-hall. Ostension is that mode of signification or semiosis whereby in place of a mediated representation by means of linguistic and other signs, the object is allowed to predicate itself and its own properties directly. Moore, instead of specifying the respective physical and agonistic properties of hare and tortoise, produces a couple of actual specimens so as to let them define themselves and show off their prowess. This is, of course, the same semiotic principle that allows the actor's body to define itself *as* a body on the stage, and so inaugurate direct iconic representation rather than discursive narration of dramatic events; and there is no doubt that Moore has an eye more to the theatrical than to the epistemological *coup*. And by the same ostensive token, the trick allows Stoppard himself to theatricalize his doctrinal material, and to squeeze improbable pathos out of the dry corpse or corpus of a spectacularly failed lecture.

The whole of *Jumpers* explores and exploits relations between visual ostension and verbal discourse. The comedy begins with a gymnastic display by a group of philosophers whose bodies in formation represent iconically the kind of analytical acrobatics which their language-oriented philosophy enacts—the linguistic turn, as it were, figured forth by a circus turn. And Moore's wife, the retired showbiz star Dotty, subjects her suffering husband, among other things, to frequent rebuses or charades in which her body and its positions and gestures act out the lexical items of proverbs, titles, and the like. As Magritte observes in one of his semiological theses, "an image can take the place of a word in a proposition."

The trouble for Moore lies in the fact that the ostensive use of an object depends on its surrendering up, as it were, its uniqueness as a single entity in order to serve as the token for a type, or as the representative of the *class* of objects to which it belongs. A pipe, or a tortoise, or a human body represent ostensively, precisely, the pipe, the tortoise, and the body to the extent that they are taken to stand for the *cultural* units in question. If this were not so, [the actor] Michael Hordern could represent only Michael Hordern rather than a potentially unlimited range of human males (and, at an extreme, even females). In *Jumpers*, the unfortunate tortoise and hare are doomed to surrender up all too literally their individual existences in the interests of Moore's ostensive display, a fact laden with a certain pathetic power since the philosopher has unwisely adopted them as pets and given them names (i.e., taken them as individuals rather than as tokens).

But the problems really arise with the conspicuously ostended body of Dotty Moore, which, apart from representing an apparently irresistible point of attraction for all the male characters, is the object of the play's central mysteries and most painful ambiguities: first, as to whether hers is indeed the hand that pulls the trigger that murders the professor that sets off the comedy's farcical whodunit main plot (whether she is, so to speak, the guilty body); and second, as to what she actually *does* with her body semiotically and erotically. Moore, among his other moral, metaphysical, and (to steal one of Stoppard's jokes) merely physical dubieties, has the probably justified suspicion that his wife enjoys a more than intellectual rapport with his philosophical rival, the arch or Archie gymnast, logician, psychiatrist, and vice-chancellor (or chancellor of vice), Archie Jumper. Dotty and Jumper spend considerable lengths of time together in the closed bedroom, with Dotty in, as they say, varying degrees of undress, on the pretext of conducting psychosomatic check-ups. But when Moore, accompanied by the play's resident sleuth Inspector Bones, enters the bedroom to discover the classic scene of Jumper kissing Dotty's hand while she is seated on the bed, his wife's absolute lack of surprise or shame raises the central marital-semiological puzzle: "It must have been one of her games," explains Moore to the astonished Inspector, who, detective that he is, proceeds to crack the suitably sleuthy saying supposedly being acted out ("softly, softly catchee monkey")—as if to say, it is not Dotty's body *as such* that is caught in so compromising a gesture, but only her body as depersonalized sign vehicle, standing innocently for an item within an innocuous game.

Moore's agonizing aporia—which is, of course, intimately bound up with the very moral uncertainties he attempts to tackle in his lecture— derives from the fact that the simple *perception* of the ostended object provides no reliable information about it until we know at what level or in what context or within what universe of discourse it is to be defined. Or as Wittgenstein would say, in what language-game it is participating (in Dotty Moore's case, the charade-game or the courtship-game). The reference to Wittgenstein here, of course, is anything but arbitrary. Moore himself relates a typical Wittgensteinian anecdote illustrating the great philosopher's unsentimental way with the treacheries of perception: "Meeting a friend in a corridor, Wittgenstein said: 'Tell me, why do people always say it was *natural* for men to assume that the sun went round the earth rather than that the earth was rotating?' His friend said, 'Well, obviously, because it just *looks* as if the sun is going round the earth.' To which the philosopher replied, 'Well, what would it have looked like if it had looked as if the earth was rotating?' "—an unanswerable conundrum that illuminates Moore's immediate and more local problem: what would it look like if his wife's body were *really* performing what it appeared to be performing?

Wittgenstein is in a real sense the presiding deity of Stoppard's semiologically reflexive poetics, the natural and recurrent point of reference for his fruitfully self-conscious "afterness" with regard to philosophical and aesthetic theory. Unquestionably, the text that best illuminates not only the pains of perception and definition in *Jumpers*, but a range of issues dramatized in more recent comedies, is the *Philosophical Investigations*, a text substantially dedicated to the very questions of ostension, the relations among objects, linguistic and iconic signs, and the business of playing language-games, that so consistently fire Stoppard's dramaturgic inventiveness. Wittgenstein's conception of the language-game itself, whereby "the *speaking* of language is part of an activity, or of a form of life," and is subject to an almost infinite multiplicity of forms, according to its ends, to the circumstances of its playing, to the kinds of non-verbal doings and objects involved: such a conception is immensely suggestive with reference to the drama in general and Stoppardian comedy in particular, which indeed might well be approached as a dynamic weave of multiple and precarious language-games within ever-shifting frames of definition.

It is, in effect, the perilous process of distinguishing one game from another, or of knowing just what it is that is being done with objects, with words, and with other signs, that most preoccupies Wittgenstein as it does Stoppard and his victims. Take the emblematic instance from the *Philosophical Investigations* of what Wittgenstein wryly terms the "It could be *this* too" game, which the philosopher introduces in order to expose the illusion of substituting one form for another or one object for another, or one sentence for another, in the hope of disambiguating its perception and definition. Wittgenstein's slogan celebrating the perpetual non-finality of definitions, "It could be *this* too," might be adapted to any number of Stoppard's ironical dramas and dramatic ironies, from *The Real Inspector Hound* ("It could be *him* too") to *The Real Thing* ("This could be *it* too"). Wittgenstein, significantly citing the creations of Lewis Carroll, provides the suitably Wonderlandish exemplum of the hybrid duck-rabbit, a gestalt condemned to eternal ambiguity and slave to the point of view of the beholder. We are back in the territory of Stoppard's tortoise-gourd or mock turtle, perceived in an instant from conflicting perspectives. "And I must distinguish," adds Wittgenstein, "between the 'continuous seeing' of an aspect and the 'dawning' of an aspect." Stoppard's perceptual hermeneutics—the hopping footballer, Dotty's enigmatic body—always catches the beholder at the moment of the dawning of an aspect; he is never allowed the luxury of a continuous seeing.

The *Philosophical Investigations* begin with a quotation from St. Augustine's *Confessions* that ushers in the discussion of ostension as a constituent part of language-games. Augustine presents an autobiographical account of his own language-acquisition as an infant by means of ostensive definition: "When they (my elders) named some object, and accordingly moved towards something, I saw this and I grasped that the thing was called by the sound they uttered when they meant to point it out. . . . Thus, as I heard words repeatedly used in their proper places in various sentences, I gradually learnt to understand what objects they signified." Wittgenstein is understandably sceptical of this account, which he defines as "a primitive idea of the way language functions," or alternatively as "the idea of a language more primitive than ours." And he proceeds to dramatize, as it were, this notion of the primitive language-game by imagining a situation in which such an ostensive language might be adequate, namely an exchange between a builder and his assistant who need only refer to the materials of their trade, and so require only a very limited repertory of denotative substantives: "block," "pillar," "slab," "beam." It is not hard to see why Wittgenstein's gestural me-Tarzan-you-Jane microdrama, which raises again the fundamental question of the referential univocacy of language in its relationship with the object, should have caught Stoppard's imagination. It is, in any event, this passage that inspires the dramatist's most explicit tribute to the philosopher, the brief text that he might well have entitled "After Wittgenstein" but that instead he labels, choosing to underline the play's second main debt, *Dogg's Hamlet.*

What Stoppard attempts, in effect, is to out-Wittgenstein Wittgenstein, applying to the latter's dramatized primitive language-game the very "It could be *this* too" principle expounded later in the *Philosophical Investigations.* If one were to witness the builders' limited dialogue, observes the playwright in his preface to the published test, one might automatically suppose that the speakers were referring to their materials, distinguished according to size and shape, etc.: the dawning of an aspect. "But this," he notes, "is not the only possible interpretation. Suppose, for example, the thrower knows in advance which pieces the builder needs, and in what order." In this case the lexical items might denote not the objects in use but aspects of the *process* of construction. Thus "plank" might in fact signify "ready," "slab," "okay," "block," "next," "cube," "thank you," etc. Stoppard declares that the purpose of his comedy is precisely to teach the audience this code, Dogg—the grunting language of Wittgenstein's builders revisited—which *looks* like English but which is semantically altogether another lorry-load of bricks. In this sense the dramatist revalorizes the language-acquisition process described by Augustine, inasmuch as the audience, through its dramatic delegate the builder Easy, has to acquire the new code through ostensive clues alone, i.e., by means of the objects and gestures that support the *sprachspiel* during its actual playing:

DOGG: Brick.
(*He positions* CHARLIE *in line with* BAKER *and the lorry.* EASY *stands next* CHARLIE *in the place where the steps are to be built. To* BAKER *and* CHARLIE.) Plank? [*Ready?*]
BAKER/CHARLIE: Plank, git. [*Ready, sir.*]
DOGG (*Calling out to* ABEL.): Plank?
ABEL (*Off-stage.*): Plank, git.
(DOGG *gives the piece of paper to* EASY *who studies it warily.* EASY *puts the paper in his pocket.*)
DOGG (*Calling out to* ABEL *loudly—shouts.*): Plank!
(*To* EASY's *surprise and relief a plank is thrown to* BAKER *who catches it, passes it to* CHARLIE, *who passes it to* EASY, *who places it on the stage.* DOGG *smiles, looks encouragingly at* EASY.)
EASY (*Uncertainly, calls.*): Plank!
(*To his surprise and relief a second plank is thrown in and passed to him the same way. He places it.*)
Plank!
(*A third plank is thrown in and positioned as before.* DOGG *leaves, satisfied.*)

Note: EASY *is going to build a platform, using "planks," "slabs," "blocks,"*
   and "cubes" so that the platform is stepped, with the steps upstage.
(*Confidently, calls.*) Plank!
(*A block is thrown instead of a plank.*)

The protagonist Easy finds the code-cracking easy indeed, mere
child's play as for Augustine's *tabula rasa* infant, and at the end of the
comedy has acquired perfect mastery of Dogg. Whether the audience attains
a similar level of competence is another matter: the sense of semiotic
inferiority is probably one of the main masochistic pleasures offered by the
play. But in any event, in reversing Wittgenstein and thereby reinstating
the deposed saint, Stoppard seems to suggest that dramatic discourse is itself
a "primitive" language-game of a kind, being necessarily tied in its production of meaning to the simultaneous presence of ostended objects, bodies, and gestures; but at the same time even a so-called primitive game may
not be all that it seems. It could be *this* too. The theatre, indeed, with its
semiotic mix of objects, images, and words is the privileged seat of plea-
surably painful ambiguity. Or is not this, at least, what the tortoise would
appear to have taught us?

Chronology

1937	Tomas Straussler is born in Zlin (now Gottwaldov), Czechoslovakia, on July 3, the second son of Eugene and Martha Straussler. Eugene Straussler is a doctor on the staff of Bata shoe manufacturers.
1939	As German invasion of Czechoslovakia appears imminent, Bata transfers the Strausslers to Singapore; either Dr. Straussler or his wife was of partially Jewish descent.
1942	The Japanese invade Singapore, prompting evacuation of Martha Straussler and her sons to India. Dr. Straussler, who remains in Japan, is killed.
1943–46	Thomas attends American multilingual boarding school in Darjeeling, where mother manages a Bata shoe store.
1945–46	Martha Straussler marries Kenneth Stoppard, a major in the British Army stationed in India; the children adopt his surname. The family moves to England, where Kenneth Stoppard becomes a salesman of machine-tools.
1946–54	Stoppard attends Dolphin School in Nottinghamshire until 1948, when he transfers to Pocklington School in Yorkshire.
1954	Stoppard leaves school and joins the *Western Daily Press* as a junior general reporter, writing play and film reviews, news reports, features and columns; he befriends people at the Bristol Old Vic.
1958	Stoppard joins the *Bristol Evening World* as a reporter and feature writer.
1960	In July, Stoppard resigns his job, free-lancing instead. Writes his first stage play, *A Walk on the Water*, on which basis Kenneth Ewing becomes his agent. The play is optioned by H. M. Tennent but not produced.
1962–63	Moves to London, where he is hired as a drama critic by *Scene* magazine. Stoppard reviews 132 shows before the magazine goes out of business, seven months after it was launched. *A Walk on Water* is produced by British Independent Television.

1964   Two plays of Stoppard's, *The Dissolution of Dominic Boot* and
        its companion *M is for Moon among Other Things* are broadcast
        by BBC Radio. Faber and Faber publishes three short stories
        by Stoppard ("Reunion," "Life, Times: Fragments," and "The
        Story") in *Introduction 2: Stories by New Writers. A Walk on
        Water* is staged in Hamburg (as *The Spleen of Riley*). From
        May to October, Stoppard participates in a colloquium in
        Berlin for young playwrights, on a Ford Foundation grant.
        There he pens a short verse play, *Rosencrantz and Guildenstern
        Meet King Lear*: "the whole thing was unspeakable," he later
        comments. Writes five episodes of *The Dales*, a daily radio
        serial; and a ninety-minute television drama, *This Way Out
        with Samuel Boot*, which is never produced.

1965   Marries Jose Ingle, a nurse. Writes seventy episodes of a weekly
        radio serial, *A Student's Diary*, for the BBC; translated into
        Arabic, the scripts are broadcast on the Overseas Service. The
        Royal Shakespeare Company acquires a one-year option on
        Rosencrantz and Guildenstern Are Dead (never exercised). The
        Drama Department of Bristol University produces his second
        play, *The Gamblers*. He is contracted by Anthony Blond to
        write a novel.

1966   The BBC broadcasts *If You're Glad I'll Be Frank*. The Royal
        Shakespeare Company stages Stoppard's adaptation of Sla-
        womir Mrozek's *Tango*. *Rosencrantz and Guildenstern Are Dead*
        is first staged by the amateur Oxford Theatre Group at the
        Edinburgh Festival. The *Observer* reviewer, Ronald Bryden,
        lauds it as "the most brilliant debut by a young playwright
        since John Arden." Stoppard's novel, *Lord Malquist and Mr
        Moon*, is published in England.

1967   The National Theatre at the Old Vic stages *Rosencrantz and
        Guildenstern Are Dead* under the direction of Derek Goldby.
        Stoppard receives the John Whiting Award from the Arts
        Council of Great Britain and (along with David Storey) the
        Evening Standard Award for Most Promising Playwright. BBC
        Television produces *Teeth* and *Another Moon Called Earth*.
        BBC Radio broadcasts *Albert's Bridge*, which is awarded the
        Prix Italia. On October 16, *Rosencrantz and Guildenstern Are
        Dead* opens in New York, where it receives the Antoinette
        Perry (Tony) Award and the Drama Critics Circle Award for
        Best Play of 1967–68.

1968   A revised version of *A Walk on Water* entitled *Enter a Free Man* is staged in London, March 28. *The Real Inspector Hound* opens in London, June 17. *Neutral Ground* is produced on Granada Television, December 11.

1969   Two radio plays, *Albert's Bridge* and *If You're Glad I'll Be Frank*, are staged at the Fringe of the Edinburgh Festival, August 29.

1970   Stoppard begins research for *Jumpers*. BBC Radio broadcasts *Where are They Now?* on January 28, NBC Television broadcasts *The Engagement* on March 8, Inter-Action produces *After Magritte* at the Green Bananas Restaurant in London, April 9. Stoppard and Jose Ingle are separated.

1971   Inter-Action produces *Dogg's Our Pet* at the Almost Free Theatre. Stoppard and Jose Ingle are divorced.

1972   On February 2, the National Theatre at the Old Vic produces *Jumpers*, under the direction of Peter Wood (who will later direct the premiers of *Travesties, Night and Day, On the Razzle* and *The Real Thing*). It receives the *Evening Standard* Award and the Play and Players Award for best play of the year. On February 11, Stoppard marries Dr. Miriam Moore-Robinson, who is the medical director of Syntex Pharmaceuticals, a company specializing in contraception, and who will become a well-known television personality as a panelist on the BBC television quiz show, *Call My Bluff. After Magritte* and *The Real Inspector Hound* are staged in a double bill in London during April; later that month, the play opens in New York. Stoppard makes *Tom Stoppard Doesn't Know* for the BBC Television series, "One Pair of Eyes." BBC Radio broadcasts *Artist Descending a Staircase*, November 14.

1973   An English version prepared by Stoppard of Lorca's *The House of Bernarda Alba* is staged in London on March 22, at the Greenwich Theatre. Stoppard directs Garsan Kanin's *Born Yesterday*, which opens April 18 at Greenwich.

1974   Stoppard is commissioned to work on the screenplay of Thomas Wiseman's *The Romantic Englishwoman* for a film by Joseph Losey. *Jumpers* opens in New York on April 22, André Previn commissions a play employing a complete symphony orchestra on stage. The Royal Shakespeare Company produces *Travesties* at the Aldwych Theatre, June 10.

1975   Stoppard writes adaptation of Jerome K. Jerome's *Three Men in a Boat* for BBC Television. Stoppard and Clive Exton write

Boundaries, a half-hour play broadcast live by BBC Television. Inter-Action produces *Dirty Linen* and *New-Found-Land* at the Almost Free Theatre in April; moving in June to the Arts Theatre, the plays open in New York on January 11, 1977. Inter-Action performs Stoppard's *The (15 Minute) Dogg's Troupe Hamlet* on the terraces of the National Theatre in London, August 24. According to Stoppard, the work "was written (or rather edited) for performance on a double-decker bus." As a member of the Committee Against Psychiatric Abuse, Stoppard addresses a Trafalgar Square Rally in August, subsequently joining a march to the Soviet Embassy to deliver a petition for the rights of Soviet dissidents.

1977   Stoppard visits Moscow and Leningrad with an official of Amnesty International, reporting what he observed in *The Sunday Times* (February 27, 1977). In February, *The New York Times* publishes a letter from Stoppard about the repression of Charter 77 in Prague and referring to official harrassment of the Czech playwright, Vaclav Havel. Stoppard travels to Czechoslovakia, meeting with the playwrights Vaclav Havel and Pavel Kohout. The Royal Shakespeare Company, together with the 100-piece London Symphony Orchestra, perform *Every Good Boy Deserves Favor,* a play with music, in the Royal Festival Hall in London, July 1. André Previn, the composer, conducts the orchestra. In another production employing a 32-piece orchestra, the play enjoys an extended run at the Mermaid Theatre in London. In September, BBC Television produces *Professional Foul,* which receives the British Television Critics' Award as the best play of 1977. In December, Stoppard is made Commander of the British Empire.

1978   *Night and Day* is staged at the Phoenix Theatre in London, a production by Michael Codron. Stoppard writes the screenplay for Rainer Fassbinder's film *Despair,* adapted from Vladimir Nabokov's novel. WNET Television in New York produces *Professional Foul* in April.

1979   *Dogg's Hamlet, Cahoot's Macbeth* is premiered by the British American Repertory Company at the University of Warwick, under Ed Berman's direction. In July, it opens in London. *Undiscovered Country,* Stoppard's English version of Arthur Schnitzler's *Das Weite Land,* is produced in June by the National Theatre. Stoppard is awarded the Shakespeare Prize of the FVS Foundation in Hamburg; writes screenplay for the film version of Graham Greene's *The Human Factor.*

1981   Declines BBC invitation to give the Reith Lectures on Radio 3. *On the Razzle*, a play by Stoppard adapted from Johann Nestroy's *Einen Jux will er sich machen*, is produced by the National Theatre in August.

1982   *The Real Thing* is performed in London (a Michael Codron presentation), in November.

1984   *The Real Thing* opens on January 5 in New York. Receives 1984 Tony Award for Best Play. Judged Best New Play of Season by both New York Drama Critics Circle and Drama Desk.

1984   *Squaring the Circle*, a television film directed by Mike Hodges about Poland's Solidarity, is transmitted by TVS in May.

Contributors

HAROLD BLOOM, Sterling Professor of the Humanities at Yale University, is the author of *The Anxiety of Influence, Poetry and Repression* and many other volumes of literary criticism. His forthcoming study, *Freud: Transference and Authority*, attempts a full-scale reading of all of Freud's major writings. A MacArthur Prize Fellow, he is the general editor of *The Chelsea House Library of Literary Criticism*.

ALLAN RODWAY is the author of *The Romantic Conflict, The Truths of Fiction, English Comedy: Its Role and Nature from Chaucer to the Present Day, The Craft of Criticism* and *A Preface to Auden*.

BRIAN M. CROSSLEY is a free-lance drama critic and Lecturer in the Department of English at Napier College, Edinburgh, who has produced many plays.

RONALD HAYMAN is the author of such books as *Literature and Living: A Reconsideration of Katherine Mansfield and Virginia Woolf, The Set-Up: An Anatomy of the English Theatre Today, How to Read a Play, Theatre and Anti-Theatre: New Movements Since Beckett* and *K, A Biography of Kafka*, as well as studies of Albee, Arden, Artaud, Beckett, Bolt, Brecht, Fassbinder, Ionesco, Arthur Miller, Nietzsche, John Osborne, Pinter, de Sade, Stoppard, Tolstoy, Arnold Wesker and John Whiting, among others.

JOHN A. BAILEY is Professor of English at Mayville State College in North Dakota.

G. B. CRUMP is Associate Professor of English at Central Missouri State University and the author of *The Novels of Wright Morris: A Critical Interpretation*.

HOWARD D. PEARCE teaches English at Florida Atlantic University.

JUNE M. SCHLUETER, the author of *Metafictional Characters in Modern Drama* and *The Plays and Novels of Peter Handke*, teaches English at Lafayette College.

JOHN WILLIAM COOKE is an Assistant Professor of English and Drama at LeMoy College in Syracuse, New York.

WILLIAM E. GRUBER is Assistant Professor of English at Emory University and the author of studies of modern drama and dramatic theory.

JIM HUNTER is the author of *The Metaphysical Poets, Gerard Manley Hopkins, Kinship: A Novel* and *Tom Stoppard's Plays.*

THOMAS R. WHITAKER is Professor of English at Yale University. His books include *Swan and Shadow: Yeats's Dialogue with History* and *Fields of Play in Modern Drama.*

HERSH ZEIFMAN, Associate Professor of Drama and English at York University in Toronto, is currently working on a critical study of Stoppard's productions.

RICHARD CORBALLIS, Senior Lecturer in English at the University of Canterbury, New Zealand, is the author of *Stoppard: The Mystery and the Clockwork.*

KEIR ELAM, a Harkness Fellow at UCLA during 1974–75 and at Yale during 1975–76, is currently a Research Fellow at the University of Florence. He is the author of *The Semiotics of Theatre and Drama* and *Shakespeare's Universe of Discourse: Language Games in the Comedies.*

Bibliography

Bennett, Jonathan. "Philosophy and Mr. Stoppard." *Philosophy* 1, vol. 50 (January 1975): 5–18.

Berlin, Norman. "*Rosencrantz and Guildenstern Are Dead:* Theater of Criticism." *Modern Drama* 3 and 4, vol. 21 (December 1973): 269–77.

Bigsby, C. W. E. *Tom Stoppard.* London: Longman Group Ltd. for the British Council, 1976.

Billman, Carol. "The Art of History in Tom Stoppard's *Travesties.*" *Kansas Quarterly* 4, vol. 12 (Fall 1980).

Buhr, Richard J. "Epistemology and Ethics in Tom Stoppard's *Professional Foul.*" *Comparative Drama* 4, vol. 13 (Winter 1970–80): 320–29.

Cahn, Victor L. *Beyond Absurdity: The Plays of Tom Stoppard.* London: Associated University Presses, 1979.

Cohn, Ruby. *Modern Shakespeare Offshoots.* Princeton: Princeton University Press, 1976.

Corballis, Richard. *Stoppard: The Mystery and the Clockwork.* Oxford: Amber Lane Press, 1984.

Dean, Joan Fitzpatrick. *Tom Stoppard: Comedy as a Moral Matrix.* Columbia, Mo.: University of Missouri Press, 1981.

Delany, Paul. "The Flesh and the Word in *Jumpers.*" *Modern Language Quarterly* 4, vol. 42 (December 1981): 369–88.

Draudt, Manfred. "Two sides of the same coin, or . . . the same side of two coins: An analysis of Tom Stoppard's *Rosencrantz and Guildenstern Are Dead.*" *English Studies* 4, vol. 62 (August 1981): 348–57.

Ellmann, Richard. "The Zealots of Zurich." *Times Literary Supplement* (June 12, 1974): 744.

Gabbard, Lucinda P. "Stoppard's *Jumpers:* A Mystery Play." *Modern Drama* 1, vol. 20 (March 1977): 87–95.

Hayman, Ronald. *Tom Stoppard.* London: Heinemann, 1982.

Hinden, Michael. "*Jumpers:* Stoppard and the Theater of Exhaustion." *Twentieth Century Literature* 1, vol. 27 (Spring 1981): 1–15.

Hunter, Jim. *Tom Stoppard's Plays.* London: Faber and Faber, 1982.

James, Clive. "Count Zero Splits the Infinitive." *Encounter* 5, vol. 45 (November 1975): 68–76.

Levenson, Jill. "Views From a Revolving Door: Tom Stoppard's Canon to Date." *Queen's Quarterly* 3, vol. 78 (Autumn 1971): 431–42.

Londre, Felicia Hardison. *Tom Stoppard.* New York: Frederick Ungar Publishing Co., 1981.

Rothstein, Bobbi. "The Reappearance of Public Man: Stoppard's *Jumpers* and *Professional Foul.*" *Kansas Quarterly* 4, vol. 12 (Fall 1980): 35–44.

Salmon, Eric. "Faith in Tom Stoppard." *Queen's Quarterly* 2, vol. 86 (Summer 1979): 215–32.

Schulman, Milton. "The Politicizing of Tom Stoppard." *The New York Times* (April 23, 1978): 3.

Taylor, John Russell. "Tom Stoppard." In *The Second Wave: British Drama for the Seventies.* New York: Hill and Wang, 1971.

Tynan, Kenneth. *Show People.* New York: Simon and Schuster, 1979.

Whitaker, Thomas R. *Tom Stoppard.* London and Basingstoke: The Macmillan Press, Ltd., 1983.

Acknowledgments

"Stoppard's Comic Philosophy" by Allan Rodway from *English Comedy: Its Role and Nature from Chaucer to the Present Day* by Allan Rodway, copyright © 1975 by Allan Rodway. Reprinted by permission.

"An Investigation of Stoppard's 'Hound' and 'Foot' " by Brian M. Crossley from *Modern Drama* (March 1977), copyright © 1977 by University of Toronto. Reprinted by permission.

"*Lord Malquist and Mr Moon*" by Ronald Hayman from *Tom Stoppard* by Ronald Hayman, copyright © 1979 by Ronald Hayman. Reprinted by permission.

"*Jumpers*: The Ironist as Theistic Apologist" by John A. Bailey from *Michigan Academician* 3, vol. 11 (Winter 1979), copyright © 1979 by Michigan Academy of Science, Arts, and Letters. Reprinted by permission.

"The Universe as Murder Mystery: *Jumpers*" by G. B. Crump from *Contemporary Literature* (Summer 1979), copyright © 1979 by the Board of Regents of the University of Wisconsin Press. Reprinted by permission.

"Stage as Mirror: *Travesties*" by Howard D. Pearce from *Modern Language Notes* (December 1979), copyright © 1979 by The Johns Hopkins University Press. Reprinted by permission.

"Moon and Birdboot, Rosencrantz and Guildenstern" by June M. Schlueter from *Metafictional Characters in Modern Drama* by June M. Schlueter, copyright © 1977, 1979 by Columbia University Press. Reprinted by permission.

"Perception and Form in *Travesties*" by John William Cooke from *Modern Drama* (December 1981), copyright © 1981 by University of Toronto. Originally entitled "The Optical Allusion: Perception and Form in Stoppard's *Travesties*." Reprinted by permission.

"Artistic Design in *Rosencrantz and Guildenstern Are Dead*" by William E. Gruber from *Comparative Drama* (Winter 1981–82), copyright © 1982 by *Comparative Drama*. Originally entitled " 'Wheels within wheels, etcetera': Artistic Design in *Rosencrantz and Guildenstern Are Dead*." Reprinted by permission.

186 • ACKNOWLEDGMENTS

"*Night and Day*" by Jim Hunter from *Tom Stoppard's Plays* by Jim Hunter, copyright © 1982 by Jim Hunter. Reprinted by permission.

"Language, Lunacy and Light" by Thomas R. Whitaker from *Tom Stoppard* by Thomas R. Whitaker, copyright © 1983 by Thomas R. Whitaker. Reprinted by permission.

"Comedy of Ambush: *The Real Thing*" by Hersh Zeifman from *Modern Drama* (June 1983), copyright © 1983 by University of Toronto. Reprinted by permission.

"*Dirty Linen* and *New-Found-Land*" by Richard Corballis from *Stoppard: The Mystery and the Clockwork* by Richard Corballis, copyright © 1984 by Richard Corballis. Reprinted by permission.

"After Magritte, After Carroll, After Wittgenstein" by Keir Elam from *Modern Drama* (December 1984), copyright © 1984 by University of Toronto. Originally entitled "After Magritte, After Carroll, After Wittgenstein: What Tom Stoppard's Tortoise Taught Us." Reprinted by permission.

Index